"LOVE AND ADMIRATION

AND RESPECT"

THE O'NEILL-COMMINS CORRESPONDENCE

"LOVE AND ADMIRATION

AND RESPECT"

THE O'NEILL - COMMINS

CORRESPONDENCE

Edited by Dorothy Commins

Duke University Press   Durham 1986

© 1986 Duke University Press
All rights reserved
Printed in the United States of America
on acid-free paper ∞
Library of Congress Cataloging in Publication Data
appear on the last printed page of this book.

The following permissions are gratefully
acknowledged.
Eugene O'Neill's correspondence and Carlotta
Monterey O'Neill's diaries are published by
permission of the Collection of American Literature,
Beinecke Rare Book and Manuscript Library, Yale
University, and the Yale Literary Property Committee.
The Eugene O'Neill and Saxe Commins letters,
Random House Papers, Rare Book and Manuscript
Library, Columbia University, copyrighted
by Random House, Inc., are published by permission.
Carlotta Monterey O'Neill's letters, housed at the
Firestone Library, Princeton University, are
published by permission of her grandson
Gerald E. Stram.
Various excerpts from Dorothy Commins, *What Is
an Editor? Saxe Commins at Work* (Chicago:
University of Chicago Press, 1978), are reprinted
by permission of the University of Chicago Press.

For my children:

Frances Ellen Commins-Bennett

Eugene David Commins

CONTENTS

ACKNOWLEDGMENTS

This book would not have been possible without the generous help of a number of people. I extend to them my most grateful thanks and here acknowledge a portion of my profound debt to them.

In the beginning my good friend Professor Richard Ludwig, of the Rare Books, Special Collections at the Firestone Library, Princeton University, recognized the validity of my undertaking the task of bringing to view the O'Neill-Commins correspondence. Professor Ludwig advised me to talk to Dr. Donald Gallup of the Beinecke Library at Yale University about my project. Dr. Gallup was not only gracious but encouraging, and wrote me to that effect.

When I began to organize my material, I turned to Louis Sheaffer, whose two volumes about O'Neill are veritable mines of information. Throughout the years of my work Louis Sheaffer stood by, advising and clarifying situations that were new to me. It was he who made it possible for me to contact Carlotta Monterey O'Neill's grandson, Gerald E. Stram. I shall ever be grateful to Mr. Stram for granting me permission to include his grandmother's letters to Saxe Commins and me during the years between 1928 and 1951.

Though Professor Jackson R. Bryer of the Department of English at the University of Maryland is a new friend, he is a wonderful one in that he has given much thought and effort to bring my manuscript to a point of excellence.

For Ruth M. Alvarez, who in her quiet way worked along with Professor Bryer and who absorbed the inner meaning of the written word, my appreciation cannot be measured.

When my manuscript was in its embryonic stage, I had the rare opportunity to talk to Professor Freeman Dyson, of the Institute for Advanced Study in Princeton, N.J., about it. He listened most attentively. Before long,

I had a letter from him, suggesting that I contact Professor Henry Petroski at the School of Engineering at Duke University. Then he added, Professor Petroski is a man of varied interests, and the subject of Eugene O'Neill would interest him.

I did write to Professor Petroski. His immediate and gracious response was most encouraging. He asked me to send him a copy of what I had done so far, and said that he would see to it that it would reach some person at the Duke University Press.

Sometime later I had a letter from Mrs. Joanne Ferguson, editor-in-chief of Duke University Press, advising me to finish the manuscript so it could be fully appraised. That of course involved a long period of work. Finally, I turned in the completed manuscript. Then came a period of waiting—it seemed interminable! But when the letter of approval came, I sat looking at it, not believing. Then the tears came. The tension was broken. For leading me to the door of Duke University Press, I shall ever remember Professor Henry Petroski's utter kindness to me.

Since then, my direct communication with Mrs. Ferguson is a privilege I value. I think I did say, Saxe Commins would have applauded her.

The Foreword that introduces my book to the reader, by Professor Travis Bogard, of the Department of Dramatic Art at the University of California, Berkeley, undoubtedly enriches my book—and I bow to Professor Bogard in deep respect and appreciation.

I shall always remember the kindnesses, to me, of the various people in the section of the Rare Books Collection at the Firestone Library, Princeton University, when I was burrowing into the O'Neill files. I salute Mr. Alexander Clark, and Mr. Alexander Wainwright, for answering the many queries I have put to them that were related to my work.

FOREWORD

Love's Labor Dispossessed: The Complexities of a Friendship

by Travis Bogard

Not every marriage is made in heaven. People may be joined together in many unlikely places, even in a publishing house, where on rare occasions an author and an editor can meet in mutual trust, bred of professional competence, friendship, interdependence, and a shared participation in a creative process. Or, as Eugene O'Neill put it, inscribing a copy of *The Iceman Cometh* to his editor Saxe Commins, in "love and admiration and respect."

The association that was to become a lifelong intimacy probably began in New York City in late 1915 and was affirmed during the summer of 1916 at Provincetown on Cape Cod, when both men were drawn into the enthusiastic playmaking of the dedicated amateurs who were shortly to form the Provincetown Players.[1] Commins went to the Cape to join his sister Stella and her husband, a young actor named E. J. Ballantine. Stella appeared in the Players' production of George Cram Cook's *Change Your Style*, and Ballantine acted in, and later claimed to have directed, their memorable first performance of O'Neill's *Bound East for Cardiff*.[2] The Ballantines were signers

---

1. In the memoir that follows, Commins dates his first meeting with O'Neill in 1914. He does not specify the place of the meeting but says that it came about through Jack Reed and Louise Bryant. Commins, a nephew of Emma Goldman, certainly knew Reed, but Bryant, Reed's mistress and later his wife, did not arrive in New York City until 1916. Cf. Barbara Gelb, *So Short a Time* (New York: Norton, 1983), p. 76. Commins describes a meeting with O'Neill in Provincetown in 1915. O'Neill, however, did not go to Provincetown until 1916. In 1914 O'Neill, recently discharged from a tuberculosis sanatorium, was living in New London, Conn., and working on a local newspaper. That fall, he attended Professor George Pierce Baker's class in playwriting at Harvard. He did not move to Greenwich Village until sometime in the latter part of 1915. Probably Commins first met him then.

2. Cf. Robert Karoly Sarlós, *Jig Cook and the Provincetown Players* (Amherst: University of Massachusetts Press, 1982), pp. 23–24.

of the first "constitution" of the Players, and, although Stella's participation as an actress was short-lived, her husband appeared in a number of the New York productions of the group. Commins's contribution that summer was prophetic. He typed Susan Glaspell's play *Trifles,* an early editorial service of the kind he was later to perform for O'Neill.

At the University of Pennsylvania, during the time of World War I, Commins inhaled the odor of ferment that was to result in the heady intellectual wine of the 1920s. Like any young man whose interests ranged beyond the ordinary goals of middle-class America, he gravitated when occasion permitted to Greenwich Village, where, it appeared, all that was new was being tested for validity in argument and art. He has not recorded the course of his *vie de bohème* in detail. He still maintained his contact with the Players; his unlauded lost play, *The Obituary,* closed a three-play bill at the Provincetown Playhouse in December 1916. O'Neill's *Before Breakfast* had been staged by the group earlier in the same month.

What drew the two men together, if indeed there was at first any special bond, can only be surmised. Commins's friendly intelligence and an eagerness to learn about many things made him attractive. As Emma Goldman's nephew, he no doubt gained entrée into the circle of radical experimenters of whom O'Neill for a time made one. In his turn, he perhaps responded to a wildness in O'Neill, an untamed masculinity that was a far cry from what he had known in the warmly communal Jewish family in Rochester, N.Y., where he had his roots. O'Neill had a remarkable aptitude for making friends among men of all social levels and interests; Commins had an aptitude for listening and for making intelligent and amusing commentaries on the world around him.[3] He had a love of literature that even in its youthful stages would have appealed to the more or less self-educated O'Neill.

The first substantial account of their association is contained in a series of letters O'Neill wrote to his wife, Agnes, when he left her in Provincetown to visit Commins in Rochester. By 1921 Commins, who had studied dentistry, had established a successful practice in his hometown. O'Neill's teeth were a disaster area. He arrived for treatments on April 21 and was taken to meet the elder Comminses, with whom Saxe lived. He found them to be "fine, lovable people." Less lovable was the process that began that afternoon. A wisdom tooth was extracted, and, although it proved to be stubborn, O'Neill at first wrote that he felt relatively pain free. "Bridge-work," Commins said, was in order, but not "plates." On Friday, O'Neill was less cheerful. He wrote Agnes that the roots of the wisdom tooth "had grown together in a bunch making the tooth larger at the bottom than anywhere else—hence Saxe had almost to call in the derrick squad before he could budge it."

3. For example, see his letter describing the meeting of the "Ghourdieffists." Letter 36.

He found that he liked Saxe's family. They are "fine folks," he said again, and he appreciated their courteous hospitality. On the day of his arrival they had received a wire from Los Angeles, saying that their granddaughter had died following a tonsillectomy. Despite their sorrow, the elder Comminses welcomed O'Neill into their home.

On Saturday the drilling for the bridge-work began, continuing on Sunday, "in spite of its being the Sabbath." On Monday Saxe extracted "some old abcessed roots . . . a frightful ordeal. . . . They had grown in under the next tooth and simply refused to be yanked out—had to be cut out bit by bit—and the anasthetic [sic] didn't work right and—well it was hell on wheels, believe me. Poor Saxe! He honestly suffered more than I did about it. I'm a fine sight—jaw all swollen—and glad you can't see me. No woman could love this face."

Commins's bereaved brother and sister-in-law arrived in Rochester, and the men moved from the family home to that of Commins's sister Miriam on the outskirts of town. O'Neill rested contentedly there in a "half farm, half suburban villa . . . nice and quiet . . . woods nearby . . . fertile . . . big orchards, etc." On Thursday, April 30, another extraction was in order, but by Saturday the bridges were fabricated and, O'Neill wrote, "five or six small fillings are still in store—and then, release! The work Saxe has done has been fine and should prove lasting.[4] It has *not* been painless—but I expected the worst anyway."

By the beginning of May, O'Neill had had enough, not only of the dental process but of the Commins world. He complained to Agnes of there being too much "family—crowds and crowds of them, seven or eight children running and shouting about—talk, talk, talk! a general pandemonium . . . all yesterday afternoon and evening. Twelve or more sitting at dinner! I nearly went 'nuts,' and writing was out of the question. But I was sort of guest of honor and had to stick it out." He stuck it out until May 4 when his treatment ended, and he returned to Agnes and the sea and the quiet of Provincetown.[5]

For O'Neill, who had never had a family nor, it would appear, significant dental work, the double ordeal of familial affection and dental extraction proved too much. Yet something beyond the Greenwich Village friendship was born in that week. The relationship between the men moved from a level of easy familiarity to a plane of personal sympathy and gratified response: "Poor Saxe! He honestly suffered more than I did. . . ." Throughout

4. Commins's work was by no means the last major dental attention O'Neill required. In New York later in the 1920s and in Paris in the 1930s he spent hours in the dentist's chair.

5. The letters from O'Neill to Agnes Boulton O'Neill are housed in the Houghton Library at Harvard University. The letters cited include those written between April 21 and May 2, 1921. Many of the letters are undated.

his life O'Neill responded to such attention as Commins paid him. All of his important friendships—as with Kenneth Macgowan and George Jean Nathan—as well as his marriage to Carlotta Monterey were based partly on a dependency, an unspoken request to be looked after and cared for. There was nothing overtly effeminate or passive in such a need. O'Neill was a man men genuinely liked. Even today he is remembered by casual laborers who worked for him on his California ranch, by Herbert Freeman, his chauffeur for many years, and by those who knew him in more fully professional ways as someone who met them as equals and treated them fairly and with reliable friendship.

However outgoing he sometimes appeared, those who knew him most closely speak of his shyness, a quality that was an outer manifestation of the deep center of his personality, that part of his being where he most fully lived and from whose fires the plays came. When he wrote, he was a different person from the friendly man for whom so many felt affection. Freeman was puzzled and a little hurt by O'Neill's occasional failure to acknowledge his greeting when they first met during the day. Sensing Freeman's concern, O'Neill apologized and told him that when he had been writing, he was not always aware of those around him.[6]

The encircling walls of his study and his own extraordinary powers of concentration walled him in physically and psychologically against intrusion. With the exception of Carlotta, no one breached those walls to enter the world of solitude and silence where the plays were created. Some, however, came near that world, and once the essential creative act was complete, were allowed participation in the final readying of the work for stage or publication. Saxe Commins was one of these few, and it is probable that no other person except Carlotta was trusted so completely or came so close to knowing the essential O'Neill. It was perhaps inevitable that he and Carlotta, whose lives were given a special meaning by their privileged service, would become rivals in their desire to protect and preserve the creative core of O'Neill's being.

At first, it was friendly assistance Commins offered—talking out ideas, suggesting source books, typing, and nonprofessional editorial chores on those occasions when they were together. Later, Commins began to stand in for O'Neill at ceremonial occasions, accompanying Agnes to first nights and once, as his memoir records, serving as priest for an astonishing confession. By 1928, however, Carlotta Monterey had entered O'Neill's life and his marriage to Agnes ended. Then the relationship between the men took on a new and ultimately more professional turn. In December 1927 Commins married Dorothy Berliner, a talented pianist of great personal charm. Soon thereafter he rebelled against the life of a Rochester dentist. A man needs no reason to

6. Herbert Freeman's comment was made in an interview at Tao House, March 23, 1983.

pack up and get out from a situation in which the profits yield nothing of the spirit. Commins wanted to write. He had recently published a collaboration with Lloyd Coleman, *Psychology, A Simplification* (1927), but thereafter his writing was largely confined to editorial suggestions and to a variety of notes and introductions.[7] Although in such a boom time as 1928 the freedom to look for more than Rochester offered was readily possible, for Commins it was almost too late. He was thirty-four, and married, and financially "settled." Yet his wife's career needed nurturing: a year studying in Paris was an almost essential preliminary to an important career as a pianist. For a would-be writer, in those years, the lure of Paris was strong. Also, a fact to be noted as the Comminses determined to set sail for France is that they were following in O'Neill's wake. O'Neill had left New York City with Carlotta in February determined to live abroad until the divorce from Agnes was final. Certainly Commins did not sell his dental practice and go to France because of O'Neill, but his friend's romance, his somewhat adventurous journey, and the example of O'Neill's cutting off old ties may have been an encouragement. Commins's break may have seemed easier because of his friend's presence in Europe.

Whatever part O'Neill's elopement played in Commins's decision, it was not long before they met. In July, Commins went to visit O'Neill at Guéthary near Biarritz. He was invited cordially but was asked not to bring Dorothy. The letters indicate that the reason given was the presumptive embarrassment of the two women over the fact that Eugene and Carlotta were, as the phrase was, "living in sin." Commins arrived on June 21 and stayed through June 30, returning to Paris with the manuscript of the recently completed *Dynamo*, which he typed to O'Neill's full satisfaction.[8] Shortly, as the letters reveal, he was performing a number of personal services for both O'Neills.

On August 20 Carlotta invited the Comminses to dinner at their Paris hotel, and from that time forward the relationship was fixed in orbit. Carlotta asked them to run more errands, thanked them effusively, and in tones of extravagant affection wooed them. O'Neill, beginning the long period of work on *Mourning Becomes Electra*, was more laconic, but his letters testify to the affirming friendship, based on affection, gratitude for services rendered, and growing trust. Later, in February 1929, when the O'Neills had returned from their cruise to the Orient, both the Comminses were received as guests, and to judge by the letters that remain, the social waters were unruffled.

7. Bennett Cerf, who lavishly praised Commins's qualities as an editor, also commented that Commins was a "frustrated writer," whose suggestions for emendations sometimes worked against the grain of authors such as John O'Hara, but who was "adored and counted on" by O'Neill and William Faulkner. Cf. Bennett Cerf, *At Random* (New York: Random House, 1977), p. 220.

8. Commins never accepted or received payment for typing or any other services he did for O'Neill or Carlotta.

Below the surface, however, Carlotta's private response to the visits at Guéthary and at the château at Le Plessis was less cordial. In her diary she refers to the Comminses only briefly, as "C" and "D," and most frequently she calls him "our 'guest,'" putting the term in ironic quotation marks. She notes on July 20, 1928, that "Gene & 'guest' talk out in garden until midnight—I retire at 11—." Although the Comminses surely did not arrive uninvited, she remarks on February 19, 1929, that "C & D turn up as house guests," and when the Comminses came to dinner in Paris as a result of the gracious invitation contained in letter 24, she notes in her diary for August 25, "Our 'guests' from Guéthary turn up! They remain to dinner." What was perhaps her most affectionate letter to Commins, letter 64, dated August 30, 1929, was in answer apparently to a letter from Commins that, in her diary entry of August 31, she called "idiotic."[9]

What motivated Carlotta will never be fully comprehensible, although Commins's "idiotic" letter may provide a clue. The letter is lost, but if its contents can be inferred from her reply, it concerned some of O'Neill's friends from the Village days, particularly the Provincetown stage director James Light, his wife, and Eleanor Fitzgerald, the former guardian and overseer of the Players. Carlotta viewed this group of old friends with suspicion and antipathy. They remembered and called to an O'Neill she had not known and brought back a time from which she had attempted to divorce the playwright. Saxe Commins, in a way, belonged to that group. What he represented to her, therefore, was at first an intruder from a past she did not wish to acknowledge. Furthermore, as his services to O'Neill increased, and as O'Neill talked with him late into the night, he appeared to be moving closer to the center of O'Neill's creative life. The ironic quotation marks of the diary entries may reveal a jealousy, a dawning feeling that he was becoming her rival.

Carlotta Monterey was a temperamental, spoiled, sophisticated, imperious, handsome woman. Her tastes, formed in New York City and London, were a defense against her origins in Oakland, California. Like many men and women, she used her marriages and her love affairs to propel herself up and out of a world she found stultifying. Her rise, although it was achieved by a different form of transport, had a similar motivation to that of Commins when he left Rochester. Her career as an actress was ephemeral and secondary to her appearances in a somewhat hazily defined social milieu. She acted in nothing but rubbish until 1922, when she was cast in the on-Broadway production of *The Hairy Ape*, replacing the actress who had created the role in the Village theatre. That the respected, uptown producer Arthur Hopkins used her in the short but crucial role suggests that she had some ability and

9. The diaries of Carlotta Monterey O'Neill are housed in the Beinecke Rare Book and Manuscript Library, Yale University.

that her name had drawing power. The theatre, however, offered her little more than a temporary standing place. It was not her future.

When she and O'Neill met again, in Maine during the summer of 1926, the acquaintance, which had earlier been fractious since she was an unwelcome alien among the Provincetown group, became warmer. Their liaison at the Belgrade lakes continued throughout the next year, and O'Neill saw in her something more than a passing summer love. He was at work on two plays that signaled a change in quality and direction from his earlier work, *Lazarus Laughed* and *Strange Interlude*. Neither could be produced with the facilities offered by the Village theatres, which to this time had been adequate to his needs. As the horizons of his playwriting expanded, he began to think of major stars as his actors—Katharine Cornell and Feodor Chaliapin, to name two. He made an alliance with the Theatre Guild, which was shortly to stage both *Marco Millions* and *Strange Interlude*. Seeking more profound forms of dramatic statement, he was entering a new world and, as he approached forty, a new life.

He came to think of Carlotta as essential to that life. What O'Neill asked of her was that she give up everything she had gained—her career, her friends, the comforts of her known world—and become his protectress, or, as he said in the dedication to *Mourning Becomes Electra,* his "mother, and wife and mistress and friend!—And collaborator!" She was to become the guardian of his creative life, as Agnes, with a more casual style of living in a more careless time, had never become. Carlotta knew well what he asked of her, and she accepted the bargain, keeping faithfully to it for so long as the marriage remained vital.

The center of the marriage was his writing. His plays became her raison d'être. They were her pride and in a measure her love. As she loved the man, she loved and served his work, making no separation between the two. To Agnes, O'Neill once wrote in some bitterness, "Excuse me for speaking so much about my plays. I realize it's tactless on my part. It's quite evident to me that you're not interested since you never mention them."[10] He would never have written such an accusation to Carlotta. She stood close to him as he wrote, moving from his side only to position herself at the gates to turn away all persons she felt might intrude on their common center. The letters reiterate her determination to create and to guard the quiet world where he could write undisturbed by any intrusion. She built homes to give him comfort and peace, and she willingly endured the lonely, mute days while he worked. She nursed him in his increasingly severe illnesses. She provided diversion when he needed it and warded it off when in her judgment it was unwelcome. The criterion *was* her judgment. There was no one else, for

10. Undated letter: "Tuesday," probably Dec. 20, 1927. Houghton Library, Harvard University Library.

O'Neill made few decisions about the outward conduct of their lives together. Thus, in her judgment, the past was distraction. O'Neill's animosity toward Agnes for not making possible a rapid divorce was intense. Carlotta set her sword against all that Agnes represented, with the result that many of O'Neill's old friends—the drinking cronies, the Village theatre people—were turned away. Agnes's children were continual problems, and, although Carlotta received them, she did so with an inner reluctance, akin to the irony with which she at first received the Comminses. O'Neill let it happen; his love for Carlotta was great and his trust in her complete.

No doubt, she felt a certain vanity at being "Mrs. Eugene O'Neill, the wife of America's greatest playwright," but she does not appear to have capitalized on her position. Instead, she entered the silence with him. Her withdrawal to France, thence to Casa Genotta in Georgia and to Tao House in California, was as complete as his. The marriage was not easy to achieve, but together they found the way to its fulfillment in the Tao House plays, which were nurtured through great physical hardship in times of national and familial stress. She was jealous. How could she not be? Jealousy is a concomitant of dedication. Nurses are jealous; mothers are jealous; lovers, wives, agents, even editors are jealous of those they love and serve.

When, at the height of his creative powers, O'Neill was silenced by the tremor that made writing impossible, the marriage lost its central fire. Carlotta then had to care only for a man who could no longer create, one who had become feeble and bitter and suddenly old. She herself was ill and stranded on a remote California hillside in a war-rationed world, forced to struggle for a living that was increasingly burdensome and meaningless.

At this point in their lives, bizarre jealousies arise, passing rumors of infidelities are heard, and the final tragic years begin. Through them all, Carlotta attempted to keep out intruders, as she had always done, but her desperation was evident, and, as her own illness drove her to excess, she became manic in her attempt to keep everyone away from the ruin of their marriage and themselves. Decisively she drove away all of the lesser guardians. His producer Lawrence Langner, his friends Kenneth Macgowan and Sophus Winther, his publisher Bennett Cerf were cast out. O'Neill's children were shut away, and he who had perhaps been closest to O'Neill's central life, the faithful Saxe Commins, received blows whose motivation he did not understand, but which scarred his well-being and his trust in human relations until his death.

The story of that relationship as Saxe and Dorothy Commins understood it is set forth in the correspondence and the memoir that follow. Commins, once he had found his true métier in the editorial position O'Neill procured for him with his publisher, Horace Liveright, became an intelligent, scrupulous professional. As the letters show, he protected O'Neill from loss when the Liveright firm went bankrupt, a service O'Neill repaid by insisting that

Commins be hired at Random House as part of the agreement he signed with his new publisher, Bennett Cerf. In his new position Commins came fully into his own. Cerf described him as "one of the great men at Random House, a wonderful man."[11] He was, in fact, one of the most distinguished editors in American literary history.

As an editor, Commins made many friends among the major authors of the time, but none was so close to him as O'Neill, after whom he named his son, and for whom he performed special chores, such as typing the manuscript of *The Iceman Cometh*, a job whose routine difficulty was compounded by O'Neill's microscopic handwriting, already palsy-twitched. His care of the manuscripts, especially that of *Long Day's Journey into Night*, was exemplary, providing full testimony to his unceasing concern for O'Neill's personal and literary welfare, even after the dramatist was dead.

Can there be two zealous guardians of the same person? Perhaps, so long as the one being guarded is able to mitigate potential friction. As O'Neill's strength ebbed, however, such control as he might have exerted became weakened, and, as the ensuing letters and memoir shockingly reveal, suddenly Commins and Carlotta were face to face, and she was brutal. Commins recoiled in moral horror from an enemy he had not known he possessed.

He had not seen in the woman who wrote letters with such effusive grace the fierce strength of purpose born of the renunciation of everything for a single good, nor did he understand the psychological strain such renunciation causes when that single good is called in question. He was not, apparently, aware of the illnesses—among others, a form of bromide poisoning—that led her to uncontrollably manic behavior.[12] He had no sympathy with the sight of a woman who, with nothing left ahead in life, clung in despair to the shards of what had been her pride—the broken, passive man she once had loved.

At the end the outcry against Carlotta from those who had loved O'Neill became full-throated in its hatred, and the picture that Commins here draws of her has attained a legendary "truth." Commins, with Dorothy at his side, undertook to take O'Neill to their home to care for him. Carlotta, long before the plan was in evidence, sensed his rivalry. Her paranoia caused in her the inexplicable, melodramatic behavior Commins describes: the mysterious disappearance of the manuscripts, her insane behavior as O'Neill with a broken leg lay helpless in a snowstorm, the obscenities, the libellous attacks on Com-

11. Cerf, *At Random*, p. 85.

12. Potassium bromide, prescribed extensively in the nineteenth and early twentieth centuries as a nostrum for nervous conditions, and still occasionally found in nerve tonics and headache remedies, is only slowly excreted by the kidneys. If taken with frequency, it can reach a toxic level in the body over a period of weeks. Among the symptoms of "bromide intoxication" are irritability and emotional disturbances occasionally leading to a form of mania. Cf. Louis Sanford Goodman and Alfred Gilman, *The Pharmacological Basis of Therapeutics* (New York: Macmillan Co., 1941), pp. 129–31.

mins's honesty, the irrational rejection of every seeming invasion of their "privacy," no matter what the occasion.

Such action as the Comminses here describe is inexcusable, but perhaps there is not so great a need for excuse as there is for understanding. At the last Commins calls Carlotta "evil," for "good" and "evil" were terms habitual to his way of thinking. O'Neill's judgment is significantly different. He said to Commins, "Try to understand. She's sick, terribly sick." What needs to be understood about the O'Neills at the end of their lives together is that in a demented and frenzied way, she was attempting to do what she had always done—serve her husband.

Two matters should be noted. After the terrifying night at Marblehead, when O'Neill was in a hospital and Carlotta had been removed for psychiatric examination, O'Neill's first concerted effort from his hospital bed was to dictate a letter to Carlotta, assuring her of his love and continuing concern for her welfare.[13] Removed from her "influence" by his friends and transferred to a New York hospital, he returned immediately to her side once he was able to travel, despite the arguments and the pleas that he leave her.

The second matter concerns his relationship with Eugene O'Neill, Jr., in whose career he had taken particular pride. The son had failed in his efforts to find a more glamorous career than teaching classics at Yale University, and had come far down in the world, jobless, drinking, relying on his father for support. Commins, who heard the account only from the younger O'Neill, implies that Carlotta prevented Eugene, Jr., from reaching his father at a time when he needed his signature as co-signer on a small mortgage note. Thus, Commins suggests, Carlotta was responsible for the fact that soon thereafter Eugene, Jr., committed suicide. There exist, however, two letters, one undated and written painfully in O'Neill's shaking hand, the other typed, presumably by Carlotta, dated February 25, 1950, and signed "Father" by O'Neill. The former was sent to the younger O'Neill's lawyer on March 7, 1949, and forwarded as its envelope attests. The second was sent on February 27 directly to the son. Both were covering letters for notes that O'Neill had endorsed. Carlotta did not interfere.[14]

After O'Neill's death, when Carlotta assumed control of his literary estate and arranged for the publication and production of *Long Day's Journey into Night*, she was again viewed as a villainess transgressing against O'Neill's dying wishes. Yet with considerable theatrical acumen, she saw that the play was carefully presented to the public. She arranged that it should first be produced in Stockholm, where the personal revelations would be of less interest than the play itself. Starring in it, and thus ensuring not only definitive

13. Undated letter, dictated but signed by O'Neill: probably Feb. 9, 1951. Beinecke Rare Book and Manuscript Library, Yale University.

14. The correspondence between O'Neill and Eugene O'Neill, Jr., is in the Beinecke Rare Book and Manuscript Collection, Yale University.

performance but an aware and interested world press, were the actors from the Swedish National Theatre, many of whom were becoming international stars through the films of Ingmar Bergman. With this rather elaborate "out-of-town tryout," she then brought *Long Day's Journey into Night* into New York partly presold by the Swedish production as an unusual work of art and saw that it had a superb cast and sympathetic direction. The production in November 1956, together with the revival at Circle-in-the-Square of *The Iceman Cometh* earlier that year, began the O'Neill renaissance, restoring him to the position he had abdicated after the production of *Days Without End* in 1934—that of "America's greatest playwright." No doubt, in a measure, Carlotta's former pride of place was also restored.

The production and her arrangement for the preservation of his literary remains was her last important service to her husband. In coincidental parallelism with his friend, Commins, who had been born six years later than O'Neill, died six years following his death. His love was unabated; his bitterness unassuaged.

INTRODUCTION

by Dorothy Commins

When the publishing house of Liveright failed in the 1930s, other publishers immediately tried to acquire its leading authors; most of all they wanted to sign up Eugene O'Neill, not only because he was a world-famous playwright, the first this country had ever produced, but because his published works—even those that had failed on the stage—always sold. After weighing various offers, O'Neill chose Random House, a relatively new publisher, but only on condition that it employ Saxe Commins, his editor at Liveright and his closest, most trusted friend. Years later, after Saxe had served as editor not only for O'Neill but for William Faulkner, W. H. Auden, Isak Dinesen, Robinson Jeffers, Sinclair Lewis, John O'Hara, Irwin Shaw, Adlai Stevenson, and other noted writers, both Bennett Cerf and Donald S. Klopfer, the heads of Random House, said that Saxe had proved as important to them as O'Neill.

O'Neill himself said, in inscribing a copy of his play *The Iceman Cometh,* "To Saxe, you know, oldest and best of friends, how deep that friendship is and what a joy it is to work with you or rather be helped by you on each and every book. Well, Here is another you got out. I hope you like it. I do. And here's love and admiration and respect. Ever your Gene, October 1946."

This almost fraternal relationship began about 1916, when O'Neill emerged as a leading member of the Provincetown Players and Saxe became involved with the theatre group through one of his sisters, who was married to an actor. The relationship would endure until the playwright's final years, when all his friends were shut out of his life by painful circumstances beyond O'Neill's control.

The letters presented here, written between 1920 and 1951, as well as the reminiscences and commentary of my husband, Saxe Commins, shed new light on the O'Neill saga, a story steeped in human conflicts as dramatic as any the eminent dramatist ever wrote.

It is not easy to evaluate O'Neill's character; even those who knew him best were baffled by the contradictions and complexities of his personality. He could be outgoing, winning, and affectionate; at other times he was withdrawn, unbending, bitter. In her memoir *Part of a Long Story*, his second wife, Agnes Boulton, asks rhetorically: "What made you what you are, what were the hidden stigmata that had wounded you, and at times bled with drops of bitterness?" Carlotta Monterey, his third wife, derided talk that he was too elusive to pin down, yet she ended by contradicting herself: "He was a simple man. They made a lot of nonsense and mystery out of him. . . . He was interested only in writing his plays. . . . He was nine or ten men in one." Again, Russel Crouse, playwright and Broadway notable, summed up the view of many when he said: "O'Neill is one of the most charming men I know, and I've known him for twenty-five years, but I can't say I understand him. His face is a mask. I don't know what goes on behind it, and I don't think anyone else does."

O'Neill's shyness and his hesitancy in speech made others feel protective toward him, as though he were unable to defend himself; but when it came to his writings, he had a will of steel—nothing and no one could interfere with his need to create. In sum, it seemed that several personalities were alternating with each other and were forever struggling to resolve the ambivalences.

In January 1958, six months before Saxe died, he began to chronicle the facts and meaning of his relationship with O'Neill. What follows is taken from his notes:

Eugene O'Neill's life, even more than his plays, was involved in tragedy. Misfortune is selective; its choice is deliberate, final and irreversible. He was, as Charles Lamb said of himself, "in a manner marked." Gene accepted that verdict without appeal or dispute because his preference was for a climate of doom.

Applauded and honored throughout the world, he gained the rewards that most men seek, in recognition, in wealth, and in devotion, but he disdained them all for the reason that he had a deep scorn for the man to whom they were offered. Torn with self reproach, tortured by fear, in perpetual nervous panic and a constantly brooding loneliness, he deliberately built barriers around himself and made himself believe that he had succeeded in shutting out a hateful world.

That world waited on the outside and moved in on him stealthily. It found ways of gaining entrance and revenge for having been excluded. Neither glory nor money could buy it off or keep it at a distance. He convinced himself that he was beyond its good or evil and beyond its praise or blame. He persuaded himself that he had been immunized against all pain inflicted from the outside, only to feel a greater self-induced anguish. The world, however, ignored these elaborate inner defenses.

The more he fled, the more he was pursued. There was no escape from the ambush within himself. The tremor in his spirit was even greater than the trembling of his hands. In his last years, its outward manifestation was in convulsive movements of his arms and legs, a quivering of his dry lips and a look of wonder and anxiety in his brown eyes. Fear haunted him. He lived under the stress of bewilderment and uncertainty about himself. His fright was called shyness by many, by himself seclusiveness and a mania for privacy. It was all that and more. The more was a gentleness that winced under the ordinary necessities of living. Constant companionship with illness and pain was the reason he gave for withdrawal.

Because he shunned people to overcome his own uneasiness in their presence, he isolated himself and became a recluse. By elaborate means he avoided public places. The manorial houses in which he lived were fenced against intruders. Only rarely would he answer a telephone call and when he did it was in a quivering voice. He would never go to a barber-shop to have his hair cut, but would insist upon having the barber bring his paraphernalia to his room. He rarely attended a performance of his own plays, nor did he visit his publisher's offices except when it was made certain that no strangers would be in sight. At rehearsals, which he supervised with minute attention, he hid in the back of the dark theatre and would convey his instructions through the director. Rather than be seen in a restaurant, he brought food to the theatre and ate it in private. Once rehearsals were over and the play was launched, he avoided the theatre and remained in his hotel room only long enough to pack his belongings and return to whatever isolated house he was living in at the time. The customary two tickets set aside for the playwright on opening nights were usually given to me, so that I could accompany his then wife, Agnes Boulton, to the premiere, and after the performance to go to their hotel apartment to report the event.

Tormented as Gene was by his past and the tragic events in his family's history, he never denied reality. Indeed, his need to confront his past and deal with it as honestly as possible was a primary impulse at the root of his art. Carlotta Monterey was, however, constantly on the alert to guard the fantasy she had created about her background. She maintained, for instance, that an aunt who had no children had set up a trust fund from which Carlotta received a lifetime annuity of approximately $14,000. In reality, the alleged aunt was James Speyer, a prominent Wall Street banker with whom she had had an intimate relationship for years before her marriage to O'Neill.

Born in California to a mismatched pair, Hazel Nielson Tharsing (Carlotta Monterey's real name) was only four when her mother left her husband; intent on making her own way as a boardinghouse keeper in San Francisco, she deposited her child with a married sister who had young of her own. From an early age Hazel showed a taste for theatricals and a bent for self-dramatization. Since she was also beautiful, her mother (who had a succession of prosperous lovers) sent her abroad once she was grown, to prepare for the stage and, not incidentally, to improve her matrimonial chances. At this point the girl took a new name—Carlotta, because she appeared Latin, and Monterey from the city in California.

Miss Monterey had three husbands before O'Neill. After finishing school in Paris and Sir Herbert Beerbohm Tree's Academy of Dramatic Arts in London (later the Royal Academy), she married John Moffat, a Scottish attorney. That union lasted only a few years. Between her first and second marriages, she made her Broadway debut in 1915. Shortly afterward, returning home to California, she married Melvin C. Chapman, Jr., also a lawyer, by whom she had a daughter, her only child. When the girl was less than a year old, Miss Monterey, leaving the child to be raised by her (Carlotta's) mother, returned to Broadway. In one of her first interviews she agreed with someone's estimate of her as "a girl of strong emotions," adding that "I am always vacillating between extremes. . . . There are times when I feel within me a calling for the primitive, the wild and the elemental in nature and in art. . . . Then at times I crave the very reverse, the exquisite and the ultra-refined. . . . It is not pleasant to be like a living pendulum swinging between two natures."

In the early 1920s Melvin Chapman sued her for divorce, at her request, so that she could wed Ralph Barton, a clever cartoonist and bon vivant who ran and drank with the smart set in New York. Like the actress's previous marriages, her third one did not last long.

Meanwhile, critics and the public had received Eugene O'Neill's *The Hairy Ape* so enthusiastically that it was decided to move the drama from Greenwich Village to Broadway. With Louis Wolheim, who had scored a personal hit, still heading the cast, the production moved uptown almost intact, except that Mary Blair was replaced by Carlotta Monterey as the neurotic society girl. This was the first time she and the playwright had ever met and, from all accounts, neither at the time showed any interest in the other.

When they met again, in the summer of 1926, a spark was ignited between them and, after a secretive courtship conducted in New York while O'Neill was rehearsing his new play *Strange Interlude*, they ran off to Europe together and settled in France early in 1928.

A few months later Saxe and I, recently wed, also left for Europe, planning to spend a year abroad while Saxe devoted himself to writing and I to furthering my studies in music. After taking an apartment in Paris, we heard from Gene, who had settled with Carlotta in a villa in Guéthary, near Biarritz.

Gene, working at the time on his play *Dynamo,* urged Saxe to visit him—he wanted his editorial counsel—and explained that he was not inviting me as my presence under the circumstances (he and Carlotta were not married as yet) "would give rise to an uncomfortable situation for all hands concerned."

Not long after Saxe's visit to Guéthary, where he spent more than a week, O'Neill and Carlotta sailed for the Far East, a voyage Gene had long dreamed of making. As we learned later, Gene suffered from sunstroke while swimming at Singapore and was not fully recovered when he and Carlotta debarked at Shanghai. One day they were spotted by a young Canadian newspaperman Gene had known in Greenwich Village, who worked at the time for the *North-China Herald.* After the chance encounter, O'Neill was glad to have the other man show him sights unknown to most tourists, while Carlotta, who loved fine clothes, found someone to take her shopping.

By now O'Neill was in an emotionally disturbed state due to several factors: relations between him and Carlotta, who had reprimanded him over some of his behavior, had deteriorated since their departure from France; the fabled Orient seen close up was considerably less romantic than he had envisioned; and, finally, he could not repress guilt feelings over his desertion of Agnes and their two small children. One night, after a round of the bars with the newspaperman, he returned drunk to the hotel and got into an argument with Carlotta, a confrontation that ended with her moving into another hotel. After he landed in a hospital from drinking while in a rundown condition, he and Carlotta were reconciled, but the dissension between them was only one of the many rows that would flare up in their twenty-five-year marriage.

Back in France early in 1929, on the Riviera this time, they rented a villa in Cap d'Ail, near Monte Carlo, where Saxe and I visited them for a week. We were greatly relieved, after reading newspaper dispatches from the Orient about O'Neill's being ill, to find him looking well. Within a few months the pair decided to move, for they wanted more privacy than the Riviera offered. Earlier, in touring the Touraine, they had been charmed by its beauty and now they decided to live in the château region. After searching around, they rented Le Plessis, a moderate-sized château not far from Tours. Vacant for a good many years, the place was rundown, but Carlotta, who had a real gift for homemaking as well as great drive and boundless energy, shortly had it in comfortable shape. Under her guidance, electricity was installed, one bedroom was converted into a modern bathroom, and, since O'Neill loved swimming, a pool was built.

We saw quite a bit of Gene and Carlotta, as they often visited Paris, and whenever we did we could expect to hear complaints about Agnes, chiefly that she was dragging out her divorce suit to embarrass them. Apparently they never stopped to consider the difficulties of her position, and how O'Neill's disappearance was sadly affecting their two small children, especially

Shane, who was almost nine. Finally, Agnes got her divorce in July 1929, with Gene and Carlotta marrying that same month.

At Le Plessis, O'Neill went to work on an idea he had had for years about a drama based on one of the old Greek classics, an idea that gradually materialized into his trilogy *Mourning Becomes Electra*. To relax from the most ambitious and difficult project he had ever attempted, Gene liked to drive at high speed in his Bugatti racing roadster around the Touraine countryside. He found another kind of pleasure in a pedigreed Dalmatian named Silverdene Emblem, an unusually bright dog whom his masters nicknamed "Blemie" and whom Gene and Carlotta loved with a wholehearted feeling neither ever gave to their children.

Soon after the O'Neill's return from Europe in 1931, they built a splendid home in the Georgia resort of Sea Island, where Gene worked on a cycle once envisioned as eleven plays, finally as nine, that dwarfed even *Mourning Becomes Electra*. They remained in the South only a few years, driven away by the heat. While residing temporarily in Seattle, where he wanted to do some research for his cycle, O'Neill won the Nobel Prize for Literature in 1936, an event that found him besieged by reporters, photographers, and newsreel men. After Seattle, forever seeking privacy and quiet, the O'Neills built a mountainside home called Tao House (the Chinese word *Tao* meaning "the right way of life") in Danville, California. Weary of his multi-play cycle, after working on it for years with the end nowhere in sight, O'Neill shelved the project to write two plays that had long been on his mind, two that proved to be his masterpieces, *The Iceman Cometh* and *Long Day's Journey into Night*. They were written just in time, for not long afterward a tremor of his hands, which had been manifest at times in his earlier years, became so bad that he was no longer able to write. It was the supreme tragedy of his life: he was at the peak of his talent and, as he told us, full of new ideas, but his hands had failed him.

After World War II, when the O'Neills prepared to come east to arrange for the production of *The Iceman Cometh*, Bennett Cerf invited them to stay at his home (the housing shortage in New York was severe at that time), but Carlotta replied in September 1945 that they would stay at a hotel and expected to see Saxe regularly. Once they were settled at the Hotel Barclay on East 48th Street, Saxe frequently went there straight from his office for working dinners, but more often wished he was not present at the altercations that immediately arose between Gene and Carlotta.

The O'Neills soon gave up their suite at the Hotel Barclay and moved into a penthouse apartment at 84th Street and Madison Avenue, which they furnished with the fine and unusual things they had acquired in their travels. At O'Neill's insistence, Saxe used to visit them several times a week, sometimes to work, more often to reminisce and discuss literary matters. Our own home was on East 95th Street, only a short stroll away, and we used to exchange visits with them.

One day in spring 1946 Gene dropped by and asked me to write out the music for two numbers that were to be sung in the forthcoming production of *The Iceman Cometh*, numbers his father had sung as a boy in Ireland. The two were "The Potato Song," current at the time of the great potato famine of the mid-nineteenth century, and "Rap, Rap, Rap," another old ditty, which Gene called the "Sailor Lad." While he sat near me and sang the numbers in a voice so muffled and low that it was difficult to hear him, I picked out the tunes at the piano. Eventually we had the tunes and lyrics down on paper.

These were quiet times, the calm before a storm; but when the storm broke, it left destruction in its wake, with Saxe's relationship with Carlotta among the lasting casualties. The details of Saxe's break with Carlotta are given in the last section of this correspondence and in the excerpts from Saxe's memoir that are interspersed among the letters. Saxe's loyalty to O'Neill never wavered during this difficult period. Even though, at O'Neill's death in 1953, they had not seen each other or communicated with one another for two years, their friendship was that of two brothers rather than that of a writer and his editor.

A NOTE ON THE TEXT

The following abbreviations describing physical form have been utilized in the headings: TLS, typed letter signed by author; TL, typed letter unsigned; ALS, autograph letter signed by author; AL, autograph letter unsigned; TL(cc), typed letter, carbon copy; ACS, autograph card signed; WIRE, telegram; WIRE(copy), telegram, copy. The numbers enumerating the total pages of the original letters refer to the pages designated by the author of the individual letter. Usually the number indicates one side of one leaf of stationery, but occasionally it refers to one side of a leaf of stationery when both recto and verso are used. Less frequently it refers to one-half of a side of a leaf of stationery, when the author numbered two pages of an individual letter on one side of a leaf of stationery. Stationery headings that appear on the originals have been transcribed in upper- and lower-case type regardless of the appearance of the original and have been printed under the description of physical form.

The position of the headings has been standardized. All dates appear at the top right of individual letters regardless of their position on the original. O'Neill's practice normally was to place the date at the top right of a letter, but later in his life when his letters were transcribed to typescript by someone else, the date usually was placed flush to the bottom left margin of the last page of the letter. Where the date or part of the date does not appear in the original, it has been supplied in square brackets, which have been reserved for editorial insertions. These supplied dates have been determined by means of internal and external evidence and with the use of a universal calendar. Supplied dates for telegrams have been determined for the most part by the dates stamped on them by the telegraph office when they were received. Superfluous terminal punctuation in dates, closings, and signatures has been omitted. Although it was Carlotta Monterey O'Neill's practice to place a period before the comma in a salutation, these superfluous periods have been deleted. The position of closings and signatures has been standardized as well.

O'Neill's habitual spelling and punctuation errors and misspellings of personal names have been retained. Obviously inadvertent misspellings and typographical errors have been silently corrected. Occasionally, a word in brackets has been supplied where its insertion is necessary to clarify meaning. The position of quotation marks with punctuation has been regularized. The length of dashes in O'Neill's letters has been standardized to one em, although his practice in typing was to use one hyphen for a dash. An attempt has been made to reproduce the unique holograph dashes of Carlotta Monterey O'Neill; they have been standardized to one, two, or three one-em dashes. The abbreviation of ordinal numbers, which are used in the correspondence, has been regularized to "1st," "2nd," "3rd," etc. However, the holograph practice of both O'Neill and Carlotta Monterey O'Neill was to raise and underline the letters. The letters "P.S." that precede most of O'Neill's postscripts have been regularized to appear on the same line as the text of the postscript. His general practice was to put the "P.S." on a separate line.

Only meaningful deletions made by O'Neill have been retained, printed in footnotes. Insignificant deletions and obliterations have not been restored in the text. Interlineal insertions and marginal material have been printed as part of the letter or placed at the end of the letter. Letters marked with an asterisk have been copied from transcripts of letters made at the Princeton University Library when they were placed there after Saxe Commins's death; all other letters have been transcribed from the original letters. The vast majority of the letters are owned by Dorothy Commins; in the few instances where letters are included that are held by a university library, the name of the university is listed in square brackets following the abbreviation describing physical form.

Most of Saxe's letters to the O'Neills have disappeared. All those that survive are printed here. All of O'Neill's letters, telegrams, and post cards to Saxe and Dorothy Commins are included, except for a handful of Christmas cards. Approximately half of Carlotta's letters to Saxe and Dorothy are included; those selected were chosen both for their commentary on O'Neill and his activities as well as for what they revealed about Carlotta herself. The excerpts from Saxe's memoir of O'Neill are presented as he wrote them, with only an occasional footnote noting errors of fact in the narrative and with inadvertent spelling errors silently corrected.

THE BEGINNINGS

1920 – 1929

Although the first piece of Commins-O'Neill correspondence dates from 1920, the men actually met in late 1915 or early 1916. Saxe had grown up in Rochester, New York, an avid reader—especially of Chekhov, whose dual careers as physician and writer inspired Saxe to enroll in the School of Medicine at the University of Pennsylvania. After his first year of medical school, his brother was stricken with tuberculosis and had to be sent to live in Arizona, thereby seriously depleting the family's financial resources. Saxe was told he either had to quit medical school or accelerate his program. He decided to transfer to dentistry, acquired his degree, and returned to Rochester to practice.

During his undergraduate days Saxe had frequently visited his sister Stella in New York, where she lived with her husband, Edward J. Ballantine, a gifted painter, sculptor, and actor. During one of these visits Saxe met John Reed, fresh out of Harvard, where he had been known as a fiery young rebel with a marked gift for journalism. Upon reaching New York, Reed had found an outlet for his gift in the New York *Globe* and the *Metropolitan Magazine,* where he wrote columns stressing the wretched working conditions of the poorer classes and the dire facts of social discrimination. Reed's columns had attracted considerable attention, including that of young Eugene O'Neill, who was intrigued and captivated by Reed's flaming idealism.

It was through Reed and his lover (later to become his wife), Louise Bryant, that Saxe first met Eugene O'Neill. His memoir of O'Neill tells the story:

It was through Jack Reed and Louise Bryant that I first met Eugene O'Neill in 1914.[1] I had encountered Gene infrequently in those days.

1. As Travis Bogard explains in his Foreword, above, Saxe's dating of his first meeting with O'Neill is probably about one year too early.

But in the summer of 1915, while visiting in Provincetown, I was invited to a party at the home of Mary Heaton Vorse. She was then married to Joe O'Brien, a newspaperman of long experience in New York. At the party were Hutchins Hapgood, his wife, Neith Boyce, George Cram (Jig) Cook, Susan Glaspell and several others. By way of entertainment there were to be readings of the new work of the summer colonists. At the time Susan Glaspell had written a one-act play and I had volunteered to type out for her the manuscript of *Trifles,* a work which later won considerable acclaim and became one of the favorite inclusions in anthologies of the American drama. Susan and I went to the party together.

There I caught a glimpse of Gene O'Neill drinking by himself in the kitchen. He was dressed, I recall, entirely in white—white sweat shirt, white duck pants and white sneakers. His hair was beginning to gray at the temples; his skin was bronzed by the sun; his brown eyes were then, as later, brooding. He was at that time and thereafter a solitary, a scrupulously tidy solitary in his thinking, in his speech, in his drinking.

When the entire group, Gene excepted, had gathered in the living room, it was Hutchins Hapgood who announced that he would read a little piece of prose just written by Gene. In substance it was an elaboration of a then current joke, dashed off as a short story about a troop of Russian soldiers descending upon an East German village on an errand of loot and rapine. The head of the German household stands defiantly in front of his family of wife, daughter and aged mother, his arms outspread in a gesture of protection. The Russians are about to descend upon them to wreak their will on the women when the father-husband-son cries out: "Take my wife, take my daughter, but do not touch a white hair of my poor mother's head!" Whereupon the old woman declares herself against this kind of discrimination by shouting *"Aber Krieg ist Krieg!"* (but war is war).

It was a childishly poor joke, a piece of juvenilia, written in a derisive mood that was not communicated and it was passed over with a few polite but forced chuckles and the halting embarrassed remarks that are usually made on such occasions. Nobody took the reading seriously or humorously. But when Susan Glaspell read *Trifles* Gene's trifle was quickly forgotten in the enthusiasm aroused by her grim and terrifying tale in one act. Gene's jocular prologue had been completely overshadowed.

.   .   .   .   .

My prolonged visit in Provincetown made it possible to spend many hours with Eugene O'Neill. Whereas in New York we saw each other infrequently and then only to exchange little more than the common-

places of greeting. While walking in the village we met quite accidentally near Francis' store and he asked me to go with him to Peaked
Hill Bar, where the abandoned Coast Guard Station was converted into
a home on the edge of the sea. He was then engaged in writing the one-
act plays which were to comprise the Glencairn Cycle. In that summer
of 1916 the first of these, *Bound East for Cardiff,* was produced at the
Wharf Theater. Jig Cook, Susan Glaspell's husband, played the part of
Driscoll and panted through its lines with the intensity of an amateur
declaiming an oration. It was Jig, however, who gave heart to the undertaking and imparted to it the zeal and fire of his own convictions and
faith. . . .

At Peaked Hill Bar Gene and I walked the dunes, paddled in his
newly acquired kayak and talked, for a good part, in quotations. Our
favorite sources were Max Stirner's *The Ego and His Own,* an anarchical
explosion of aphoristic generalities, defiant and iconoclastic, and Nietz-
sche's *Thus Spake Zarathustra,* all heady stuff, diluted a little with the
milder wine of the romantic poets.

While Saxe's dental practice flourished in Rochester, after that 1916 encounter in Provincetown Gene's career as a playwright also grew quickly. His
one-act sea plays were done by the Provincetown Players in Greenwich Village in 1916, 1917, and 1918. In 1919 the first important published collection
of his plays appeared, *The Moon of the Caribbees and Six Other Plays of
the Sea.* And early in 1920 his first full-length play, *Beyond the Horizon,*
opened at Broadway's Morosco Theatre. It was enthusiastically received by
both critics and audiences, ran for 111 performances, and won for O'Neill the
first of his four Pulitzer prizes. On April 12, 1918, Gene had married Agnes
Boulton in Provincetown; in 1919 their son Shane was born.

Even though Saxe was extremely busy with his dental practice, he continued to make frequent weekend trips to New York so he could spend time
with the writers he admired. And it was with Eugene O'Neill that he would
most often spend his vacations. The absence of letters from the time Saxe
and O'Neill met until 1920 may be explained by the fact that they met at
different times and places during which their friendship became rooted and
burgeoned through discussion and exchange of opinions. Whatever early
correspondence may have existed does not survive. Their correspondence
begins as O'Neill has had his second major success of 1920, *The Emperor
Jones,* which opened in Greenwich Village at the Playwrights' Theatre on
November 1; it was so successful that plans were made to move it to Broadway at the end of December. Saxe had seen it on a visit to New York and
had written O'Neill to tell him how much he liked it. O'Neill, who by
this time had converted the abandoned Coast Guard station at Peaked Hill
Bar into his home, replied.

1. To Saxe Commins from Eugene O'Neill. TLS 1 p.

Provincetown, Mass.
Dec. 4, 1920

My Dear Saxe:

I am more than grateful for your letter. Real appreciation is a rare and thrice welcome event; and praise, when you feel yourself that the work in question is really part of your best, and when you know that the praise is sincere and not prompted by any alterior motive, is one of the finest incentives to keep on and "hew to the line." So more power to your writing hand, and may I continue to deserve more of such letters in the future!

As for the sage Greenwich Village chirpings about the ending, it is a funny thing but none of that bunch ever thought of making the criticism until Haywood Broun went on record with it in his Tribune article.[2] All of which goes to show that their superior scorn of what the newspaper critics say is not quite as sincere as it might be. The poor boobs are quoting Broun, that's all. As for the worth of the criticism itself, I think it is just a piece of carping stupidity—and I am glad you agree with me.

I haven't an extra script, Saxe—nor any script at all. I sent the last one to the Theatre Arts Magazine which is going to publish "The Emperor Jones" in their next issue. Comes out sometime this month, I think. If you can't get a copy in Rochester, let me know and I will get one for you at once—that is, I mean as soon as it appears.

When you wrote last for a script of "Gold" or "The Straw," I was in the same position. Between agents, managers, and Boni and Liveright[3] I usually am copyless until the play is published.

"Gold" and "The Straw" are to be produced in New York sometime this winter and I hope you will be able to get down for them. As to when or where they are to go on, remember that I am only the author and so will be the last one to get that information.[4]

Agnes[5] joins me in our very best to you, Saxe. Come up and see us if you ever get a chance.

And thanks again for your corking letter!

Gene

2. Writing in the New York *Tribune* for Nov. 4, 1920, Heywood Broun had praised *The Emperor Jones* as "truly a fine play," but he felt that the final scene should have been stronger, that Jones should not have died offstage.

3. O'Neill's publisher.

4. *Gold* opened on June 1, 1921, at the Frazee Theatre, *The Straw* on Nov. 10, 1921, at the Greenwich Village Theatre.

5. Mrs. Eugene O'Neill.

---

2. *To Saxe Commins from Eugene O'Neill.* ALS 1 p.

Provincetown, Mass.
March 12, 1921

Dear Saxe:

I feel no end of gratitude for your kind invitation and I'm sure going up to Rochester the first real chance I get. Can't make it now, however, or for some time to come. Tyler[6] threatens to start rehearsals for my "The Straw" any day now so I have to be "on call." The rehearsals will mean four weeks of being on the job every minute, as you know. So I can't make any certain predictions to you at this moment.

You'll find you'll have an awful amount of work coming on me. My teeth are in frightfully dilapidated shape—what there is left of them! I don't believe I've really been to a dentist—except for extractions—in the past eight or ten years. Most of that time, I couldn't for some reason or another—and since I could, I've been half-afraid and half-ashamed to go. So you see what you'll be up against! I warn you to polish up all your racks and thumb screws, for I'll probably need them all.

I'll be only too tickled to death to stay with you. Your cellar, however—I regret to state—is no inducement any more as I have sincerely taken the w. k. New Years oath as far as these U.S. are concerned.[7]

I'll let you know more definitely when I can come when more definite dope on "The Straw" reaches me.

All thanks and best wishes. Agnes joins me in same.

Gene

---

3. *To Saxe Commins from Agnes Boulton O'Neill.* TLS 1 p.

Provincetown, Mass
March 30th [1921]

Dear Saxe:

I am writing for Gene, as he is up to his ears in work (trying to get done so that he can hie Rochesterward) and he wants to get this letter off to you at once.

The plans are this: we are going to move over to the outside first and get settled there. Then about the 18th of April Gene will come to you, stopping

6. Producer George C. Tyler.
7. O'Neill is referring here to the fact that he has stopped drinking.

off at New York for a glance at the dress rehearsal of *The Moon*,[8] but not staying there more than a day or two at most. So that will bring him to you about the 20th. How is that?

I could be *exact* as to date if I knew just the day of the dress rehearsal—but I am writing to Stella[9] now to find that out. Will let you know then.

Gene is looking forward to seeing you. Treat him tenderly. You'll find you will have quite a dental job on hand I'm afraid. He says he knows you won't do what other dentists seem to delight in—look at his teeth, shake your head and sigh: "Dear, dear! Terrible!"

I wish you could plan to spend a week or so with us this summer. We'd love to have you. Do you know, Saxe, when Gene would get your rare letters about his work, he would say—here's somebody that knows what I'm trying to get at. He thought more of them than of any he received. I don't blame him. They were fine.

Agnes

---

4. To Saxe Commins from Eugene O'Neill. ALS 1 p.

Provincetown, Mass.
Saturday
[May 6, 1921]

Dear Saxe:

Well, I did miss that damned connection in Boston. On account of daylight saving they had switched the train to 6.30 instead of 7.30 and our train was half an hour late. 'Nuff said. I had to bum around a hotel until 3.30 in the p.m.

Your wish for fine weather for me is losing by a mile. It rained Thursday, yesterday, and is pouring today. Wind right in from old mother Ocean, surf roaring in our front yard all wild and wooly. But it's great to lie back and rest, safe in the knowledge that I have no appointment to have my teeth beaten up today. They feel fine, by the way, and eating is again becoming the popular indoor sport it used to be of yore.

I am enclosing notes for you to give to your Mother and Miriam.[10] I feel enormously grateful to all of you for your corking, "homey" spirit of hospitality to a guest who bounced in at such an unfortunate time. You can bet

8. O'Neill's *The Moon of the Caribbees* was being revived by the Provincetown Players in New York; it opened on April 25, 1921.

9. Commins's sister, married to actor E[dward] J. "Teddy" Ballantine, who had appeared in many Provincetown Players productions.

10. Commins's sister.

your house and your folks in general will be among my dearest memories of fine human beings as long as I live.

And as for you Saxe, I can't say all I feel for you of friendship and gratitude for fear it would sound "sloppy." It's simply that you are my friend, in the finest sense of the word, and that it means a hell of a lot to me that you are.

Be sure to try and make the opening of "Gold"!!! Write via Stella and let me know. Agnes and I are going down on Tuesday, I guess.

This letter probably won't be mailed until Monday. I am going to stick out here until then and there isn't any chance of the Coast Guards going in in this weather to act as postmen for us.

Agnes sends her kindest—and I all my best to all of you.

Gene

---

5. *To Saxe Commins from Eugene O'Neill.* ALS 1 p.

Provincetown, Mass.
June 19, 1921

Dear Saxe:

I have been meaning to write you every day since God knows when—but you know that procrastinating "tomorrow" stuff. At any rate, here I am at last.

I knew when your "Gold" wire arrived that you had just about hit the nail on the head.[11] Your dope just fulfilled my expectations after suffering through three rehearsals. The sad part was that there was nothing I could do. You have to have brains associated with you in order to get any reaction. And brains were sadly lacking about the Frazee—with the exception of Teddy and Marion.[12]

But let the dead past skin its own skunks, so to speak. Hopkins has taken "The Old Davil," Pauline Lord is to play in it, and Jones do the sets.[13] So the future holds promise of a fine and lasting association with the best people in our theatre. Not to speak of my hope that Hopkins will take my Fountain of Youth play[14] when it is finished, have Ben-Ami[15] act in it, and Jones again for its ten scenes. I have just started on the dialogue. So why stop to repine

11. *Gold* had closed after only thirteen performances.

12. Teddy Ballantine and George Marion had created the roles of Ned Bartlett and Butler, respectively, in *Gold*.

13. Producer Arthur Hopkins had recently optioned O'Neill's sea play, later to be called *"Anna Christie,"* and had signed Pauline Lord to play the lead and Robert Edmond Jones to design the sets.

14. *The Fountain,* completed in Oct. 1921 but not produced until 1925.

15. Actor Jacob Ben-Ami, who later played the lead role of Michael Cape in O'Neill's *Welded* (1924) but was not in *The Fountain*.

for poor "Gold" when all this—and plans for much more—are before one? There is only Tyler's "The Straw" to face with fortitude as a possibly very unpleasant experience.

When are you coming up? We haven't started on the beer yet—can't get a crock for love or money hereabouts. We'll have to try Boston, I guess.

My very affectionate regards to your Mother and all the others of your's—and remember me to your brother and his wife when you write.

Agnes sends all best. She will answer your letter soon.

All luck,
Gene

―――――

6. *To Saxe Commins from Eugene O'Neill.* ALS 1 p.
On stationery headed: Eugene O'Neill / Provincetown, Mass.

July 29, 1921

Dear Saxe:

A million excuses for not having answered your letter sooner. I've really been so "up to my ears" in the new play[16] I'm slaving at that I've sort of re-signed from every activity but that.

By all means come up any time in the latter part of August. That will be fine for us. Give us a warning a few days in advance, because mail doesn't reach us every day, and I'll meet you.

So Stella & Teddy are up there with you? I thought, when "Gold" closed so precipitously, that they might have had time to make the trip to England they had planned earlier. By the way, did Teddy ever get his money from Williams?[17] I've heard rumors the cast wasn't paid. I never knew the play had closed until a clipping came! I had actually sent two passes to people for the next week! One of the parties accused me of playing a raw joke and was quite irate about it! God damn Williams any way!

Agnes is going away to visit her folks in Conn. next week but will be back by the time you arrive. We'll sure be glad to see you again, and I think you'll enjoy it over here.

Give our best to Stella & Teddy if they are still with you. And all my kindest to your family. Be sure and come—and let me know when.

Gene

P.S. Why don't you send me a bill, you old Nut?[18] Honestly, I can afford to pay and want to! It isn't fair to you and yours for you to forget this. If I

16. *The Fountain.*
17. John D. Williams, who had produced *Gold.*
18. Commins had never billed O'Neill for the dental work he had done for him in April.

were up against it, it would be different. So, please. I feel so good and well now—and so full of gratitude to you.

---

7. *To Saxe Commins from Eugene O'Neill.* ALS 1 p.
On stationery headed: Eugene O'Neill / Provincetown, Mass.

August 26, 1921

Dear Saxe:

Supposing you date your arrival via the Dorothy for Friday the 2nd instead of the 1st? Will that make any difference to you? Thursday is our worst day to greet a guest, being the one on which our woman takes her weekly 24 hour vacation. If this upsets your plans any, let me know, and come as per your schedule on the first. It really is a minor matter so don't hesitate to do the more favorable thing from your end. But if I don't hear from you, I'll meet the boat on Friday, 2nd.

Don't worry about interfering with my work, you old chump! It's going to be a great pleasure to have you here, and I hope you'll enjoy being here half as much as we will having you. And I promise to shoo you into the sun and ocean to amuse yourself whenever I'm taken with labor pains.

All my kindest to all of your's. See you soon.

Gene

---

8. *To Saxe Commins from Eugene O'Neill.* ALS 1 p.

Peaked Hill Bar
Tuesday [September 1921]

Dear Saxe:

No, of course I'm not offended at anything, you old Nut! Just been lazy, that's all, in the sort of apathetic state of calm I get into after I've finished a long stretch of work. Haven't written a line of any kind. My cold hung on until about a week ago and made me feel pretty rotten, too.

Bobby Jones has been up here for a couple of days. He says "The Claw" caught on fine in Boston and promises a long run in New York when it gets there. Fine for Teddy![19] It's about time his luck changed.

19. Teddy Ballantine, after the failure of *Gold*, had landed a role in *The Claw*, adapted from the French of Henri Bernstein, produced by Arthur Hopkins, and starring Lionel Barrymore. After a successful run in Boston, it opened in New York on Oct. 17, 1921, and ran for 115 performances.

"The Emperor Jones," after failing quite miserably in Baltimore, jumped from there to Chicago and has made a big hit there—one of the two or three exceptions out there which are playing to business. Very fortunate for me financially! If it had been taken off, I would have been in a hole.

Much rumor of "The Straw" and "Anna Christie" starting their rehearsals but no definite call yet. It's a terrible season in N.Y., folks say, and I don't anticipate making a nickel from either play.

I'll write a lot more when I get back my energy. My mood now is abysmal inaction, mental & physical.

We are all fine. Agnes joins me in all best. Be good! Remember me to everyone.

Gene

---

9. To Saxe Commins from Eugene O'Neill. ALS 1 p.
On stationery headed: Eugene O'Neill / Provincetown, Mass.

Dec. 2, 1921

Dear Saxe:

I owe you a million apologies for not having written sooner but you can imagine how hectic things were with me in New York, and since my return here a week ago I've been under the weather with a cold—and the after-effects of much bad booze I absorbed during the last ten days in N.Y. But accept my belated gratitude for your wire and letters. I was darn sorry you couldn't manage to get down for either opening. You'll never see "The Straw" now for it closed a week ago. No business in spite of some fine notices it got. Everyone was afraid they'd catch T.B. by entering the theatre, I guess.[20]

"Anna Christie," on the other hand, promises to develop into a success. Here's hoping! Business there has been steadily picking up. But it's an awful year in the theatre and one doesn't dare prophesy.

No, the play hasn't been set up yet and I don't know whether B & L will do it separately or in a book with other plays.[21] But rely on me to send you an advance copy whenever it is off the press.

Nothing definite about "The Fountain" yet. Hopkins will do it—but when, how, with whom, I don't know. If he has made any plans, he hasn't divulged

20. Set entirely in a tuberculosis sanatorium, *The Straw* was based on O'Neill's six-month stay in such an institution between Dec. 1912 and June 1913.

21. O'Neill is probably referring here to *"Anna Christie"; The Straw* had already been published in April 1921 by Boni and Liveright. *"Anna Christie"* was published in July 1922 by Boni and Liveright, in a volume with *The Hairy Ape* and *The First Man.*

them to me. At present he's busy rehearsing Ben-Ami in the "Idle Inn."[22] Ben-Ami has too much accent for "The Fountain," Hoppy[23] decided as soon as he read it—and he is right.

After all the worry and bustle of rehearsals, openings, I'm all in—very much of a nervous wreck—and glad to be back up here where noone can talk theatre to me. For the nonce, I'm fed up on that subject.

Good'bye for this time. Agnes sends her kindest. Where are we going to get together again—and how—and when? Let's make it soon.

All my affectionate best to you and yours

Gene

---

10. *To Saxe Commins from Eugene O'Neill.* ALS 1 p.

36 West 35 St.,
N. Y. City,
Feb. 14, 1922

Dear Saxe:

Just a line in much haste. By all means, come down for "The Hairy Ape." I'll never forgive you if you don't. Sure I'll be here. And "The First Man," which you read last summer, is to be produced by Augustin Duncan down at the Neighborhood about the same date.[24] I'm again in a frenzy trying to get to two sets of rehearsals at the same time. Am doing most of directing for "Ape" to boot. Some hectic life! Believe me, I am tired—dog tired—and I'm going in for a long rest period, without thinking a thought or writing a line, after this spasm is over. I'm sick of the business of having plays produced, honestly. Not that I'm in bad spirits—quite the contrary. But it is wearing, this theatre.

Shane[25] is in P'town and fine as silk. Agnes got the "flu" almost her first day in N.Y. Was pretty sick for a time but much better now.

I hear from Stella—(Agnes & I had dinner with her at Broads tonight)—that you have been under the weather. You need a vacation, that's what. R.[26] is a sweet and lovely city—but not for so long at a stretch. So come down! "The Hairy Ape" is a grand tonic!

All best to all of yours from all of us!

Gene

P.S. "Ape" will probably open three weeks from yesterday.

22. A play adapted from a Yiddish folktale by Peretz Hirshbein.
23. Producer Arthur Hopkins.
24. *The First Man* opened on March 4, 1922, at the Neighborhood Playhouse; *The Hairy Ape* opened at the Playwrights' Theatre on March 9, 1922.
25. The son of Agnes and O'Neill.
26. Rochester, where Commins lived and practiced dentistry.

Saxe did attend the opening night of *The Hairy Ape,* using Gene's ticket to accompany Agnes. To quote again from Saxe's memoir:

> *The Hairy Ape* was produced on November 9th, 1922,[27] at the Provincetown Theatre in Greenwich Village with Louis Wolheim in the role of Yank and Mary Blair as the society heiress who causes his downfall. Agnes O'Neill and I had arranged to meet at the theatre shortly before the performance.
>
> When the curtain fell for the last time, the play was given a standing ovation; there were no fewer than a dozen calls for the cast. The audience cheered Louis Wolheim and cries of "Author, Author" continued while the actors were taking their bows. Even when the lights came on, the calls for the author came insistently from all parts of the auditorium. Finally when the audience realized that he was not present, it drifted slowly out into the street.
>
> Agnes and I sat silently and sadly through the demonstration, all too aware of the pathetic errand Gene was on at the moment when the applause and the clamor for his appearance were at their height. He had gone to Grand Central Station to claim the coffin containing his mother's body, shipped from California where she had died the week before. It was under the care of Gene's older brother, Jim,[28] who had travelled across the country on the same train.[29]
>
> Agnes and I made our way out of the theatre, hailed a taxi, and drove to the hotel. From the lobby we telephoned Gene to announce our arrival. He asked us to wait where we were, and in a few minutes he appeared. It was shocking to see the ashen color of his skin under the usual sun-burnt bronze. A tremor shook his body and he seemed to have lost control of his hands. His lips were two lines of blue and when he tried to talk the words had the sound of grating, as if they scraped past a

27. Saxe misdates the opening of *The Hairy Ape,* which occurred on March 9, 1922. Ella Quinlan O'Neill died in Los Angeles on Feb. 28, 1922.

28. O'Neill always referred to his brother as "Jim," but his mother and father addressed him as "Jamie," and so did most of his friends.

29. Actually, though Agnes and Saxe never knew it, O'Neill had not gone to the railway station. He had recruited William P. Connor, one of his parents' oldest friends, to go with him, but as the time approached, he became increasingly agitated. He lost his nerve and telephoned Connor that he was not equal to the ordeal. Connor insisted, but to no avail, that it was his duty; in the end Connor had a nephew of his accompany him. At Grand Central they found Jim in a drunken stupor, incoherent, almost unconscious, and with difficulty they located the mother's coffin. After making the necessary arrangements for the coffin and depositing the brother in a hotel, Connor, in a voice cold with reproach, telephoned a report to O'Neill. From O'Neill's account later, Agnes and Saxe assumed that he had met his brother's train.

rough lump in his throat. Finally he asked Agnes to go upstairs while he and I would go for a walk in Central Park.

That walk began shortly after midnight and continued until four in the morning. As we entered the park I tried to give him an account of everything that had occurred at the opening performance of *The Hairy Ape*. He was not interested. In fact, he interrupted in anger with an outburst: "For Christ's sake, cut it! I don't give a damn." I thought naively that I could override his impatience and went on talking about the play and the reception given it only an hour or so earlier. I recalled the number of curtain calls for the cast, told of the wave of surprise that ran through the audience on seeing the fire in the furnace in the stoke hole and the highlighted waist-bared figure of Louis Wolheim shoveling coal. I quoted snatches of conversation and comments of many people in the audience, expressing their astonishment and delight, and how they reacted to the scenes on Fifth Avenue with the mannikins talking in a stylized manner; in the I.W.W. headquarters and the zoo when Yank tore open the bars of the cage and gave the gorilla his freedom only to pay with his life in its crushing embrace. All this I had hoped would distract Gene from brooding about his mother's death, Jim's collapse into drunkenness, and his own gruesome search in the dark cellars of Grand Central Station.

I might have been talking to myself. If he had heard anything I had been saying, it meant as little to him as the other night noises in the park. My account became repetitious, but that did not matter because he was not listening. Balked by his inattention, I stopped my droning. We trudged on in silence. We found ourselves walking behind the Metropolitan Museum of Art and turned westward when we reached the reservoir. Thereafter we followed a winding path around a playing field and over a bridge that spanned an artificial lake. We were walking aimlessly and now silently.

Perhaps a half hour later as we retraced our steps, that silence was broken by a remark by Gene that had no relevance to what had happened or had been said. "It doesn't mean anything," was all he said. I had no answer to this cryptic observation. I waited for him to expand it, but there was another long silence. Then he repeated those four words as a kind of cue to himself by which the dikes of his reticence would be opened. Slowly and tremblingly at first, he began to talk with long pauses between words and sentences, and then, as if all the barriers were down, with the eloquence of bitterness. Now he wanted to talk and, above everything else, he wanted to purge his mind with a flow of words of his dark memories of his family.

He told of his mother's school days in a convent in Indiana and of her sheltered, innocent life until she met his father. He represented the antithesis of everything she had ever known. He was a famous actor, a matinee idol who for thirty-odd years proclaimed the lines by which he was identified all over America "The world is mine," from his perennial vehicle, *Monte Cristo*. There were times when he forgot that it was a quotation and considered it a reality. Certainly *Monte Cristo* became the dominant fact in their lives; they were chained to it.

Year after year James O'Neill toured the country, playing the same part, but wanting to shed it so that he could undertake something new and more challenging to his great gifts as an actor. Booth had once acclaimed him as his successor. But quick and sure money overrode ambition and as Joseph Jefferson could only play Rip Van Winkle, so he could only remain Edmond Dantes by public edict.

While on the road with one of his troupes, James O'Neill met, courted and won Ella Quinlan. She, a stranger to the theatre, began her yearly wandering across the country, enduring the agonies of one-night stands, the shabby accommodations and the improvised food of theatrical hotels. Only the summer brought a respite. Then they did not live in trunks, but in an actual home near the sea in New London. They could drive around the countryside in their high-perched Packard automobile and forget for a few months the rigors of the road. Then my father was "at liberty" and could talk of new roles he could someday undertake, once he had accumulated enough money. To get it a little quicker, he invested in wildcat mine stocks and even wilder real-estate gambles. Each new speculation meant greater parsimony and bitter quarrels. At the end of each summer, James O'Neill was again on the road and again crying out, as if it were the literal truth, "The world is mine!" to the delight of American audiences who thronged to the theatres and always applauded this wildly exaggerated, climactic line.

Bitterly, Gene said "Imagine! He played that part more than six thousand times, no wonder it made an addict of her."

There followed a long, tormented recital of his mother's struggle against the habitual use of drugs. His speech was no longer slow and hesitant, but it poured out of him as if at a confessional. *The Hairy Ape* was forgotten. It was not as if it had been played for the first time that night, but belonged to another life and to another person. His mother was now the central figure of the tragedy and in the telling of her history his compassion and natural sense of the dramatic, fashioned a figure of loneliness and longing and disillusion. The world, Gene said, sardonically, was certainly not hers and she had to seek another in a faraway narcotic dream.

But most bitter of all was Gene's denunciation of Jim and his long record of disgraceful behavior, climaxed on this night of drunkenness on what should have been an errand of mourning. Yet even in his fierce excoriation of his brother, there was a note of pride and affection and even of envy. Jim, in Gene's eyes, was the talented, the gifted one, but the one who had committed the great sin against the Holy Ghost; he had wasted his talent, thrown it away casually and mockingly for a cheap audience of fools and parasites. Jim was too attractive, too richly endowed, and yet he squandered himself on what he called the "Main Stem" where the showgirl is the supreme symbol of love and her bed her altar.

Jim could have had anything he wanted, according to Gene, especially women, and he had them for the asking. He could overwhelm them with his quick wit and his flattering attentions. His pleasure turned bitter with every petty triumph, but he turned to his philandering time after time, more to renew his belief in his cleverness than to earn the tinsel of their admiration. His behavior was shameful and yet there was a kind of quixotic victory in his conquests; he had a province of his own which he knew he could always either govern or subdue. Jim could have been a fine writer, a poet and certainly a barbed satirist or a romantic actor in the best tradition or even, highest in Gene's esteem, a clear and persuasive thinker. But no, Jim was too bedazzled by Broadway, by round-heeled women, by his auto-intoxication with his own boasting while his sycophants urged him on. Praise and drink and applause for his sharp wit were enough for him, and his young brother was a fool to want anything else, and there was some truth in that. It was foolish to want anything except whatever was natural and easy and pleasant. On that score Jim had everything Gene lacked and yet he considered it nothing at all. He could squander his resources casually and jokingly, a newly coined wisecrack on his lips and a shrug of disdain on his shoulders. But Jim was a wastrel with his talents, rich as they were, and that was his unresolvable sin. If only he, Gene, had Jim's gifts, then perhaps the O'Neills might be redeemed, especially redeemed from the father who allowed himself to be trapped by success. The old man was a Sisyphus and *Monte Cristo* was the stone he was condemned to push uphill in hell.

The recital of reproach and abuse, yet with an overtone of pride continued. I had sense enough to let it go on without interruption and I did not refer again to what had happened at the theatre that night. In any case my edgewise words could not have dammed the flood. Besides, he would not listen.

We walked along the dark paths of the park, I holding on to his arm and feeling the tremor that shook through his coat sleeve. Several times I mentioned the damp air and suggested that we return to the hotel. His answer each time was "Stay with me."

I stayed with him as we plodded aimlessly through the park, neither of us aware of fatigue so intent was he on revealing his family history and I on listening. At that hour of the morning there were few park loiterers and we had the darkness to ourselves. We walked through it as if in a sleep, compelled to go on toward no goal, but talking in acute wakefulness.

Finally our steps took us toward an exit on 59th Street and we left the blackness of the park behind us. In a few moments we stood in the glare of the hotel lobby. Then Gene, realizing the lateness of the hour, became concerned about my loss of rest and urged me to go home, assuring me the while that he felt better for the walk. We parted with a handshake and an embarrassed embrace.

————

11. *To Saxe Commins from Eugene O'Neill.* TLS 1 p.

Provincetown, Mass.
Sept. 5, 1922

Dear Saxe:

We were certainly damned sorry that you couldn't come—and this latest news that after all it turned out you didn't have to go to New York is too bad. I hope it didn't result in your being cheated out of all vacation and that you did manage to get in a day or so somewhere. You certainly must need it after such a long stretch on the old job.

As for "The Fountain" I can't give you very definite news. All I know is that it will follow that John Barrymore–Hopkins production of Hamlet— which will probably make it sometime in the first part of December.[30] It was to have gone on sooner but the plans have been changed—and I am just as well pleased because I have no stomach for undergoing the ordeal of rehearsals in New York while the hot weather lasts. And also this present plan will give me a month more up here.

August up here was pretty hectic and I'm glad its over. My other son, Eugene,[31] was up here for three weeks, and Jim[32] was here and Agnes' youngest sister.[33] We were pretty well crowded the first part of the month

30. Producer Arthur Hopkins, whose critically praised and highly successful Broadway production of *Hamlet*—starring John Barrymore—opened in Nov. 1922, had optioned *The Fountain* and hoped to get Barrymore for the lead. He was unsuccessful and did not produce the play.

31. Eugene, Jr., was the offspring of O'Neill's first and brief marriage to Kathleen Jenkins; they never lived together as husband and wife, and their son did not know until he was nearly twelve that O'Neill was his father.

32. O'Neill's brother, James O'Neill, Jr.

33. Margery Boulton.

and I find it hard to stay concentrated on anything with so many people flitting about. I've done a lot of rewriting on "The Fountain," as I believe I wrote you before. I think I have improved it immensely. At any rate, taken altogether, I've worked harder on it than on any play so far, and I hope it brings adequate results.

Just what I'll start to work on now I don't know yet. I feel in a sort of scrambled mood and will have to wait until the right moment comes for resuming the drama. There are a lot of things I want to do but I don't seem to be able to make a decision which to tackle first.

I'm glad to hear Teddy and Stella will be back soon. I hope Teddy is going to be in "The Fountain."

The kodak had done some good work for us. It is a dandy. I'll send you some samples when we have copies made. No, the Times photo is one taken by a Boston Post photographer for an interview in that paper. They sent it out, I guess.

All our best to all of you. See you in New York when Fountain time comes around. Remember!

Gene

---

12. *To Saxe Commins from Eugene O'Neill.* ALS 2 pp.
On stationery headed: Peaked Hill Bar / Provincetown, Mass.

August 7, 1923

Dear Saxe:

It was sure good to hear from you. I'm damn sorry you won't get up this summer but perhaps its just as well. Things up here promise to be uncertain from now on—I mean I'm liable to be called away for this or that. For one thing my brother Jim is now in his second sanitarium of the year. He was "nuts complete" when taken there but is sane again now but very sick with alcoholic neuritis.[34] Also *he is almost blind* from bad booze and the *best* they hope for is to get his sight back to *50 percent normal only.* What the hell can be done about him is more than I can figure. He'll only get drunk again, I guess, after he gets out and then he'll be all blind. In the meantime his antics have tied the estate up more than ever and I begin to doubt if we'll ever get a cent out of it.[35]

I believe I remember the Calhern you speak of. Didn't he play in "Roger

34. James O'Neill, Jr., a bachelor deeply attached to his mother, committed suicide the slow way—through drink—after her death. Within two years of her end, he achieved his own on Nov. 8, 1923, at age forty-five.

35. Through the death of his brother, O'Neill inherited the entire family estate, which amounted to over $100,000.

Bloomer"?[36] If so, I thought he was damn fine, although the play itself carried its study of adolescence to the extent of being adolescently badly written and thereby bored me, for I came expecting to see something. However, the evening was made well worth while for me by the performance of the actor who played the Yale man. As I remember his name was Calhern or Calhoun or something similar. If that's your friend, I'm all for him.

It's great news about Stella![37] Teddy wrote me about it. Your Mother must certainly be pleased. How is she now? Fine, I hope. Give her all my most affectionate best—also to your father, your sister & her husband—and to all your family who were so kind to me when I was there.

When I wrote above "just as well" you can't get here, I meant you can come to Ridgefield[38] instead. You can surely arrange to manage that for a week-end, if for no longer. We'll be settled there by "Fountain" time.

I've a favor to ask. Our playful heir has lost the bulb to our kodak—unscrewed it on beach and its in the sand somewhere. Now its impossible to replace here and I don't know where to write exactly. Could you ask them to send one C.O.D.—also a portrait attachment for that sort of camera & a tripod. I wouldn't trouble you but I've lost their booklet which came with the kodak and am all at sea. Now I don't want you to go to any extra trouble about this—just wait till you happen to be around an Eastman supply place and tell them to send collect.

All best to Charlie Kennedy. Has he found any place in Rochester as good as Gilhooleys?[39]

I'll promise to send you some snapshots when we get some good ones—if you'd like them.

Agnes joins in all best to you!

Gene

————

In 1924 O'Neill, together with Kenneth Macgowan and Robert Edmond Jones, reorganized the Provincetown Players and presented plays at both the Provincetown Playhouse and the Greenwich Village Theatre, in New York. The "triumvirate," as they were called, presented the premiere productions of several of O'Neill's own plays, among them *The Ancient Mariner* (opened April 6, 1924), *All God's Chillun Got Wings* (May 15, 1924),

36. *Roger Bloomer*, with Louis Calhern in the cast, was by John Howard Lawson.
37. Stella Ballantine was pregnant with her first child.
38. With proceeds chiefly from *"Anna Christie,"* the playwright in 1922 had purchased Brook Farm in Ridgefield, Conn., a thirty-acre estate with a handsome colonial-style residence.
39. Charles O'Brien Kennedy, an aide of Arthur Hopkins, who was in Rochester for dental work by Commins. Presumably, Gilhooley's was his favorite New York speakeasy.

Desire Under the Elms (November 11, 1924), *The Fountain* (December 10, 1925), and *The Great God Brown* (January 23, 1926).

The O'Neills continued to spend their summers on Cape Cod; but in 1924, rather than going to Ridgefield for the winter, they rented a home in Bermuda. There, on May 13, 1925, their daughter Oona was born. They decided to sell Brook Farm and buy a permanent home in Bermuda. Accordingly, they bought Spithead, a nineteenth-century estate, and while they were renovating it, rented Bellevue, a large mansion. There Gene worked on his new play, *Strange Interlude,* and there Saxe visited him in April 1926.

At the invitation of Gene O'Neill, I visited his home in Hamilton, Bermuda, in April 1926. He was then living in an old eighteenth-century mansion, surrounded by spacious grounds.

During the two weeks of my stay, Gene and I frequently discussed the work upon which he was engaged, as we had done before, on my previous visits to Provincetown, Massachusetts, and Ridgefield, Connecticut. On this occasion, Gene had begun the groundwork for his play *Strange Interlude.* He wrote undisturbed during the mornings; our afternoons were spent bathing and bicycling; and in the evenings we went for long walks.

At that time *An American Tragedy* by Theodore Dreiser had attained immense success and was being discussed everywhere. I recall our talk, on one of our walks, of that book and Gene's first reference to his new play, afterwards named *Strange Interlude.* He said that Dreiser had written the novel of an unexceptional man, whereas he was at work on a novel in dramatic form of an exceptional woman. His play, according to the very meticulous outline contained in his notebooks, indicated the manner in which he would extend the device of masks used in his previous play, *The Great God Brown,* to the use of asides which would indicate the duality of thought and spoken word of his characters.

It was the working out of this problem that he devoted himself to at the time of my visit. I was shown several drawings of the proposed stage settings which O'Neill had made in his notebooks. The manuscript of every one of his plays contains such drawings, as a help in orienting his characters on the stage. I recall, too, our discussions concerning the revolutionary length of the play.

13. To Saxe Commins from Eugene O'Neill. TLS 1 p.

Hamilton, Bermuda,
June 18, 1927

Dear Saxe,

The book[40] arrived shortly after I got back down here. There is nothing to feel badly about. When I saw Ruth[41] I didn't know that the book had been published yet until she showed me her copy. I am very anxious to read it, but I haven't had a chance yet, as I am going over "Strange Interlude," and outside of that my brain is wobbly. I anticipate a good deal of pleasure when I do tackle it. It is damned fine that you have really got down to writing at last. You know I have been telling you for years that you ought to, and I look upon this first book of yours with a very fraternal affection.

Why don't you come down and see us? I mean this seriously. Any time from now on. Bermuda, you know, is becoming a bit of a summer resort. It isn't really any hotter than it is most of the time in the country in the States. And where else can you find bathing like ours? You would be interested in seeing what we have done to Spithead, I know. If the bankroll holds out we will have a fine place. Try and come!

Give my best love to your mother and remember me affectionately to your sister and brother-in-law, and everyone else I know there. I always remember my visit to your home in Rochester with a very warm appreciation.

Yes, all is well with Shane and Oona and Gaga[42] and everyone. We are all in the pink and we'd like to see you.

As ever,
Gene

Contrary to O'Neill's sentiments in his June 18, 1927, letter to Saxe, all was not well in his household. After working through the spring of 1926 on *Strange Interlude* and his next play, *Lazarus Laughed,* he had taken his family to Belgrade Lakes, Maine, for the summer. There he remet Carlotta Monterey, whom he had not seen since her appearance in the Broadway pro-

40. Saxe, who was interested in Freudian theory, wrote *Psychology: A Simplification* with Lloyd Ring Coleman, a friend. It was published in 1927 by Horace Liveright, Inc.

41. One of Saxe's sisters.

42. Mrs. Fifine Clark, housekeeper, cook, and virtually a member of the family, went to work for the O'Neills when Shane was born and was practically a second mother to him. Shane called her Gaga.

duction of *The Hairy Ape*. Carlotta was now free of her third marriage and set out to win O'Neill. When the summer was over, Agnes was fully aware that O'Neill's interest in Carlotta was not transitory.

During the rest of 1926 and 1927 O'Neill put the finishing touches on *Strange Interlude* in Bermuda, returning to New York on several occasions to confer with officials of the Theatre Guild, who were going to produce his play. During these visits to New York he also secretly pursued his relationship with Carlotta. Early in 1928 he made plans to run off with her after the premiere of *Strange Interlude,* scheduled for January 30, 1928. Saxe received an invitation to the premiere, which he attended and O'Neill did not. After the performance he confided his plans to Saxe; on February 10 O'Neill and Carlotta sailed for Europe and settled in France, where they waited for Agnes to file for divorce.

Meanwhile, Saxe and I had also remet in 1927, after not having seen each other for several years. (We had first encountered one another when he was in medical school and he had taken me to Roosevelt Hospital to see an operation performed.) After a brief courtship, we were married on December 24, 1927.

---

14. To Saxe Commins from Eugene O'Neill. WIRE 1 p.
(F New York NY 23 204P)

[January 23, 1928]

Dr Saxe Commins
838 Mercantile Bldg Rochester NY
Invitation first performance of *Interlude* will be next Saturday instead of Sunday see you then

Gene

---

15. To Saxe Commins from Eugene O'Neill. ACS 1 p.

[March 28, 1928]

Dear Saxe:
I'm settled down here and at work again after an interesting motor tour through France. The address is Villa Marguerite, Guéthary, B.P., France. Drop me a line when you get a chance but keep the address under your hat.[43]

43. Fearful of scandal and of being flushed out by the press, O'Neill gave his address to only his most trusted friends and cautioned them against divulging it to anyone.

Have been having a grand vacation. This Basque country is great stuff. All best to your wife and you.

Gene

———

16. *To Saxe Commins from Eugene O'Neill.* TLS 2 pp.

> Villa Marguerite,
> Guéthary, B.P.
> France
> [after June 21, 1928]

Dear Saxe:

This is just a line to say I got your letter and was damned glad to hear from you. I have been meaning to write ever since you wrote me before—but you know how it is.

Don't let anyone know the above address. I have left here a long time ago as far as anyone knows. But it will be a favor if you will advertize it that you have heard from me from Berlin or Vienna or Prague or any other town provided it isn't in France.

Would it be possible for you to separate yourself from your happiness for a few days and come and visit?[44] I would sure love to see you and you would be as welcome here as the flowers in June. Let me know if you can come and when. I would ask both of you but, after giving it careful thought, I am sure that under the present circumstances that would give rise to an uncomfortable situation for all hands concerned. I know you will appreciate what I mean. Later on—and I hope this will be in the not too distant future—when this present mess with Agnes is cleared up it will be grand to have you both any time you can come. I intend to stay here until October 1st.

The fair Aggie's broken heart was transformed over night into a gaping money greed.[45] This is liable to result in a rotten mess because she has engaged a firm of shark lawyers and they are trying to blackmail me—legally, of course—out of so much as the price of a divorce that it would leave me in financial slavery for the rest of my life. This after all I have done for her and hers in the past ten years and the promise on which our marriage was based that either would free the other if they ever fell in love with someone else; strikes me as pretty yellow. Also, for the sake of my own future freedom from financial worry, I have got to fight her demands. I offered her an agreement that guaranteed her from six to ten thousand a year—more than I can

44. Saxe had ended his dental career, and he and his wife had sailed for a year's stay in Paris.

45. Trying to cope with guilt feelings over his abandonment of wife and children, O'Neill had begun to picture Agnes to himself and to others in a most unfavorable light.

really afford—and the only thanks I get is demands for a lot more! Can you beat it! She thinks because I am having a big year that she ought to have it, forgetting that I had to live all the year previous and fix up most of Spithead on my savings and borrowed money.

But enough of that. Outside of the worry and rages this has caused me I have been happy and free as never before and have done about two-thirds of Dynamo and am well satisfied with it. And my health has been good outside of a two weeks lay-up with flu.

Let me hear from you soon. Please try and get here for a few days—and please understand why, for the present nonce, I think it would be uncomfortable and strained stuff for your wife as well as on this end. But I know you will. There's a hell of a lot I'd like to talk over with you and a visit from you would be a big help. Biarritz or La Negresse would be the best stations for you and I would meet you at either. The swimming is wonderful here.

All best, Saxe! Write that you're coming!

Gene

P.S. (over)
P.S. Clippings I've just got from Harry[46] show that Agnes has given a very snotty interview to one of the tabloids![47] She's sure making a cheap fool of herself!

---

17. *To Saxe Commins from Eugene O'Neill.* ALS 2 pp.

Villa Marguerite
Guéthary, B.P.
France
July 9th [1928]

Dear Saxe:

Your letter arrived this a.m. and I was sure damn glad to hear you're coming! You better book through Cooks as soon as you get this as the season is on now and the trains for Biarritz are crowded. We motored here from Paris so I'm not up on the trains. I'd advise you to get a day one and get a look at the country, arriving at Biarritz or La Negresse (these stations are only a mile or so apart—both equally convenient, about eight miles from us, I'll meet you in car) in the evening. There's an all night train getting in at some ungodly hour in the a.m. which I advise against for your sake—and my own! Let us know a couple of days ahead.

Here's one thing, Saxe—and mind you heed it or I'll be sore! The trip here

46. Harry Weinberger, O'Neill's lawyer.
47. The interview had appeared in the New York *Daily News* on June 21, 1928.

is expensive and I absolutely insist that I stake you to the fare! You shouldn't afford it and this is a fat year for me—that is, until Aggie's lawyers finish with me (if I let them get away with it which I'm not going to!) So remember!

I think I can guess the line of bunk that Agnes must have peddled to Stella and Teddy. She has really been pulling some pretty yellow tricks on me, Saxe, and acting as one might expect a chorus girl wife to act, trying to blackmail me out of all she can get just because I'm having a good year.

But never mind that now. It's grand you're coming! Give my best love to Dorothy and my gratitude for giving you up for a few days.

Gene

18. *To Dorothy Commins from Saxe Commins.* ALS 1 p.

[postmarked
July 27, 1928]

Darling,

Here is another letter to mail.[48] Its after one in the morning—I've been up reading the play.[49] It's magnificent, another enormous stride forward in his inexhaustible genius. Just you wait. Mark my prophetic words: it will be a tremendous sensation, greater than any of the others, or I quit as prophet.

How do you feel? This is the time I worry so much about you. By all that's fair, I should be at your side. And here I am basking in this sunlit Utopia without a single care. It isn't right. Assure me at once that you are not ill. If the slightest thing is wrong, wire me and I'll come by the next train. Please.

I love you
Saxe

48. The O'Neills asked Saxe and Dorothy Commins to mail letters for them from Paris so that no one would be able to trace their whereabouts.
49. *Dynamo.*

19. *To Saxe Commins from Eugene O'Neill.* ALS 2 pp.

> Villa Marguerite,
> Guéthary, B.P.
> France
> Friday
> [August 1928]

Dear Saxe:

Your letter arrived yesterday and the script of the first scene this morning.[50] I've glanced through the latter and it sure looks fine to me. But don't break your back getting it done! If it's as hot in Paris as it is here, it's no weather for forced labor! Yesterday and today have been hellish and I feel like a wet rag.

There's no news to speak of. Before the hot spell hit us I had the Fast Blond[51] out for a couple of practice spins and it sure is a grand little boat! But there's no fun driving in this weather and I've laid off it.

The nifty loose-leaf book hasn't arrived yet but suppose it will tomorrow. As for a clamp book, that will be quite O.K. in cardboard so go ahead and get one.

I'm glad to hear the studio is developing so well—also that my dragging you off down here at least had some recompense for Dorothy and inspired her to composition. I'd love to hear it and hope I'll get the chance in Paris.

We're so tickled you enjoyed your visit here. It was sure grand to have you! I'm sorry we couldn't have had more of the Blond's company together—but she'll be here next time.

This is only a note. I'm dissolving in sweat. The humidity is vile with not a breath stirring.

Much love to you both!

> As ever,
> Gene

P.S. Don't say anything of my motors to Fitzie![52] It's better not. If A.[53] knew I had a car she'd raise the ante 100000 out of pure spite! I meant to warn you of this. For public consumption, I have bought a bicycle!

50. When O'Neill expressed reluctance to entrust his handwritten script of *Dynamo* to a stranger to be typed, Saxe volunteered for the task.
51. A blond Renault roadster.
52. M. Eleanor Fitzgerald. Her nickname was usually spelled "Fitzi."
53. Agnes.

20. *To Saxe Commins from Carlotta Monterey.* ALS 6 pp.

Aug. 9th 1928

Dear Saxe,—

Your more than kind letter reached me & I *blushed* when reading your un-deserved praise. Oh—Saxe, one dreams of *creating* & *being* the perfect lover,—friend & human being,—one *craves* & *yearns* to be just "this" or "that"—but how short we fall!— At least—such is *my* case! Sometimes all strength seems to leave me— —and then there is nothing but a knowledge that even *physical* strength isn't there to fight—and smile—hope!—

The parts of "Dynamo" arrive—Gene asks me to thank you—& also to send a *special* thanks for the photographs of you & Dorothy that you so kindly sent!— — Work goes on.

I am busy getting a villa for next summer in Biarritz—a more modern house—One's servants can do so much more if they have the wherewithal to work with.

The "water pipes" in the kitchen range were *at last* repaired—which neces-sitated the sweeping of the chimney (which I *know* hadn't been cleaned since the time of Napoleon I!) & my God! had you but seen Villa Marguerite. We were "soot" from top to bottom! Houses *must* be modern I have dis-covered! —At least for cranks like me who hate dirt—!

Let me know what Calmy[54] says re "Interlude"—

Gene has only gone out in the Canary[55] once since you left. We simply haven't had time!

The teeth are all re-done—& *seem* most satisfactory! All the front re-done with the Steele facings (?)![56]— — *That* has taken two or three afternoons.—

I am busy now arranging all the Hong Kong business[57] so Gene will have no thought of *that.*— When we leave here in Sept. there will be no debts or strings— just an "adieu!"— I listen to tales of *debts, confusions,* & *indecisions* & really I can't understand such half wittedness![58] My parents would have had me locked up for weak mindedness had I ever seemed so uncertain of my desires & ways & means!— —

Oh—well,— —*someday* there will be *peace*—& Gene and I will be able to

54. Monsieur Calmy (first name unknown) had been commissioned to translate *Strange Interlude* into French.

55. The Renault roadster.

56. O'Neill, whose teeth were in poor shape, frequently underwent dental treatment over a long period of years.

57. From childhood onward, O'Neill had yearned to visit the Orient, and now he and Carlotta were planning such a trip.

58. An attack on Agnes.

take each other by the hand & go out into the sunlight & forget the "miasma" of the Past!

It makes us glad to hear of your & Dorothy's happiness—but I know you two have earned it! Bless you both!

No more gossip— But our love always,—

Carlotta

---

21. *To Saxe Commins from Carlotta Monterey.* ALS 3 pp.

[postmarked Guéthary
August 16, 1928]
Sunday—

Dear Saxe,

Gene has asked me to answer your letter as he is busy. I am to say *"yes"* to Calmy's suggestions of one year's option (!)—in regard to "Interlude." I *do* hope he does a job of it,— because I want my adored "Lazarus"[59] translated.— But the man who does "Lazarus" must not only know (in the *finer sense*) French & English—but he must be *in his bones* a poet! A *real* poet! I do not know this Calmy—perhaps he is all this!——

Go in any shop & ask for their *best* petrole, (what is burned in lamps!) here—in this particular vicinity—the most rarified, answers to the name of "Luculine"! Do *not* put on too much—but see that it gets *in* to the scalp! Let it rest for a bit, if you wish, & then wash your hair. Putting lemon juice into the water acts as a harmless softener! If you rub all the oil (possible) out of your hair with an old cloth first—it makes the washing easier. This is a marvellous *cleanser* & *tonic* for the head!—

"Things" still go on—sometimes maddeningly—but Gene & I are *"put"*— so the "miasma" does not go beyond causing *nausea!*—[60]

We are still searching houses—but saw a divine chateau *not* for sale, & valued at 2,000,000 francs. It would have been a perfect setting for our love!

God bless you both—
Carlotta—

59. *Lazarus Laughed*, completed in June 1926 and published by Boni and Liveright in 1927, had never been produced on Broadway. It had received its first professional stage production in April 1928 at the Pasadena (Cal.) Community Playhouse, where it ran for twenty-eight performances.

60. O'Neill and Carlotta were upset and angry that Agnes still had not filed for a divorce.

22. *To Saxe Comins from Carlotta Monterey.* ALS 4 pp.

[August 1928]
Saturday Night

Saxe dear,—

I hope you got my wire telling you of the safe arrival of the scripts. They were very well done. Gene is in the dining-room now blue pencilling etc.— We will both be glad to get them finished & out of the house.

Saxe I want to get something for Gene & am afraid I won't have time when we get to Paris— I want a book for him to write his next play in— but— I want lined (good) paper the *size* of the enclosed sample,— & 300 sheets—*bound in brown tooled leather!*— The tooling *in gold!*— Brown-gold *end-papers!*— The paper must be decent to write on, that is *most* essential—it needn't be *too* thick or two thin! I feel certain you know the kind of thing— I also feel certain you know what I mean.

Enclosed 1000 francs—if you need more let me know. I want this to have a dignified, solid design of tooling—not too "chi chi"—

It has been rather warm for two days—but "God is Love & all is divine"— & my heart sings,—in spite of—the heat!—

Don't let the gnats annoy you dear Saxe.

Work—& live—& love & keep your head in the stars.

Gene is well and I know will be glad to start away on our great adventure—, and new work—& new Life.——

Hope Dorothy is well,— and that you two keep your own world complete— paying no heed to the outside envious ones.—

Our love always,—
Carlotta

23. *To Saxe Commins from Carlotta Monterey.* ALS 3 pp.

Tuesday, A.M.
[August 1928]

My dear Saxe,—

Gene asks me to write and tell you that all is well—& that he is working hard—.

Poor dear— he is trying to finish "Dynamo" before leaving for Paris— and I know to *finish* a play must be hell!— For one becomes depressed about it all—uncertain—and (so I *imagine*) *fed up* with the subject! However, I must add that my Lover looks extremely well, is dear beyond words—& I adore him! (News for Saxe!)——

The weather has changed completely—from dry, hot, sun-shiney weather we have dull, cloudy, grey skies! But pleasurable!——

Enclosed is a letter Gene wants you to please post for him.—

I wrote to Louis[61]—gave him your address & told him that you wished to hear from him!

My time is occupied now in making "lists" of all the things to be attended to—to close this house & get off on our journey—! I *know* it will bring a great deal to both Gene & me.—

We will see you soon now—and as soon as I finish up my "business affairs" will look forward to a pleasant evening with you & your charming wife. I am *more than anxious* to know her!—

With love to you both—from Gene and

Carlotta

---

24. *To Dorothy Commins from Carlotta Monterey.* ALS 2 pp.

"Villa Marguerite"—
Guethary, B.-P.
Aug. 20th, 1928

Dear Mrs. Commins,

I would be so pleased if you & Saxe could dine with Gene and me at the Hotel du Rhin, Place Vendôme, next Saturday evening at eight o'clock.— I am also asking Mr. Kalonyme so it will be just a family dinner. I am looking forward, with such pleasure, to meeting you!

Very sincerely,
Carlotta Monterey

---

25. *To Saxe Commins from Carlotta Monterey.* ALS 2 pp.

Wednesday
[September] 5th 1928

Saxe, my dear.—

Just a hasty line before we fly into town. Gene says to tell you the "linen envelope" arrived. —nothing else!—

I—too—am alive with "Dynamo"—but Gene at the stage of wondering if it

61. Probably Louis Kalonyme, also known as Louis Kantor, a free-lance journalist who used to run and fetch for O'Neill in Greenwich Village and Provincetown, whom Saxe also knew from his visits to New York from Rochester.

is *rotten* or *what not!* A perfectly healthy re-action at this stage for the Creator! I understand & soothe—! This Lover of mine is also my child—& living beside him thro' Fire & Beauty has greatly developed & enriched the inner me;—so that he will get back—*thro' that*—greater love & understanding *from* me—thro' *our* love! My God—have I made that sound complicated? It really is *so* simple—I just love him—that's all!—

Dear Saxe, please pay *no* attention to letters from *anyone!* The "failures" in this life can't bear seeing others bear fruit!—— My dear—*smile*—& hug Dorothy!

The process of elimination is necessary but difficult, dear child;—we must separate the sheep from the goats! God bless you both—our love—

Carlotta

---

26. *To Saxe Commins from Carlotta Monterey.* ALS 2 pp.

Friday
[September 1928]

Saxe dear—

Gene asks me to thank you for your very nice letter—"Pete's"[62] letter—& the translation—which he thought pretty good. You were a darling to go to all that fuss.

Enclosed dear—two letters for the post. —Please.

I want to thank you for your dear letter to me & also say how very grateful I am to you for ordering the book. —I hope—Saxe—to be able to do commissions for you some day!

I am doctoring my child[63] thro' a case of liver—a worry period—(damn that half wit woman!)[64] and a little anxious moment regarding the Guild's opinion of "Dynamo"! I understand it all so well & thank God for the privilege of looking after him—for *in spite of her would-be revenge* & the battle of Life he *blossoms!*—Of course we say nothing of this!

Here's the post man—

Our love to you & dear Dorothy—

Carlotta

62. Pete Gross, an employee of Liveright's.
63. The relationship between Carlotta and O'Neill was in some degree a mother-son relationship. She used to say, "I was his wife, mistress, nurse and secretary."
64. Agnes.

27. *To Saxe Commins from Carlotta Monterey.* ALS 3 pp.
On stationery headed: Messageries / Maritimes

Sunday Oct. 7th '28

Saxe-dear-dear person,

Your wire touched me more than you will ever know!

After the boat had left I went in Gene's cabin to help him arrange his things & *there* & *then* we found the cable from the *Guild* saying they *accepted* "Dynamo"—*all of them,* & wished Gene Bon Voyage!—I had worried so long & was so *at end* I wept like a fool & could have died! But it was a divine send off & Gene is resting & relaxing & is his dear *un*-worried self! God—what a lovely soul that lover of mine has—what a fortunate woman I am!—And God knows I appreciate him & only pray to God I'll be able to make him happy & give him Peace! We are passing thro' the Straits of Messina. Divine weather & smooth sea—— I'll write later of the boat etc. It is all amusing & French!

God bless you & Dorothy—

Live your own lives!—

Love from Gene & Carlotta

28. *To Saxe Commins from Eugene O'Neill.* ACS 1 p.

[postmarked
October 15, 1928]

Dear Saxe:

This written just as we're in the act of getting East of Suez. I'm fine. Good weather so far. Getting hotter. C. has written you about the Guild cabling acceptance "Dynamo." So that's that and a weight is off my mind!

Much love to you both & much gratitude for your sensitive kindness!

Gene

29. *To Saxe Commins from Eugene O'Neill.* ACS 1 p.

[postmarked
October 29, 1928]

Dear Saxe:

This place in French Somaliland desolate but interesting. Am writing this on the Indian Ocean. Arrive Colombo, Ceylon tomorrow. Have been working all morning every day in cabin on "It Cannot Be Mad,"[65] getting it ready to do. Good, this! A poor uninteresting crowd on board—petty officials off to their jobs—very depressing to look upon in the tropic heat.

C. joins in all best to D. & you.

Much love
Gene

---

30. *To Saxe Commins from Eugene O'Neill.* ACS 1 p.

[November 1928]

Dear Saxe:

This Saigon is quite some town—the most interesting so far! I'm a bit under the weather—got a touch of sun in Singapore—and C. is also suffering from the tropic heat. We're here for a few days—then on to Hong Kong where we hope the higher latitudes will soon return us to "the pink."

Love to you & D
Gene

---

31. *To Saxe Commins from Eugene O'Neill.* ACS 1 p.

[November 1928]

Dear Saxe:

Have decided not to stay here.[66] Not interesting and climate damp and enervating—bad for work. So on to Japan! We'll probably settle there. Let you know. Feel punk. Bad cold. Tropics wore me out.

Love D & you,
Gene

65. O'Neill originally planned *Dynamo* as the first play in a trilogy that would, as he explained in an Aug. 26, 1928, letter to critic George Jean Nathan, "dig at the roots of the sickness of Today as I feel it—the death of the old God and the failure of Science and Materialism to give a satisfying new one." The "other two plays," he added, "will be 'Without Ending of Day's' and 'It Cannot Be Mad.'" Though he later dropped the idea of the plays as a trilogy, he wrote the middle one under the title *Days Without End* (1934); he never completed the final one.

66. The picture on the front of the card is captioned "Aberdeen, Hongkong."

32. To Saxe Commins from Carlotta Monterey. ALS 4 pp.

Villa "Les Mimosas,"–
Boulevard de la Mer,
Cap d'Ail (A.-M.)
France
Jan. 30th 1929

Saxe dear,–bless your darling heart–you **mustn't** believe what you **read** in the newspapers! Good *or* bad!–Seriously speaking **Gene** & I both had bronchitis in Shanghai,–but *he* had been naughty & insisted upon going in swimming in Singapore,–there he got a touch of sun–which was not good for nerves!– We, unfortunately, ran into riff raff reporters in the Orient,–they *snooped*–& Gene was driven crazy having to do things he detested doing trying to keep *my* name out of it! *I* could have murdered them!– When the boat reached Manila we went thro' the same thing! I do not know why Americans can't mind their own business! Other nations (in the newspaper world) seem so much more civilized & even, if curious, have better manners!– But–the trip East was a *marvellous* experience & we will always be glad we went![67]–

Gene is busy trying to get arranged as to papers & work,–I also as regards house etc.–

We will be in Paris before you leave & look forward to seeing you & Dorothy[68]–

What is all this about your being ill? Saxe dear, I am afraid you allow "people" to worry you.– Never will you be *really* happy until you set yourself on the mountain tops with your beloved–& forget the outside world!– That makes work easier too!– Gene is *blooming*–! He has gained so much. I sit back & admire & adore! What happier lot for a woman?–

Please keep well–

Our fondest love to you both–. When Gene gets to writing letters you will hear from him. At present I am the letter writer!

God bless you both–

Carlotta

"Strange Interlude" opened *one year* ago to-night!

67. The trip to the Far East was more turbulent and distressing to the pair than her report suggests. In Shanghai they fell out so violently–shortly before O'Neill, suffering from the flu and alcoholism, was taken to a hospital–that Carlotta moved to another hotel. After a reconciliation, dissension between them flared again so badly, as they were sailing back to Europe, that she left the ship for another. Before long, though, they once again were reunited.

68. With their year's stay in Paris about over, Saxe and Dorothy Commins were set to return home in spring 1929.

---

33. *To Saxe Commins from Carlotta Monterey.* ALS 2 pp.

[February 28, 1929]
[Cap d'Ail]
Thursday

Dear Saxe,

We are both delighted to know you enjoyed your few days with us.— I am particularly happy that Dorothy came with you—for it gave us an opportunity to see each other *as we are!* I know you are intelligent enough & fine enough to appreciate what Jehovah has given you.—

My life goes on. No variation. Gene is working & we wait for a new car— & mean while plan our future *home.* In America!

Keep well & don't forget to eat vegetables!! Poor you!—But it *was* good for you!

Tell Dorothy I am sending, under separate cover, the blue skirt I neglected to give her before she left. I had spoken of it to her.—

With fondest love to you both,

Carlotta

---

34. *To Saxe Commins from Carlotta Monterey.* ALS 2 pp.*

[postmarked March 2, 1929]

Saxe dear.—

Thank you so much for the photos—but if you don't write & tell me *truthfully* how much I owe you for them I will never ask you to do anything for me again! *There!—* Don't you be such a silly over money—you give it so much importance in one way & not enough in another!

Scolding over—now to abject apology.— When Gene looked over the photographs he destroyed all of me (but the one sitting on the stairs with him)— & some of him, & those of Dorothy that he thought did not do her justice! Also the *films!* So I can't send you the films—I *am* so sorry dear.—

I sacked the cook & now we have a really good one. So come again before you leave & I'll give you both *really good food!* It was terrible when you were here before.—

Gene is working—and well & I think not too perturbed over fools not understanding what "Dynamo" is about! Thank God the opinions of the Masses means nothing to him.[69]

Love to Dorothy & you dear Saxe from us both—

Carlotta

---

35. To Saxe Commins from Carlotta Monterey. ALS 2 pp.

[postmarked March 4,
1929]

Saxe dear.—

The snaps arrived & I think some are excellent. Good God,—I knew I had a long nose—but as I grow older it gets worse. When I am sixty I will look like an ant eater!——

Gene feeling more settled & we have commenced our really work regime—. Up at eight etc.—

The "Transition"[70] arrived—many thanks—It sounds like a college paper (to me) after reading Spengler!

The criticisms from N.Y. stupid—& have meant nothing to G. Only time can tell! ("I" feel that *25 years from now* the real questions will be answered.)

My love to Dorothy.— The sun shines—but the wind still blows.— I think of you both so much. *Try* elimination Saxe— it gives one more love for the few! And strength too! (Forgive my punctuation.— Gene has made me so self conscious about writing letters—but *you* understand I am sure—it's just *me*—not a writer!—)

Best love always to you both—
Carlotta

---

36. To Eugene O'Neill from Saxe Commins. TL(cc) 3 pp.

March 15, 1929

Dear Gene,

At the risk of seeming to be under the influence of hop or trying to kid you with a fantastic tale, let me describe some of the strange antics Dorothy

69. *Dynamo* had opened on Feb. 11, 1929, at the Martin Beck Theatre and had been harshly criticized by most reviewers; it lasted for fifty performances.

70. Founded and edited in Paris by Eugene Jolas, *Transition* (1927–1938) was a leading avant-garde periodical of its day.

and I witnessed at a meeting of a group of Ghourdieffists[71] last night. You may find some material in it, if you can disentangle my report. My own recollection of the affair being as if I had seen it through a glass darkly.

At the invitation of Margaret Anderson[72] we wandered over to a very elaborate apartment on the Quai Bourbon, Isle St. Louis. On entering it, we saw a man, more or less, contorting for the benefit of a few indeterminate ladies. He was practising the first part of the Ghourdieff rites, which, as we were to learn a little later, were a method for releasing the three centers, physical, emotional and intellectual, synchronising them and lifting them toward the planets beyond the milky way, seven in number by actual mathematical calculation on the part of Mr. G. But the exercises themselves were led by a lady who might have closed the gym a minute before in the Y.W.C.A. She led the count and watched lest the aspirants toward perfection did not sneak anything over. Hands must be fixed, palms in, arms making the perfect geometrical design traced by the master by which harmony of movement ushers in a universal harmony of the world. When done privately these exercises must be timed to phrases like these: "I want to be glad." "I can work." "My sorrow is past." We were given to understand that these exercises are not calisthenic nor are they meant to give greater suppleness to the body or greater strength. They are solely the means by which the physical center is brought into equilibrium and are based entirely on the rhythmic meaning of the new planes in which *the* method leads the aspirant.

For two hours 10 ladies and one so-called man cavorted. Occasionally there were complaints but these were silenced quickly by the tender solicitude of a sweet young gal who would caress away the hurt or by the hard-boiled Ghourdieff recruit sergeant who held up the shining example of the master. As for the dancers, one glance at them would make any wavering young woman a confirmed hetero. A second might lead her to the excesses of nymphomania.

While "cutting the air as with a pair of scissors," one hand over the other on the top of the head, a girl had the temerity to complain "But this doesn't seem abstract to me." A few dirty looks silenced her. The lone man said something about the "higher consciousness" and continued to do his stuff with the seriousness of an advanced pupil. He was wonderful when he cut the air as with a scissors right over the top of his bald head, and everyone ad-

71. Disciples of George Ivanovich Gurdjieff (1877–1949), founder and high priest of a cult, based in France, which held that serenity and self-control could be attained through a system of exercises performed to music.

72. Founding editor of the *Little Review*, begun in Chicago in 1914. This important "little magazine" published Joyce, Eliot, Yeats, Pound, Hemingway, Marianne Moore, Wallace Stevens, William Carlos Williams, and Hart Crane, and had moved to Paris after World War I. In 1962 Margaret Anderson published *The Unknowable Gurdjieff*, giving the history of her devotion to the cult.

mitted him to be the leader of the class. That baby was good, and if he can swing his emotional and intellectual centers as effectively as he can "the first circle which represents the physical" he is on his way to grace.

Finally Jean Heap[73] arrived. No need to picture her. Realism becomes caricature. Busily she hung up a few charts on the wall and began her little chat. The charts represented the spectrum, from the seven colors of which the seven notes of the scale are drawn ending finally in the note "sol," which is sun. The octave is the plan of the universe and one must work one's way up from *do* to whatever point our mean little equipment will allow. The bald fairy was somewhere near Fah. So was the line of the real world under which were ranked the invertebrates, and believe me, they have a ranking that would stagger the ghost of Huxley.[74] To hear Jane put pigs and rhinocerouses and poets and polar bears into their categories according to the musical scale is something that had never been dreamed of in my philosophy.

Having disposed of the solar system and the civilization of the lost Atlantis, she went on to talk about writers, calling on the class to recite the five categories of writing and to give examples of authors as they fit into each class. I took the trouble to remember this fantastic mummery and Dorothy will bear me out that this is an exact transcript of what was written on the blackboard:

1. Tubercular   Keats, Stevenson, all romantics
2. Venereal   Joyce
3. Alcoholic and Sex   Defoe, Poe
4. Epileptic   Dostoievsky
5. Constipated   Shaw, Dreiser

I'm not kidding. When someone asked why Joyce was considered a venereal writer, Jane snapped back "Everyone knows he has syphilis." Annoyed for the first time sufficiently to stop laughing, I challenged her, saying she had no right to make such a statement unless she was pretty certain of her facts. "Well," was her priceless remark "To what else can we attribute the trouble with his eyes." A man is a constipated writer, Shaw being the example, because it seemed to Jane that he had to squeeze to make it come out. These, understand, are inflexible categories, the result of the master's long contemplation and mathematical inquiries. The list originally numbered some diseases that Osler[75] never thought about, but higher cogitation brought the number down to the irreducible minimum of five. There is also a most ingenious arrangement of "the higher motivating forces," which to my be-

73. Miss Anderson's assistant editor on the *Little Review*, who, after it moved to Paris, increasingly assumed editorial responsibility for the magazine.

74. Thomas H. Huxley (1825–95), the English biologist and exponent of Darwinism.

75. Sir William Osler (1849–1919), an outstanding Canadian physician, medical historian, and teacher in Canada, the United States, and Britain.

nighted brain looked very much like the old-time instincts of the psychologist. Oh no, they are a curious group of adjectives that describe what ordinary people used to call modifiers. The word "lying" is something or other special in this group and faithful and fierce and passive or what have you, to make some mystic number that fits in a circle and can be multiplied by seven or divided by the line under Fah in the scale, which is the plane on which disorganized centers are cavorting in the name of present day living. Something like that. I'm not drunk.

Inquiry about Mr. Ghourdieff revealed that he is not a Russian but a Greek "A black Greek with an overwhelming eye," he is writing a three volume book in four languages all at once, speaks 36 dialects and manages to keep an international cult busy paying him reverence and whatever else he can get besides. Rasputin[76] could have learned a few tricks from him. Apparently his chief disciples are Orage[77] and Ouspenskai[78] of Tertium Organum fame. Jane claims the honor of being his right hand man, so to speak. A little farther along the line are the gals we met last night, straight from Fontainblau.[79] You should have seen some of them; imagination never could picture them. One little gal looked like a five months old foetus, the kind that they keep preserved in alcohol in a Fourteenth Street Museum. It was she who talked a great deal about the vibrations of her consciousness, giving it electrical waves and trying to figure out how the current effects the "higher motivating centers of sex and fear and self pity."

No good to attempt to add confusion on confusion. If you get a portion of the picture, its more than enough and more than should be inflicted on you. I thought before last night that I had seen how sterile a cult could be. But now I know how sterile and funny it can be. A dictaphone record of the proceedings would be a piece of data valuable beyond price. As it was, I felt like a bit of a sneak, horning in where I didn't belong. But my curiosity is satisfied now. The general conviction I have is that the emotional, physical and intellectual centers can be located somewhere below the belt.

But, what the hell?

76. Grigori Yefimovich Rasputin (1872–1916), the illiterate, corrupt Russian monk who had a malign influence—during the World War I era—over the Empress Alexandra Feodorovna.

77. Alfred R. Orage (1873–1934), at one time editor of the British periodical *New Age* and a disciple of Gurdjieff.

78. P. D. Ouspensky (1878–1947), author of *Tertium Organum* (1911), and a Russian émigré philosopher, novelist, and writer on the occult.

79. A château in Fontainebleau, called the Institute for the Harmonious Development of Man, was the headquarters of the Gurdjieff movement.

37. *To Saxe Commins from Carlotta Monterey.* ALS 2 pp.

> *Monday night*
> [March 25? 1929]

Saxe dear,—

Gene had intended writing to you himself but is up to his ears with proof reading—& signing special editions etc.— So——he has asked [me] to tell you how we enjoyed & giggled over your very amusing letter. My God—what cripples those poor dears are! To me they are pathological cases! But "each to his own," said the old lady, etc.—& that's that.

François[80] is on his way down from Paris with our new car[81]—so that's that! Am glad it is settled—. This Foch funeral[82] must be a very impressive thing. But (perhaps it is wrong for me to say so) I feel that the Germans were *starved out*—poor devils—much more than beaten by War tactics! But then I loathe war—from *any* & *all* classes & Nations!

I am already in negotiations for our house in Touraine—at which place I hope to be set for some time—I am weary of this eternal moving—& it's so terribly expensive!—

Love to Dorothy & you & God bless you both—

> Love from Gene too!
> Carlotta

38. *To Dorothy Commins from Carlotta Monterey.* ALS 3 pp.

> [postmarked April 1,
> 1929]

Dorothy dear,—

Thank you *so* much for the two lovely records. If you see—(*hear*) any good Debussy records would you be kind enough to order them for us—or *Bach*— Oh,—I *do* wish you & Saxe were here now. You're both such dears & I love you—& the sun shines & the cook is good. And Gene seems at peace & *at last* honestly happy from *every* point of view!

I have *fallen* & gone to Molyneux's & ordered 2 evening dresses—2 coats &

80. The couple's chauffeur.
81. A Renault sedan.
82. Ferdinand Foch, marshal of France, who was supreme commander of the British, French, and American armies in the final year of World War I, died on March 21, 1929, and his funeral took place on March 27, 1929.

skirts, & 2 afternoon frocks! (Gene says it's good to see pretty things & know he won't receive the bill!) Now I'm set for a longtime!

Our love to you both—
Carlotta

We *adored* Saxe's letter!

---

39. *To Saxe Commins from Eugene O'Neill.* WIRE 1 p.

[April 7?, 1929]

1181
Saxe Commins 11 rue
Schoelcher Paris 14—
    CapdAil 421 38 7 8 30—
Have been writing new scenes into Dynamo for publication Have you time and do you care to type these If so will mail to you immediately This is business Best from us

—Gene—

---

40. *To Saxe Commins from Eugene O'Neill.* ALS 1 p.

[April 1929]
(Two carbons will be
plenty)

Dear Saxe:

Herewith are the first two scenes I have written in. I'll mail you the third one in a day or so. Much gratitude to you for offering to do this! I don't know what I'd do otherwise.

I'm doing all this labor on *Dynamo* not because of any of the boob critics outcry of bunk, as you well know, and not because of its failure as a production, but simply because, ever since I read it over after my return to Europe—too late to do anything for the production—I've felt extremely dissatisfied with it. One of my main ideas in the play—what the treachery of his mother does to him in taking his father's (and his father's God's) side against him, his obscure concealed from himself longing for her and what the news of her death does to him, and finally how he finds her again in the *Dynamo*—the God Mother—who demands the sacrifice of the girl's life because he has been untrue to Her—all this got completely lost in the obvious-religious struggle in the latter portion of the play and left it dehumanized and unconvincing to me. It is this I am trying to clear up and emphasize in my rewriting so that it can at least be what I hoped for it in the book and when it is produced over here. I want it to be above everything the story of that human boy and the psychological mess he gets into and his mad solution via a combination of his deep inner yearnings, his Fundamentalist upbringing, and the popular science books.

As for instructions, Saxe, there ain't none. You can follow where it's thought and where speech easily enough.

Of course I'm greatly cutting down and simplifying the rest of the play to make way for these new scenes. It needs this cutting in any event.

Have finished Act One of the new one[83] but have had to lay it aside for this work.

Much love to Dorothy and you! I hope we'll be able to get to Paris before you leave. It's quite probable as we're going to Touraine house hunting soon. (Keep Touraine under your hat)

Gene

---

41. *To Saxe Commins from Eugene O'Neill.* ALS 1 p.

[April 1929]

Dear Saxe:

Herewith are the last two segments of the new version. I've clipped them seperately so you won't get mixed. One is an entirely new scene between Rueben & Mrs. Fife which opens the third act. The other is an insert later on in the act to condense the old elements in accordance with the new development of theme.

All best from us both to both of you!

Gene

P.S. If you're still on what I sent you before, you will note that since I wrote them I am changing "generator" wherever found to "dynamo" so as not to confuse readers and you might follow that change in those last scenes of Act Two.

---

42. *To Saxe Commins from Carlotta Monterey.* WIRE 1 p.

[postmarked April 12, 1929]

Saxe Commins 11 rue Schoelcher
Paris 14—
CapdAil 13 17 12 1020—
Hold second installment script until you see or hear from us

Carlotta—

83. "It Cannot Be Mad." See letter 29, n. 65.

---

43. *To Saxe Commins from Carlotta Monterey.* ALS 2 pp.

April 12th 1929

Saxe dear—

We will be in Paris to bid you farewell!— Did you receive my wire asking you to *hold* the second installment of the script?— "If" you have time in the midst of all your packing etc., will find out how many plays of Lenormand's have been translated into English and order same for us.— We will collect our books from you—so they will not have to be sent.

Heaps of love to Dorothy & you from us—

Carlotta

Don't you two attempt doing too much—.

---

44. *To Saxe Commins from Carlotta Monterey.* WIRE 1 p.

[April 1929]

Urgent Saxe Commins 11
rue Schoelcher Paris 14—
Urgent Guethary 164 12 7 14 25—
Scripts arrived Splendid job Love—

Carlotta

---

45. *To Saxe Commins from Carlotta Monterey.* WIRE 1 p.

[postmarked April 20, 1929]

Saxe Commins 11 rue Schoelcher
Paris 14—
De Tours 5771 14 20 1620—
Telephone us Hotel du Rhin Sunday eight evening—

Carlotta

46. *To Horace Liveright from Eugene O'Neill.* ALS 2 pp.[84]
On stationery headed: Hotel du Rhin / 4 et 6, Place Vendôme / Paris

April 21st [1929]

Dear Horace:

The bearer, Saxe Commins, tells me that, in spite of being one of your authors, you don't know him very well—so this note is by way of being a reintroduction to you. Saxe has been one of my oldest and best friends for a great many years, and I recommend him to your friendship because he is most certainly one of the whitest human beings that I have ever met!

Also, as you know from his book on psychology,[85] he can write and think!

The special point of all which is that Saxe is returning to the States, after a honeymoon year in France, to pick up the loose ends and start the daily bread battle again. If you could find something for him around your place, I'm sure you'd find him of great value. (Pete Gross knows Saxe well and will add his voucher to mine.) But if you're full up, then all I want to say is that anything you can do to lend him a hand in getting started again will certainly be appreciated as a great personal favor by

Your's as ever,
Gene

47. *To Saxe Commins from Carlotta Monterey.* ALS 2 pp.

May 1st 1929

Saxe dear,—

The Lenormand book of three plays[86] has arrived—many thanks—. We are in that unsettled state of planning to move—going over the lease etc., with a lawyer & I making endless lists of what nots! Oh—it will be such a joy to be *put—really* put—for a bit—.

But—to know you and Dorothy are *not* in France will be horrid.

However—time passes and you will come back to us.—

I want to take this opportunity to thank you & Dorothy for your charming *giving of friendship* to me! I know so well how difficult it is to take a new person in the house of an old friend—& you have been so *generous* & so *mannerly* in your giving & understanding. Some of G's friends have not been so—(they have not been in our house) but I really don't mind—because I

84. O'Neill gave this letter to Saxe as an introduction to his publisher.
85. See letter 13, n. 40.

have no desire to know them—or give even courtesy to them!— So that is that! Life goes on—& with it only Beauty in all things,—at least—only the Beauty remains. I wish you both so much happiness and success. And *please* wrap yourselves in each others love and understanding,—& only pity the "failures" who would, by destructive criticism, besmirch your lovely home—, your perfect understanding. Remember wherever Gene & I are you both are welcome & always have your place with us.— Also know *we know* we have our place with you.

Jehovah bless you both—

With love from Gene and

Carlotta

The records haven't arrived yet—but thank you so much for sending them. We'll listen to them and think of you.

———————

48. To Saxe Commins from Carlotta Monterey. ALS 3 pp.

May 6th 1929

Saxe dear—

I am still *goose-flesh* from listening to the Bach & Beethoven records you & Dorothy so kindly sent. The Debussy *would* have been lovely only, unfortunately, it was broken in its sending!—A *thousand* thanks! I can't tell you the pleasure I shall get from hearing these over & over again.— Gene loved them too. Gene is writing you too—so this from me only my thanks & my love & bon voyage.

Bless you both always—

Carlotta

For *me* please,—give any one who makes a facetious remark about Gene— a good *kick in their sit down!* These cowardly ones who have *sat on the fence* until they were certain his [and] my love was a sincere & lovely thing! These would-be old *friends!* Show them the door dear.—(in your heart).

86. Probably *Three Plays: The Dream Doctor, Man and His Phantoms, The Coward,* translated by D. L. Orna, published in 1928 by Payson and Clarke of New York. Henri-René Lenormand was a French playwright with whom O'Neill had become friendly.

---

49. To Saxe Commins from Eugene O'Neill. ALS 3 pp.

> Villa Les Mimosas,
> Cap d'Ail, A.M.
> April 6th 1929
> [May 6, 1929][87]

Dear Saxe:

Well, I've been thinking over what services I can burden you with in God's (?) Country but I don't seem to grab on to much—except I can give you a line of what brand of chatter to hand out to all and sundry of my friends who are doing so much heavy worrying about my domestic future and the state of my artistic soul, etc. Of course, as far as how I am happy, etc. you can simply tell them the truth—that I am happy and doing no re-pining. My plans for living abroad henceforth you can divulge but not where I intend making my home. Say that I am undecided about that but probably it will be France. Don't say anything about my gorgeous Renault—make it a small Renault. As for my plans for this coming summer, say that C. & I are planning a honeymoon trip somewhere—probably to Greece—that was the last you heard. Say that I'm on a new play—not one of the trilogy—and you've heard the idea for it but it's a dead secret. Add that although I may have it finished by next season, it is doubtful if I shall want it produced then as I am determined to give more time to my stuff in future. Add to that whatever you may have gotten from all I told you that night as to the change in me in regard to living and working. Say that the failure of *Dynamo* left me cold—that I was not satisfied with it when I read it over on returning from the East and have worked on it for the book, putting in two new scenes I had originally planned for it. Lay emphasis on the change in my state of mind—my new-found content, etc. I rely on you, Saxe, to do all you can to set the boys right on all the bunk that has floated about.

You can let the P. P.[88] bunch know that I feel fairly sore at them because not a damn one has written to me. Jimmy,[89] for example, has owed me a letter for ages.

87. Although O'Neill dated this letter April 6, 1929, the reference to the Lenormand books having arrived and Carlotta's reference to "Gene is writing too" in her May 6, 1929, letter indicate he misdated it.

88. Provincetown Players. O'Neill subsequently learned that Carlotta had begun intercepting letters to him from friends of his she disliked, many of whom were associated with the theatre group that had discovered O'Neill on Cape Cod in July 1916; cf. Louis Sheaffer, *O'Neill: Son and Artist* (Boston: Little, Brown, 1973), p. 329.

89. James Light, who had joined the Provincetown Players in New York in 1917 and who directed many productions of O'Neill's plays—at the Provincetown and in revivals elsewhere.

You remember meeting Norman Winston[90]—a damn fine guy. I wish you'd call on him and give him my best. His address is Kahler Shoe Co., 15 West 44th Street. Tell him about me what I've outlined above.

Give Manuel Komroff[91] my fondest—also Horace[92] & Pete Gross. Tell Gross I hope he is keeping my Interlude, Jones, Hairy Ape specials & first eds. safe for me. I will be sending for them soon. And ask him to send me three complete sets of my plays in the ordinary edition. Also tell Horace I'd regard it as a boon if he'd ship me whatever of their present catalogue books he thinks would interest me and charge same to me.

My affectionate best to Ruth, Stella & Teddy, Ian[93] & your father & mother!

Get hold of Kenneth Macgowan[94] at the Harvard Club and give him all my greetings. He is the only one to whom I have written the truth about my future plans so you can be quite open with him.

Well, I guess that's about all—except to lay emphasis on the fact that Carlotta and I are to be married as soon as the final decree comes out.

Oh yes, it would be a favor if you would see Dick Madden, my agent— Richard Madden Play Co., 33 West 42nd and tell him all of this. Don't tell him I won't have any play for next season, however—and don't tell any of the Guild bunch that either. Oh, you might drop in on the Guild for me and give them all my best—say I've been intending to write but too damn lazy. Be sure and meet Bob Sisk, their press agent when you're there. He's a fine scout and we've done a lot of corresponding. Any news you pick up around any where I'd like to hear. So I'll look forward to a long letter from you after you've been the rounds. Tell anyone my address is care of Guaranty Trust Co., 50 Pall Mall, London until further notice. That's where you had better write me, too. I don't know the exact dope on the P.O. situation in Touraine yet.

Much love to Dorothy & you—and bon voyage! Come back to us soon. And realize, Saxe—which I'm sure you do—that if ever you need me for anything just cable and I'll cable back. Don't hesitate about this, you hear me!

The Lenormand book arrived just before I received a present of the same volume by mail from him (He had had to go back to Paris where we are to meet later) He inscribed the book to me as follows "au grand poète du théâtre, au novateur, avec toute l'admiration" which sounds as if one col-

90. Wealthy New York shoe manufacturer and backer of the Provincetown Players.
91. An editor at Liveright's who became a best-selling author with his novel *Coronet* (1930).
92. Horace Liveright.
93. Teddy and Stella Ballantine's son, who grew up to become a leading book publisher.
94. Drama critic and director who had been part of the triumvirate (O'Neill, Robert Edmond Jones, and Macgowan) that had produced plays in the mid-1920s at the Provincetowners' Playwrights' Theatre and the Greenwich Village Theatre.

league, at least, had some unenvious appreciation of my strivings. This is no end gratifying to me because I have a real deep respect for him & his work.

Again Godspeed—and good luck in New York—and love to you both from us both. We are sure going to miss you in France.

Your friend,
Gene

---

50. *To Saxe Commins from Carlotta Monterey.* ALS 2 pp.

Château du Plessis,
St. Antoine-du-Rocher,
Indre et Loire,
France
[May 1929]

That, Saxe dear, is our *confidential* address[95]—I need say no more!

Am giddy with standing on my head in boxes packing.— So no letter today—.

We leave here Friday—motor to Paris,—will have three days wild shopping—then off to Plessis to get that in order—(a *job,* believe me) then to find & get a place ready for G. in August—on the sea shore in Brittany!! And then they ask me how I spend my time!—

Heaps of love to you both—
Carlotta

---

51. *To Saxe Commins from Eugene O'Neill.* ALS 1 p.

[May 7, 1929]

Dear Saxe:

Another favor! Will you mail enclosed script to Madden—express recommandié? Don't want it to go from here.

You got the scripts bound wonderfully. Thanks!

Looking forward to seeing you & Dorothy again. Keep day open for motor trip to Chartres.

95. Part of a 700-acre estate, Le Plessis, a moderate-size château about ten kilometers from Tours, was scarcely one of the showplaces of the Touraine. O'Neill and Carlotta rented it for three years in spring 1929 for only thirty thousand francs a year, about $1,200 in American currency at the time.

Tell Calmy,[96] Guild have foreign rights "Interlude" for year & half more. Any producer would have to negotiate with them—or I would have [to] get their O.K. on anything I did. Translation is different matter. Have written Helburn[97] he was doing that.

But "Marco"[98] is all mine & much simpler.

All best!
Gene

––––––––

Saxe and I were delighted at the thought of joining Gene and Carlotta in the trip to Chartres. We met them at the Hotel du Rhin, where they stayed whenever they came to Paris. After a quick lunch, we were on our way with Gene at the wheel. The distance from Paris to Chartres is about fifty miles. We touched on some old towns that bore the mark of earlier centuries, the steep narrow streets paved with cobble stones, the houses so close to their neighbors' across the street, one could almost touch them with outstretched arms.

Soon we were in sight of the tapering spires of the two towers of the cathedral, which is situated on a slope overlooking the Eure River. As we approached the cathedral, it seemed unreal because of the veil-like mist that enveloped it.

We entered the cathedral by way of the Royal Portal, so named because of the many sculptured figures of kings and queens that frame the portal. As we stepped into the nave, the immediate impression was one of awe, the noble grandeur of its ribbed vaulting, its height and breadth, the magnificence of its stained glass windows and a prevailing serenity that seemed to shut out a troubled and anxiety-ridden world.

The mist outdoors was lifting and the windows became suffused with the radiant light of the afternoon sun. In response, the colors in the windows began to sparkle like jewels. They seemed to have a life of their own, for they kept transforming into stylized patterns that were reflected on the stone floor.

Enchanted, we stood watching this play of light, when through the nave and carried aloft toward the arched ceiling rose the sounds of the organ. The player had just begun the superb theme of Bach's G Minor Fugue.

When the music came to a close, we just stood there fixed, no sound crossed our lips. The emotional effect of the music in such an environment released within us some hidden desire for spiritual values.

96. See letter 20, n. 54.
97. Theresa Helburn of the Theatre Guild's board of managers.
98. *Marco Millions,* the first O'Neill play produced by the Theatre Guild in Jan. 1928.

In silence we made our way to the car. It was broken when Carlotta suggested that we stop at some outdoor cafe for tea or coffee. While waiting to be served, Gene turned to me and asked, "What was that the organist played?" I told him. "It's magnificent, it's magnificent," he kept repeating. Then, after a pause he added, "I have never been exposed to that kind of music."

---

52. *To Saxe Commins from Eugene O'Neill.* ALS 1 p.

[early May 1929]

Dear Saxe:

Will you mail enclosed to Madden? Sent script to you to mail to train this a.m. If there is time, mail them from Mauritania on Saturday.

All best!
Gene

---

53. *To Dorothy Commins from Eugene O'Neill and Carlotta Monterey.* WIRE 1 p.

[ca. May 10, 1929]

Madame Saxe Commins Paguebot
Cleveland Boulognesm
—6° MonteCarlo 636-18-8-1150
Bon voyage and our love to you and Saxe

Gene and Carlotta

---

54. *To Saxe and Dorothy Commins from Carlotta Monterey.* ALS 4 pp.

May 14th 1929

For days, my dears,—I have been thinking constantly of you & wanting to write—but (you'll understand as you've just gone thro' it!) I am in the midst of boxes, lists, arrangements, getting more servants—seeing to Gene's things & packing as well as my own—And——the birds!—

I know you'll have a really nice voyage back to America. For the German boats are excellent.— Once in New York you'll be busy seeing old friends & getting "put"! Don't get *too* "put"—come back some day! I feel certain you'll want to.—

May 15th 1929

Dear Dorothy & Saxe.,

I was interrupted yesterday & today brings your thoughtful letter from the boat.—

Yes dears, it *will* be nice to receive news thro' you—for there will *not* be silly sickening (thinking to play up to Gene) sentimentality— or dishonest *mis*representation. Your honesty & loyalty is what I love & respect so in you both.— Am afraid some of Genes *so-called* friends have not always been in the *best* of form! Or *quite* as honest *behind* his back as they were *loving* in their letters! We have learned much—& it is good,—it helps for elimination & gives us more time for those we love—& who really love us!—

Write & tell me you are both happily settled & that all goes well.

If certain of G.'s friends tell you G. *wants* them to have his address—just *smile*—for he *doesn't*. Those we want we will especially ask!—

If they say I'm ruining G. & spending all his money—say "yes," —& that I'm planning to *eat* his children & my own! The sillies!

Come back to us some day—We always want you—

> Jehovah keep you,—
> Our *love always*
> Carlotta—

---

55. *To Saxe Commins from Carlotta Monterey.* ALS 6 pp.

> Le Plessis—
> St. Antoine-du-Rocher,
> Indre-et-Loire,
> *France*
> June 9th 1929

Saxe dear,—

So many thanks for your charming & kind letter. My great regret is that you & Dorothy could not have stopped with us here before returning to *vibrant* N.Y.! Here I could give you comfy & large enough beds—two for each if necessary—& such peace & beauty. G. is already feeling at home— thank God—& he looks *so much better*.

Saturday we went for a walk on *our* place—& found a stream—& if that Irishman didn't take off his clothes & swim under the sunlit trees! I *was* pleased—because it was a youthful & happy act.

I arranged his workshop first,—now I tear (it's really miles a day in this big house) from one end of the place to the other—trying to advise plumbers, painters & cleaners. But it will be nice when finished.

Since the old Marquise du Plessis's death no one has lived here—& you know how dust & moths & what not collects!—

Tell no one of our home,—(unless G. does!) unless they insist—& then give them the *description* of a *peasant's cottage*!—

Our darling canary "Bozo" died. We buried him,—in a Chinese box, —under a big tree in the garden—with a mound & head stone. All this in the pouring rain—. We were quite cut up about it.— I shall become a farmer's wife—big feet & broad hips—but I don't care,—it is all so natural, beautiful, serene, & of the sweet, smelly earth. At last we're at peace—in spite of outside troublesome American things.— *We* are *put!*

Am so happy you & D. saw your dear mother.— I have great respect & love for her—that's why I dislike your aunt so!—Your mother has *created*—your aunt *attempted* to destroy—to re-make to *her* pattern! Look at your mother's eyes & tell me if the Mother-of-God quality is not there!—But has your aunt that? I am certain she has *not*.—Forgive me—I shouldn't say such things— but it is only *my* way of loving your mother—& I am one of those extremists— *all* for—or—against!——

As so glad you chose Gramercy Park—it is the last square of quiet in N.Y. City—I want to know more of Dorothy's Concert & your plans.—

I already miss your not being in France! G. is going to write his greatest play here—! I feel it!

Our best love always, to you both—

Carlotta

Pardon haste but I have heaps of business letters to write.

---

56. *To Saxe Commins from Carlotta Monterey.* ALS 3 pp.
On stationery headed: Le Plessis / Saint-Antoine du Rocher / (Indre-et-Loire)

June 19th '29

Saxe dear.—

Thank you so much for your nice letter—Gene was interested & amazed re Mr. *Quinn's*[99] suicide attempt. His thorough preparations as to calling for the police etc.—lead one to suppose he was suffering, at that time, from some mental aberration—for (from what Gene has told me of him) he is not the

99. Edmond T. Quinn, a prominent sculptor whose works included heads of both O'Neill and Agnes, the Booth Memorial in Gramercy Park, and also a head of Dorothy Commins, attempted suicide by poison on May 12, 1929. On Sept. 12, 1929, his body was found floating in New York Harbor.

cheap type of human being who seeks publicity and the limelight! One never knows what is deep within another's heart—maybe he has been unhappy for years!——

I am so delighted to know that you & Dorothy are having such a *rich* visit with your mother. I am still tearing about Saxe dear, digging out dirt—moths, —getting dark grey paint washed into white—(or near white) this place is huge & old & neglected. But if you & D. were only here,—it annoys me so that you can't be—because *you'd love it*—& I'd love so having you.—

The "lady"[100] is playing up in her last lap! She *refuses* to go on, altho' the time is up, *unless* she has the signed agreement *in her hands* before.— Of course that is *impossible*,— because she has never been known to keep her word in anything,— & she suffers from that complaint where people cannot distinguish a lie from the truth,—so the agreement must be carefully kept in other hands than hers *until* she has gone thro' with *her* part of the bargain— She is doing damned little (*considering everything*) to be insured support as long as she lives! For *what?*— Her children always— & the best— but I can't understand her lack of pride &, at least, an *attempt* to prove her independence.

However—Life & Humans—we all have our failings— God knows *I'm full of them!*

G. working—punching the bag—driving the "Blonde Canary" (we got it from Biarritz). We had to sack Francois & discovered he [had] been a naughty boy—not *too* honest!— The cook also!— So you see I have that too—to arrange, & not too simple in the country! But somehow with a little effort, things fit in! We miss our darling Bozo so—I go to his grave each day—he was a dear bird.— G. sends love as always. This is a stupid letter—but I have had to chase out so often to answer various questions. We're having a wee concrete swimming pool put in—so in about two weeks G. will be complete.

Jehovah bless you both—

Love always—
Carlotta

---

57. *To Saxe Commins from Carlotta Monterey.* ALS 2 pp.

June 20th '29

Saxe—angel child—

If I had you here I'd *spank you!* For God's sake *don't believe* anything you see in the paper re G.—his travels,—health conditions,—ideas on Life, Love, Children, Wives, Adultery—Murder etc.—*I am here—! When* there

100. Agnes.

is trouble I will look after him—& will let you know *at once.*—He is well—*bloom*ing—his one desire is to keep out of *papers* & *courts!* To be left severely alone—in peace——! He is at work on something *I* like! And we both love you— & D.—

A pat & a hug—

Bless you—
C.

---

58. *To Saxe Commins from Carlotta Monterey.* ALS 3 pp.
On stationery headed: Le Plessis / Saint-Antoine du Rocher / (Indre-et-Loire)

[postmarked July 13, 1929]

Saxe dear.—

I couldn't answer your charming letter of the 26th of June because it arrived the morning we were leaving for Paris (we had to go to town for two or three days!)—& your other charming letter of July 3rd arrived this morning—Yes— we knew of the divorce, of course[101]—& funnily enough we weren't moved by it. We've waited too long & been thro' too much from that end! We *did* get a laugh tho' about the "lady's" remark for publicity as regards her divorcing G. according to a pre-marriage contract! Her memory is short—re her 18 mos. of lies—blackmailing—selling scandalous interviews—double crossing etc. —"I" say she's a liar—G. says she's just a damn fool! The marriage will only mean a "ceremony" to us too!— We have, in actuality, been too long married & faced too much trouble & worry together to be excited by Mrs. O'Neill's tardy recognition of her own *generous* nature! May she be happy in her belief of her noble behaviour—but—may she & her friends & Gene's would-be friends leave us in peace & in ignorance of *her* existence, *her* plans or *her* life!———"Gaga" is dead too.—[102] Gene was upset about that because he feared she did not receive the care and attention due her!— But we can do nothing now—altho' Gene *had sent* money especially for her.—And Life goes on.—Gene Jr. is expected here next month.—This plagiarism suit[103] drives Gene mad & well I can understand it.— I don't see

101. On July 3, 1929, Agnes had been granted a divorce in Reno on the grounds of desertion.
102. Mrs. Fifine Clark had died on July 6, 1929.
103. On May 27, 1929, a woman who wrote under the pen-name George Lewys had filed a suit in a New York court charging that *Strange Interlude* was plagiarized from her novel *The Temple of Pallas-Athenae*, which had been privately published in 1924. After a week-long and much-publicized trial in March 1930, Lewys's suit was dismissed

why the Dramatist's League doesn't take this as a test case & do something to force a change of laws regarding blackmailers!— Of course they *don't dare* do that in Europe.—The penalty is too great against them—.

Gene & I just long for peace—to see *no Press reports,*—to be able to live & work apart from gossip—criticism etc.

Saxe dear—this is a dull letter—I'll be better next time.— With a world of love to you & Dorothy & I *do* so wish you could visit us here—perhaps next year?!—We've bought a *radio*—& an orthophonic Victrola—I also bought a wirehaired fox terrier—"Billy" by name!—

> God bless you both—
> Carlotta—

---

59. To Saxe Commins from Carlotta Monterey. ALS 4 pp.
On stationery headed: Le Plessis / Saint-Antoine du Rocher / (Indre-et-Loire)

July 27th '29

Saxe dear.—

Thank you so much for your letter of the 16th recd this morning—Saxe dear—I have no fear for Gene's work—nothing could take from him *what he has* & *what he is!* God knows he has gone thro' hell enough in his life— but *his work went on regardless*—& *it always will!* You see we are away from all gossip (thank God) so we have—I *think*—a calmer viewpoint than formerly. We only see those we have a desire to see— & that too is a luxury—. Selfish, perhaps—but one can do these things as one gets older!—

Life means a battle—but with each encounter one *should* learn something— if only when to say no—or be silent. I have never seen Gene look or feel as fit as he does now—. We are both regaining our sense of humour too. One thing that amuses us is that after eighteen months of hell—worry & G. spending much money to be rid of her—his friends are simple minded enough to write news of his ex-wife if only to say they have *no* news of her! We can't figure out how they can imagine we are interested! But they must cling on to all that old life & attempt to keep it alive when he G. has done everything a human *can* do to get away from it.— However it is of no importance— & they will one day be inspired as to what & what not is an interesting subject!—

I don't like you & Dorothy being in New York—Surely some how you will

---

as "wholly preposterous," and she was ordered to pay O'Neill $7,500, the Theatre Guild (producers of the play) $5,000, and O'Neill's publisher $5,000—none of which was ever collected, as she had no money.

come back again—& I hope live in the simple french life not that of Paris—
The former is so much more interesting & helpful to work & health.—

I bought a fox terrier for us & ye gods—what a responsibility.— Worse than
a baby—! I have him in the tub continually as he adores rolling in the filth
of the universe—but, as I say to Gene—"It's his nature to be so!" He goes
wild with excitement when Gene is in the swimming pool & also swims with
Gene.— He's fun & company as well as being a pest.—

We expect Eugene Jr.—here in August—& the visit will do both father &
son a lot of good.— I have always wanted a son—so now I can adopt Eugene
"if" he finds me compatible—!

All our birds look so much better & sing better—the country agrees with
them—.

I feel my letters to you sound almost simple minded—but we live so simply—so naturally—so with the earth & simplicity that I have no exciting news
or gossip to tell you.—

Now that our "trouble" is over we look forward to peace & work—we are
even going to *dis*continue the press clipping bureau!— That means making
a new world—cutting loose the rotten drift wood & building afresh—.

Our dearest love to you & Dorothy & how happy we'll be when you write
to say you're coming back to us.—

> Jehovah keep you—
> Carlotta

––––––––

60. *To Saxe Commins from Eugene O'Neill.* WIRE 1 p.

> [July 23, 1929]

NA6 Cable—Paris 19
LCD Saxe Commins—
11 Gramercy Park South NewYork—
Grand news Carlotta and I married yesterday Love from us—

> Gene

––––––––

61. *To Saxe Commins from Carlotta Monterey O'Neill.* ALS 6 pp.
On stationery headed: Le Plessis / Saint-Antoine du Rocher /
(Indre-et-Loire)

> *Aug. 2nd 1929*

Saxe, my dear,

Thank you so much for your letter and the clippings.— We *are* grateful
& happy that *that* is now ancient history & pray to Jehovah to inspire every-

one to keep their opinions of *ap*proval or *dis*approval to themselves as to whether either Gene or I have made an unwise move in our lives,——& to spare us from gossip,—& just *forget us* so that we may rest in peace & work. And the friends *we desire* we'll keep in touch with—those we *don't* desire should take the hint (when they do not hear from us!) & leave us in peace!— Gene & I both suffer from those (let us kindly say) "well meaning" ones (?!) who would know our plans—how we live—what we intend writing—where going—what we spend—if our ex-husbands & ex-wives are compatible—what our plans regarding our children are etc., etc.,—and——we are both getting a little "fed up" about it!— We are old enough—God knows—to look after our own affairs & need no outside assistance!

As to this damnably unfair plagiarism suit I *do* think the Author's League are missing a marvellous opportunity to make a *test case* out of this Interlude affair. But—am afraid—Geo. Middleton[104] is too busy writing dialogue etc.— in Hollywood to think of this.—And there is a tendency among us humans to only think of "things" when we ourselves are *personally* concerned. And Geo. is not—in this—were it a play of *his*—the whole thing would take on a different color. Mr. Weinberger, naturally, keeps Gene well informed as to the progress of each move & it will not come up for some time—according to present rulings!—I, personally feel that men *or* women who go about tearing down other people's reputations—personal or otherwise—should be *publicly flogged!*— I have no "God is Love & all is Divine" in my nature—. To me "an eye for an eye & a tooth for a tooth"—in the good or the bad sense.— Humans have become so without guts these days there are few "haters,"— in consequence few "lovers."— If people *got* what they *gave* these world would have fewer parasites and weaklings.— But now the humans sit back & acquiesce lest they loose something. We are becoming a race of spineless nothings.— It is for you Jews to *keep your Faith* & give an example of perseverence & determination to us weakling so-called Christians! I am a great admirer of the real Jew—to my mind nothing has touched him. I have known the best—& marvelled at the "some thing" *within* that gave *courage, faith* & that colourful sense of beauty—. No noise about it—just *example in living!* I am not speaking of the Broadway cult—but the Hebrew!—

Forgive my ranting on in this way—but I love you—therefore you suffer from my loquaciousness.

Gene is *marvellous*—and pays me the great compliment to be *really proud* & *happy* that he can say "this is *my wife!*" What greater compliment could he pay me after a *life* having been lived thro' in 18 months!—

Did I tell you we had a wire haired fox terrier "Billy" who swims with Gene every day in the pool! How you & Dorothy would love this place,— never a day goes by that I don't wish you here.—

104. A prolific writer for the stage and screen who was president of the Dramatists Guild and busy campaigner for the rights of authors.

Our love always,–& don't worry if you find *some people* not "friendly" towards *us*–(they'd be the first to lick Gene's boots if we returned!) & we *don't want them* or *to hear about them*–& that goes for some that might surprise you!——This is a *new life*–we have *cut from the old* with just about five left–

Our love always dear to you & D.
Carlotta–

---

62. *To Saxe Commins from Eugene O'Neill.* ALS 2 pp.
On stationery headed: Le Plessis / Saint-Antoine du Rocher / (Indre-et-Loire)

August 4th 1929

Dear Saxe:

As usual I have been meaning to write you for a dog's age and kept post-poning it, knowing that Carlotta was keeping you privy to the news. But I've been damn glad to get your letters although sorry to hear you've been having bad breaks in the search for a job. Still I hope you are making allow-ances for the fact that you came back at a particularly unpropitious season. Especially as regards the publishing business. Nathan,[105] who visited us for a few days, tells me the publishers are viewing their situation with alarm and retrenching. Once the summer is over you ought to have no trouble landing somewhere. As for Liveright and the Vanderbilt, there's probably a lot to that that doesn't meet the eye—in more ways than one! The lady (?) is no end of a sexual scamp, I believe—and a Vanderbilt comes under the head of advertizing, anyway.

I am glad you set Manuel[106] right about me. I like him a lot and value his friendship and I wouldn't have him giving ear to any of the malicious tattle of the envious—and, worse, the mourning jeremiads pulled by acquaintances who pose as my intimates, and the pleased condolences of false friends. It seems to be a terrible blow to some of this ilk that I should be happy—an attitude that gives away what their hopes were.

I note what Manuel says about Liveright's failure to advertize the older works and I'll give him a jab about it when next I write him.

Yes, what you gave Atkinson[107] was all right—except that I'm not off the other two plays of the trilogy for good—will certainly write them after a year or two. They're too good to let go. But it's true I am off of having the

105. George Jean Nathan.
106. Manuel Komroff.
107. Brooks Atkinson, drama critic of the New York *Times.*

three considered as a trilogy, as I told you. Probably noone but me would ever see the trilogy relationship, each is so entirely different from the others. My rating them as a trilogy was my mistake.

I've been working for the past two months—off and on, between necessary interruptions—on an entirely new conception that has come to me. I've got most of the preliminary work done and shall be ready to start in on actual dialogue soon—not too soon because I want to wait until Eugene's visit is over and several other forthcoming breaks of trips to Paris that have to be made are through. Then with a clear nine months ahead of me I'll sail in. No, it's not any idea you've ever heard. It came to me since I arrived here. I won't go into details but I'm tremendously enthusiastic! It's by far the biggest thing I've ever tried to do, I assure you of that! And it will take a lot of time and a lot of doing. I can't tell you how enthused I am about it! It's the sort of thing I needed to come to me—one that will call for everything I can give it—a glorious opportunity to grow and surpass everything I've ever done before![108] So I'm cheering! I've put aside the play I worked on this winter that you and Dorothy know about[109] in the new ones favor. For one thing this is greater in scope, gives me more of a chance. For another thing the middle part of the other wasn't ripe yet although the first and last thirds were clear enough. It will gain by being left to stew in the unconscious for a year or so. I say a year but this new work may take longer—and will get whatever it demands in the way of time and work. It has the possibilities of being the biggest thing in modern drama—not barring anyone's plays! Whether I'll have enough stuff to realize the said possibilities is another story. I have my hopes, at least. And, at any rate, I'd rather fail at the Big Stuff and remain a success in my own spiritual eyes than go on repeating, or simply equalling, work I've done before. Life is growth—or a joke one plays on oneself! One has to choose.

My "renunciation" of the theatre consisted in my mentioning in a letter to my New London agent that I intended living over here because I was sick of the "show business." Their confusing theatre with show business in this instance is merely an example of the fact that they always do just that!

The Quinn suicide puzzles me. Why, for the love of Mike? I get no answer.

I needn't tell you how happy and at peace Carlotta & I are in our marriage. By God, we earned ours! And this Plessis home is even better than our hopes for it. It's ideal! I never felt such a sense of fitting into a house and land. It's a real home! I sure hope you & Dorothy can visit us sometime! You'd both love it!

All love from us both to Dorothy & you! If there's ever anything I can do,

108. *Mourning Becomes Electra.*
109. "It Cannot Be Mad."

let me know. I'm sorry my note to Horace produced no better results but the breaks in so many ways turned out against it that it's no criterion. You may land there yet.

As ever,
Gene

---

63. *To Saxe Commins from Carlotta Monterey O'Neill*. ALS 3 pp. On stationery headed: Le Plessis / Saint-Antoine du Rocher / (Indre-et-Loire)

Aug. 24th 29

Saxe, my dear,

Thank you for your letter of the 13th inst.—

Am glad your sister is recovering nicely from her operation. I had "mine" removed & the after effects are, sometimes, *not* very pleasant! I wonder is it always necessary to remove an appendix? I always feel mine was not the cause of my discomfort! However—that's past!

Yes—Dorothy *is* flesh, blood & *soul!* One feels that—and you *are* fortunate & you *are* worthy! I wish a few of Gene's friends were as tactful as you! Per Gene's orders I "edit" all the clippings sent from the clipping bureau—&, in consequence, he sees about five out of a hundred! I can't edit his letters tho'— & "some" seem determined to *not* believe he is content & happy,—& equally determined to keep his entire past alive before his eyes! They'll tire of all this bye and bye please God!?!

Eugene Jr.—arrived yesterday—& I can pay him no higher compliment than to say if my Cynthia is as fine a woman at nineteen—as he is a man—I will be a very proud & happy mother. Gene owes a great debt to Eugene's mother—& I hope he will never loose sight of that fact.— His (Eugene's) mother's example and care & love show in his manner—his thoughts—& his viewpoint of life!

Gene also rec'd a letter (which pleased him) from Mr. Komroff.— Mr. Nathan wants to be called as a witness in this disgusting case also!— I never will understand *why* the law permits such outrage. We—as a Nation—have much to learn! We need *discipline* not freedom!—

Never mention this but I was interested (tho' *not* surprised) when none of the Provincetowners sent Gene any word of good wishes etc., on the occasion of his marriage to me![110] They can't use him any more—!!!! Gene was

110. In reality, many of his friends in Greenwich Village and Provincetown wrote to congratulate him on his remarriage. See Louis Sheaffer, *O'Neill: Son and Artist* (Boston: Little, Brown, 1973), p. 333.

more embarrassed on *my* account than on his *own—why—*God knows.— Because I have heard all along of their disloyalties.—& for some reason they hold *me* responsible for Gene's remaining abroad—! I wish I could say I had that much influence over him;—if anything it is *their rotten behavior* & *others like them* that makes him want to remain away—(even going to the extent of another country)—from them all! And I am *delighted* they were stupid enough to show their real colours! *Please mention this to no one—not even your sister!*

Gene looks *so* well—& since our marriage has *blossomed!* As he says—"it is a new development!" My fondest love to you & dear Dorothy.

—Carlotta—

Gene is upstairs working.

---

64. *To Saxe Commins from Carlotta Monterey O'Neill.* ALS 8 pp.
On stationery headed: Le Plessis / Saint-Antoine du Rocher / (Indre-et-Loire)

Aug. 30th 1929

Saxe dearest,

Because I have such a deep feeling of affection for you (*not* because you're Gene's friend—but because you are *you!*) I want to be perfectly honest & I know you will understand, & thank me for it & destroy this letter & forget it!—

Gene, very kindly, gave me your letter to read yesterday. And this A.M. I rec'd a letter from Mr. Weinberger (answering mine in which I had thanked him for his good wishes etc., re our marriage)—in which there was *more talk* of Miss Fitzgerald & Jas. Light! If I but had the words to tell you how *very, very* fed up we are with news of these two individuals! And now people are running to Miss F. & telling her Gene is "hurt" because she sent him no letter or cable when he was married! That is a *lie*—he was *not* "hurt!"— He was surprised at their lack of even *tact*—considering their endless asking of favours in the present & their having accepted so many in the past!— It is not very much of a compliment to Gene (that his other friends pay him) to think that he—(Gene)—wishes *letters,* or *thought* or *friendship* from *anyone* who must be *asked* for it! *God! such English!* Now I am going to be brutally frank—because Gene never will—he always trys to save their feelings—But as *you* have *nothing* to do with this I can honestly get all this out of my system & never mention it again—. We would be *delighted* if we never heard a word *from* or *about* these people again. (And several others!)—They have proved what they are——& *that is that!*

As Gene expressed to me the other evening—he is going thro' a *new devel-*

opement—new *pleasures*—new *richness*—new *subjects of study*—are coming into his life,——the old skin is being shed! And with it the old parasites—I hope!— We are living in *Europe*—in the *country* to isolate ourselves from people we don't want—& yet the mail brings news of them every week or so—. It's like a curse!—

Both Gene and I want to make a *clean cut* & *go on!* You are one of the few old ones we *want* to see!— But, if you love Gene,—don't worry about these others—*know nothing*—*hear nothing*—*see nothing*—regarding him & them. People are so aggressive—that idiot Winston[111] keeps embarrassing Gene by *asking* if he can't visit us & a thousand & one other things! If he hadn't the hide of a rhino he'd *know if* he were *wanted* he'd be asked--If Mr. Light asks you if we will be here in Nov. *don't know*—we may be in Arabia (to him!)—Saxe, we are praying for *freedom*—to *be left alone*—for *work*— For *peace!*— One either goes forward or backward in life—there is no standing still!—

Eugene Jr.—is here. A nice youngster & my God—such *tact!* He has mentioned *no one's* name since he arrived!— We discuss books, music, architecture, & abstract things—which makes his visit doubly enjoyable.—

My constant regret is—that I can't look up, from this, my writing desk, & see you & Dorothy enter the room. It's so beastly in life—a perverse thing— Those we *want* to have with us so much we *can't* have & those we don't want—do all but walk in on us!—

Forgive all this—but it is a prove of my affection for you— ("strange" you say? Perhaps!) and I must be honest & give you a chance to know just what our desires are!— Gene wouldn't write anyone like this—but he'd suffer thro' *wanting to!* He'd think I was unkind to write this—but I can't figure that out! You have been our staunch & loyal friend,—& sometimes a point is reached where *silence* is a greater proof of friendship than *explanations* (to outsiders!) —Oh,—you understand don't you, Saxe?—

Gene is *so* well——& in my next letter I'll send you some snaps of him & Gene Jr.—& Billy—the dog!—

We work, read, listen to Beethoven—Bach—César Franck etc., on our very good Orthophonic (is that the way to spell it?)—& play. The two Eugenes & Billy swim once or twice a day.—Life goes on—calmly & surely—with Beauty always trembling in the air—and the desire to reach up—into the completeness and fulfillment of Life & Art!

Mr. de Casserres[112] spoke so nicely of you in a letter to Gene— He sounds an honest & independent one!

Nathan visited us & was a *charming* & *lovable* guest—I was amazed to see that side of him!

111. Norman Winston.
112. Benjamin de Casseres, a writer whose works O'Neill admired.

With my best love to you & Dorothy. Let my bluntness bring us closer together not drive us apart— As ever

—Carlotta—

---

65. *To Saxe Commins from Carlotta Monterey O'Neill.* TLS 1 p.
On stationery headed: Le Plessis / Saint-Antoine du Rocher /
(Indre-et-Loire)

Sept. 21st 1929

Saxe, my dear,

Thank you for your most understanding letter. I have just got Gene all settled and wrapped warm (this is a real Autumnal morning) in his study, and have taken Billy down in the vegetable garden to arrange things with the gardener—(ate an ice-cold tomato covered with dew, from the vine!) and picked the enclosed wee fleurs from under the trees for you as I came back to the house.

After much heavy sultry weather the Autumn seems to have really arrived. The mornings are crisp and exhilerating. We are gradually *settling in* so to speak. "The Hairy Ape"[113] opened last night in Paris—but Gene with some necessary firmness escaped the usual interviews and publicity and sociability that most people of the theatre adore and scheme for. I saw in the paper the other day where Mr. Quinn finally *did* kill himself——I carefully hid the article from Gene as things like that depress him and start a strain of thought that leads to depression and all the rest of it. If he *should* know it that is another thing. The same thing as keeping from him that his ex-wife had a drunken party at her house and had to pay—at Point Pleasant—a fine of some Johnny who went after "something" in her car and ran into three cars and knocked a policeman off his bicycle!!!!! (The fine was $451.00) And she must pay the damage of the cars!!!!! These things only upset him.

I enclose three snapshots but they are very *of the family*. But feel that you will like them. It grieves me that you and Dorothy are so far away—we speak of you so much and *want* you here. With our dearest love to you both, as ever

Carlotta

113. A French-language version produced by Georges Pitoeff.

---

66. To Saxe Commins from Carlotta Monterey O'Neill. ALS 6 pp.
On stationery headed: Le Plessis / Saint-Antoine du Rocher /
(Indre-et-Loire)

[ca. November 15,
1929]

Saxe dear,

We have been in Paris for three weeks—otherwise I would have written before this. And returning two days ago finding my desk piled high with household books, bills etc.—I have been digging in ever since.—Just beginning to see light so will take a few minutes off to chat with you.—I do hope you are both very well & also that you have settled into something, if only temporary, to keep you busy and not give you enough spare time to analyse yourself too often or too much!——

Berlin *hated* "Interlude"! Boston thought it *"dirty"!* A gentleman got up in the *"House"* in Copenhagen & denounced it! Gene is really a great person to have such virulence thrown at him! But I much prefer all that which is *im*personal & comes to all people in public life who's personalities or work attract attention—than to an "apologia" in the New Yorker written by Kenneth Macgowan thinking he was doing a friendly kind thing— I was *furious*.[114] Not knowing the author's name (as the article was not signed but stated to have been written by a friend *who had visited us!*) I wrote to N.Y. to find out *who* had written this thing & expressed my opinion freely!—

I nearly dropped dead when I found out Kenneth wrote it. I have written & told him, quite frankly, what I have said & what I think—. Gene's friends are free to write what they wish about Gene *personally* or his work—(that is *his* & *their* affair) but I happen to be *one half part of the home of the O'Neill's,—in a cold blooded business proposition. It is costing me thousands a year* and no publicity can be given thro' *friendly* channels without consulting *me!* That is only *honest* & *just!* I need no apology to the public or Gene's old friends or acquaintance whether I am living in 30 *rooms* or 3. I pay as I go—& it's nobody's damned business!— Gene is not married to Agnes Boulton now but to Carlotta Monterey—&, as far as his *personal* & *home* life is concerned it makes a *great difference!*——I have sat quietly in the back ground now for nearly two years—listening to insult & unfair criticism re

114. "The Talk of the Town" (*New Yorker,* Sept. 28, 1929), in which a "friend of O'Neill just returned from a visit to him" reported that "Flamboyant descriptions of the château he has rented in France have exaggerated its grandeur. It is not a show place, simply an old residence on an estate owned by three noble ladies who rented it to the O'Neills furnished, for about half of what a four-room apartment rents in New York. It is without electricity and has but one bath."

myself, my family—my financial position—my morals & every other imaginable thing. Meanwhile I have gone on paying out money—giving out energy & care—while these Provincetown people—& other of Gene's parasites have nearly driven him & me crazy. My patience is *exhausted*. Gene, at least, owes me protection from these gossiping idiots—if he can't give it to me—I'll see what I can do.—

Now—to pleasanter topics—

The trees are golden now & the air nippy. We go to bed by fire light—a thing I love,—to lie & watch the shadows dancing on the walls & ceilings—! The house is beautifully warm and I feel certain we'll be able to stick out the Winter here.—Then Gene will be able to work without interruption. I have worked so hard to get this huge place in smooth running order that I'd hate to have to pop off to some other place for a few months.—

I heard Mengelberg direct the Paris symphony in Paris—and thought our American orchestras so much better. The Paris one seemed thin & not well disciplined. We also went (for the first time since leaving N.Y.!) to the theatre to see Lenormand's "Mixture." Mme. Lenormand was playing in it. It was well done—*in a way*—! We had luncheon with the Lenormands & met the Pitoëffs. Interesting people—sincere—. She is *charming*—has such *beautiful* eyes—but is oh! *so, so* tired. They have *seven* children & *not a son!* There's trouble for you!—And they work continually. Life is an amazing series of experiences—of hurts—with just enough happiness thrown in to give us the courage to go on & search for more. And yet look at the parasites—they seem to do nothing but *absorb others!* Yet there *must* be some sort of *Law* somewhere, somehow!—I will write again soon—this is a stupid letter—But it carries our love to you—always—Give Dorothy a hug for me!—

—Carlotta—

---

67. *To Saxe Commins from Carlotta Monterey O'Neill.* ALS 4 pp. On stationery headed: Le Plessis / Saint-Antoine du Rocher / (Indre-et-Loire)

[postmarked
November 18, 1929]

Dear Saxe,

I wrote to you a few days ago—but *your* letter just reached me this morning. No, we are not ill—either of us. But very well—& Gene hard at work—. I should have written you before but have had so many things to see to, with this establishment, that days pass & letters go unanswered. Always remember "no news is good news"! As I *never* speculate & have advised Gene never to,—

neither of us were hurt in the Wall Street drop.[115]— All that trouble was caused by the *wise ones* using Wall Street as a roulette wheel to gamble on & further their get-rich-quick schemes. These people who know nothing of finance & refuse to work for a living. Unfortunately this has hurt rich men & corporations, & banks have suffered. It is not true that the rich are resting easily back dragging in the gold.—My financial advisers are the old style conservative bankers who never speculate or allow anyone in their firm to speculate. They told me a year ago this would happen owing to the speculation & extravagance in America—So many people live beyond their means, are in debt head over heels,—mortgage their homes to buy automobiles— diamonds, fur coats—all on installment plan!—It is stupid as well as vulgar.— If one uses the Market as an investment it is safe—& makes the country's financial position so much more solid.— Enough of money—! It's a bore!—But I loathe the ostentation of the nouveau riche—the gaudiness & continual discussion of what they have! They don't deserve money—For they don't know the responsibility of it— Oh—Oh.— — —

Sunday

The sun is out & the air crisp—Gene in his tower working—. The birds singing & my dog asleep at my feet.—The house-books balanced up to date— & all in order.—

You would shriek with laughter to see Gene & me on bycycles going along country roads! I always smile when I think of what "love" has done to Carlotta!—

Don't worry about us ever Saxe dear.—We are both in the best of health & if we weren't I'm really very good as a nurse etc.—That's your Jewish good heart & "family spirit,"—a noble quality—unfortunately we so-called Christians possess none of it!—

Am glad Dorothy is well & busy—That's the only thing I miss here. Not being a woman of affairs—so to speak.—For in New York I was always so very busy,—and each hour, each day & each night taken—But *my* activities will come again later.—

Did you read "The Incredible Marquis"?[116]—I found it good reading—

Gene sends his love to you and Dorothy—as I do—always—

Carlotta

---

115. The first major drop in the stock market had occurred on Oct. 29, 1929, signaling the beginning of the Depression.

116. *The Incredible Marquis: Alexandre Dumas* by Herbert Gorman (New York: Farrar & Rinehart, 1929).

68. To Saxe Commins from Eugene O'Neill. TLS 2 pp.
On stationery headed: Le Plessis / Saint-Antoine du Rocher /
(Indre-et-Loire)

Dec. 5th 1929

Dear Saxe:

I was delighted to get your letter with its good news![117] I had been hoping that you would eventually land a job of that sort that you could get some satisfaction out of. I know you are better pleased than you would be with a higher paid job that would bore you to death.

I had written to Harry[118] previously telling him to offer you a job for me in connection with this plagiarism suit—that is, digging up similarities to her book or Interlude in modern drama and novels, and following up whatever suggestions along these lines Harry got from Nathan or Mencken or T. R. Smith[119] or whoever could help with any. I thought, if you were still jobless, that this might appeal to you and help a mite in tiding you over. I left it to Harry to fix up details with you. He probably didn't get my letter until a day or so ago. Yes, I think Harry is riding on his oars too much but then the case won't come up until God knows when and I suppose there is plenty of time. However, I am going to keep after him from now on. It is quite possible—this is confidential!—that later on I may get Henry Taft, the famous corporation lawyer with a grand respectable reputation for honesty, to act as my head one. His name, I figure, would help a lot to direct attention to the injustice of such cases in general and might be of service in getting the law revised. I have made inquiries and discovered he is willing to act for me although it is out of his line. But I've not decided definitely yet. It might look as if I were taking the suit too seriously.

I am working like the devil these days and getting a lot done. After a couple of bad starts I am now off on the right foot and it is coming grand.[120] At this gait I may get through the first draft of it by the middle of February. There is a devil of a lot of labor in it but it will be worth it. No, I'm not going to tell even you anything about it—not because I know you wouldn't keep it confidential but simply because I have a personal reaction against saying a word about it until I have it completed and it can speak for itself. It is the most ambitious thing I have tackled, I'll say that much, and it doesn't involve any further experiments in technique. It is so strong in itself that the less technique is apparent the better, it would only be in the way.

117. Saxe had landed an editorial job with Covici-Friede, a recently formed publishing house.

118. Harry Weinberger.

119. Head of the editorial staff at Liveright's.

120. *Mourning Becomes Electra.*

We are both fine and happy. The fall here is a bit rainy but mild. I love the place. I wish you were in Paris now so that you could come and visit. You would love it—and Dorothy too. I turned in my B.N.C. to the Bugatti, got a great bargain on it, and for comparatively little more dough got a Bugatti eight cylinder new model racing-roadster. They advertize it as the fastest roadster in the world and I guess it is—guaranteed to make one hundred and seventy kilometres—one hundred and six miles an hour. It is a bear! It has good suspension and double shock-absorbers and good uphoalstery so Carlotta can ride with me in comfort. I think I shall have a lot of fun out of it. The B.N.C. was too uncomfortable. On my farewell ride, when I drove it to Paris, I made from here to Chartres—150 kilometres—in an hour and fourty minutes—not a bad average when you consider there are several good-sized towns to pass through en route and that the twelve kilos from the house to Tours are over a narrow winding and mostly dirt road. I had her up to 120 k an hour at times—the fastest I ever made in it. Well, she was a good little fast blond but her motion was hard on the small of the back—in which she ran true to form for fast blonds! The Bugatti is black with a red trim—very pretty. It is only rated at 13 horsepower but the motor turns up to 5000 revolutions—a beautiful piece of work. It is the same motor practically as you saw perform at San Sebastien.[121]

I suppose you think I am a motor bug. Well, I am. I get more out of a beautiful fast car than out of most things—going to the theatre included!

The Berlin critics turned loose an anti-American barage on the opening of *Strange Interlude* there—accused me of imitating everyone from Schiller to Shakespeare. Got mad because Charlie says in Act One that "Europe is dead, etc." Accused me of saying so, of course. No end of similar silly bunk. You would have thought Interlude was an enemy alien. Didn't do much good, however, because the play has now been running almost two months and, by reports I get from the management, is one of the few hits of the season. The same anti-American rot greeted The Hairy Ape in Paris. Not as bad however. "This American playwright, etc" The same boys rave about "Mary Dugan."[122] Like us when we're cheap but we mustn't dare infringe on Europe's private property, the Arts. Very timid stuff on their part. Shows a deep anxiety complex working underneath.

Well, that's all. Good luck to you. Carlotta joins in much love to you and Dorothy.

As ever,
Gene

121. The Grand Prix auto races at San Sebastian, Spain.

122. *The Trial of Mary Dugan,* a melodrama by Bayard Veiller that had been one of the hits of the 1927–28 Broadway season, having run for 310 performances.

69. *To Saxe Commins from Carlotta Monterey O'Neill.* ALS 2 pp.

Dec. 11th 1929

Saxe dear,

Thank you for your letter. Am glad you are at work. Never mind the wage now,—it is so much easier always to get the *second* job after one has had the first.—And all this experience is precious for future work.— I read Gene about the "suggestions" of printing "To-Morrow"!—[123] How unjust a demand—not in a *business* way (for they *knew* that it was out of the question!) but from a *social* (if one may use the word in that sense?) viewpoint. It embarrassed you to ask Gene—*knowing* he would say "No"!—However that is over—so forget it!

Yes,—we always take the "Times" & so are able to follow the news. The Guild must be either stunned by success or become lazy!—

Gene is writing magnificently—but not hurrying. *Not* the play he outlined to you.— We are so happy to be away from New York,—it's noise, it's gossip,—and it's strife.—

We are becoming peaceful & middle aged & selfishly content with our lot.— We are both busy & the days glide by.— But as Gene so often says, "Carlotta, we have *earned* our happiness."!—

Christmas will soon be here & we have about 25 to 30 men, women & children to remember. *My* job—but it will make them happy!

Am delighted to hear your mother is radiant—bless her.

My dearest love to Dorothy—*there's* a woman for you!—

Our love always,—
Carlotta

123. The only short story by O'Neill ever published (*Seven Arts,* June 1917), "Tomorrow," is biographically important, for it gives a detailed picture of Jimmy the Priest's, the waterfront saloon and flophouse where the future playwright hung out, and of some of its denizens, story material that O'Neill would use in *"Anna Christie,"* The *Iceman Cometh,* and other works.

A CHALLENGING DRAMA

1930 – 1932

During nearly all of the 1920s, plays poured out of O'Neill—to list only the better ones, *"Anna Christie"* and *The Emperor Jones*, *The Hairy Ape* and *All God's Chillun Got Wings*, *Desire Under the Elms*, *The Great God Brown* and *Strange Interlude*. Unlike most authors, he practically never suffered from writer's block or from a dearth of story ideas. Indeed, he used to say that he had enough ideas to keep him writing for the next ten years, a situation that would remain true of him to the end of his career.

However, after the failure of *Dynamo* in 1929—both the critics and the public disliked it—he decided to take more time for his scripts. "Looking back," he wrote a friend, "I find I've written eighteen long plays in the past eleven years! Too much! At least seven of them shouldn't have been written—at least, not as they were written!"

No one could charge him with scanting time and effort on his next work. He was to spend two-and-a-half years on his most challenging and difficult project to date: a drama based on one of the old Greek tragedies but set in America and employing contemporary insight. "Is it possible," he had asked himself several years earlier, "to get modern psychological approximation of Greek sense of tragedy into such a play, which an intelligent audience of today possessed of no belief in gods or supernatural retribution, could accept and be moved by?"

After looking over the classical field, he chose the *Oresteia* trilogy of Aeschylus. Its basic theme, he felt, "has greater possibilities of revealing all the deep hidden relationships in the family than any other" of the ancient tragedies. Since the Aeschylus work deals with an adulterous wife who murders her husband and then is slain by her son at the urging of her daughter, it appeared, from O'Neill's remark about "the deep hidden relationships," that he regarded family life as, essentially, an internecine struggle.

A trilogy in thirteen acts in O'Neill's retelling, *Mourning Becomes Electra* underwent major changes between its first three drafts. After two years of writing and rewriting, O'Neill felt that he had *Electra* in finished shape, but he continued to revise it, and he and Carlotta returned to America for its production by the Theatre Guild. When he won the Nobel Prize for literature a few years later, the universal opinion was that he had won it chiefly for *Mourning Becomes Electra*, even though the prize is given for a writer's body of work, rather than for a particular piece of writing.

Not long after the couple's return to America in 1931, they built a handsome Spanish-style residence—they called it Casa Genotta, a contraction of their first names—in the exclusive resort of Sea Island, Georgia. The cheers for his *Electra* had hardly subsided when O'Neill went to work on his next play, *Days Without End,* which was, like so much of his writing, basically autobiographical.

---

70. *To Saxe Commins from Carlotta Monterey O'Neill.* ALS 2 pp.

Jan. 10th 1930

Saxe dear,

Thank you so much for your charming letter.

Don't fuss about what you have to do relative to the person you work for. There you have no faith, race or colour!—Just a *sense of humour*—& *tact!*— "He"[1] had that illustrator King[2] write & ask for the same thing—holding out as a bait that King would make *marvellous* illustrations for said work!— "He" must think we're half-witted not to see thro' such things.—Personally, I think King's illustrations for Gene's things were "mis-cast".—He doesn't get into the soul of what it's all about!!—But——don't mix up *your personality* with your work.—They are two distinct & separate forces.—

Dear, dear Saxe, one Jew tried to change men & was crucified!— Act accordingly—

Now *smile.*——

We have two marvellous dogs now that keep me busy—& more birds, that sing divinely—& last night the chef showed us a 5 week old piggie he'd bought to fatten & slaughter for us!— This house is becoming absolutely Russian!—— We had a dear Christmas—I purchased personal gifts for all the servants indoors & out—& their wives & children. I had a wee tree for

1. Possibly publisher Donald Friede or editor Pascal Covici.

2. Alexander King, who illustrated special editions of *"Anna Christie,"* The Emperor Jones, and *The Hairy Ape.*

Gene—& it was sweet. The servants were so generous to us in return, I was almost embarrassed—but it was charming—all of it—& so new to Gene & enjoyable.—Our life is a dear, quiet, rich & pleasant thing,—all our past hurts we are forgetting in our love & thought for each other.—Gene working each day.—

> Our best love to you &
> Dorothy
> —Carlotta—

---

71. *To Saxe Commins from Eugene O'Neill.* WIRE (copy) 1 p.   [Yale]

January 27th, 1930

COPY

Saxe Commins
  1 Gramercy Park, New York City
Would be glad to give Gruenberg[3] Opera rights Jones but there are temporary complications stop Ask him see Madden[4] and arrange situation with him stop Best to you and Dorothy

> Gene

---

72. *To Saxe Commins from Carlotta Monterey O'Neill.* ALS 4 pp.
On stationery headed: Le Plessis / Saint-Antoine du Rocher / (Indre-et-Loire)

March 31st 1930

Dear Saxe,
    I would have written before but we have been tearing about the country—making a real tour de France. We had intended going to Italy but had been kept in Paris for so long that we did not feel up to it.— While in Paris Mr. Light & his wife[5] turned up. I have my own opinions as to Mr. Light's loyalty to Gene the year Gene left New York. These opinions I have not kept to myself.— But, as Mr. L. is no friend of mine (or does he pretend to be!) it really does not matter *what* I think. But when he (J.L.) wrote to Gene asking to see him I told Gene I should be pleased,—in compliment to Gene,—

3. Louis Gruenberg, Russian-born opera and film score composer whose adaptation of *The Emperor Jones* opened at New York's Metropolitan Opera House in Jan. 1933.
  4. Richard Madden, O'Neill's agent.
  5. James Light and his wife Patti.

to receive Mr. Light at dinner at the hotel & be as polite as I knew how—but I would *not* receive his wife! His wife, the "Fitzie" woman, Miss Blair[6] & Mrs. Throckmorton[7] were all very fluent in their conversation concerning me during a certain time—& said things not only stupidly untrue—but *ridiculous* had they *looked into things!* Also they were so "sorry for" & "sympathetic with" another person who was drinking continually & having an open affair with a cheap newspaper man.[8] Even Gene's lawyer wasn't loyal enough to use this as a means to an end!—But all this is ancient history. "I" did *not* receive Mrs. L. nor *will* I ever.— Or the other three ladies mentioned above.— Mr. L. asked if Gene wouldn't see his wife. So I arranged to be out while she was brought to the du Rhin to tea one day.—*That* is the story—in case you hear other versions!—— Not that it is important—but I *never* forget the *good* or *bad* from anyone! It was *shocking* the way some of *Gene's so-called friends* covered up things to spare *another person*—when by being *honest* (nothing more) Gene could have been spared so much worry & humiliation— Their ideas of *loyalty* & *decency* I do not understand. Needless to say—in some corners—there are now regrets!—

Enough of that nonsense——. So glad your job gives you enough pleasure to make up for the rubs! Dorothy sounds the busiest of people.—I sometimes wish I had something I could do here. Of course I am never idle—there is a great deal to look after here, as the house is much too big for us—but a *personal* interest would be nice.—

When we eventually settle I will go in for some hobby—I have many to carry on with.—

Spring is in the air. Trees are budding—flowers in the woods.—

Gene returned to schedule this morning.

I would have liked to have seen Mei Lan-Fang.[9] We hear much of "Green Pastures"[10]—Have the play here but haven't read it as yet.—I always take the New York Times & that with the clipping bureaus we are kept fairly well informed as to news in U.S.A. "Anna Christie" got marvellous notices.

6. Actress Mary Blair, who had created the leading female roles in *Diff'rent* (1920), *The Hairy Ape* (1922), and *All God's Chillun Got Wings* (1924) and was known as "the O'Neill actress." When producer Arthur Hopkins moved *The Hairy Ape* from Greenwich Village to Broadway, he replaced her with Carlotta Monterey. Carlotta and Mary Blair thereafter never liked each other.

7. Wife of Cleon Throckmorton, scene designer for many Provincetown Players productions.

8. A slur at Agnes.

9. China's foremost actor, who had recently opened on Broadway in a program of short plays designed to show his artistry and versatility.

10. Marc Connelly's play, adapted from Roark Bradford's book dealing with biblical episodes as viewed through the imagination of blacks, was the sensation of the 1929–30 Broadway season.

Garbo must be excellent.[11] What *lies* are published in the papers—regarding *personal news!* And even newspaper people seem to believe their own fables!

Gene sends best love to you & Dorothy.

Bless you both
Carlotta

---

73. *To Dorothy Commins from Carlotta Monterey O'Neill.* ALS 1 p.
On stationery headed: Le Plessis / Saint-Antoine du Rocher / (Indre-et-Loire)

April 5th 1930

Dear Dorothy,—

Gene was generous enough to let me read Saxe's letter in which I learned the news of the *"baby"!* I flew to my Corona & sent a cable. I hope you rec'd it.

Saxe is going to have this baby with you—I feel certain—and what a father he'll make! But you must be severe or he'll spoil it—(says Auntie).

Seriously,—we are very happy for & with you for we know what a welcome mite this one will be.—

God bless you, Saxe & the Babe—

Dearest love,
Carlotta

---

74. *To Saxe Commins from Eugene O'Neill.* TLS 1 p.
On stationery headed: Le Plessis / Saint-Antoine du Rocher / (Indre-et-Loire)

April 29th 1930

Dear Saxe:

As usual, I have meant to answer your two letters long before this but have kept putting it off. The news about your coming heir—or heiress—is certainly glad tidings. Grand stuff! My most affectionate congratulations to you both! As for your wishing my unworthy name on this helpless infant—

11. Although O'Neill considered Greta Garbo "damned good in her work," he never saw her talking film debut in *"Anna Christie,"* suspecting that it would be "all to the Garbo and very little of the O'Neill left in it" (letter to Grace Rippin, April 4, 1930); actually, the film was quite faithful to the play.

if a son—why if he will stand for such an outrage it is certainly just too good with me!

Your dope of the lady-bitch who is suing me is certainly interesting.[12] I had heard she was that type. Of course her claim is a ridiculous hold-up that would never be permitted in any other country but our land of free blackmail, but still she has already spoiled a movie sale that would have netted me thirty-seven thousand and will have cost me nearly fifty by the time the suit is over. And there is always the danger that one will be up against a judge that doesn't know a book from a rabbit. So her damn suit doesn't add to the joy of my life at all. I am sure she stole her own book bodily from some sources, probably French erotica, and if you run across anything or hear of anything resembling it you will be doing me a big favor.

I am hard at work on the beginning of the second draft of my new stuff.[13] It keeps growing and I am well pleased with it. But there is a hell of a lot still to be done and I doubt very much if it will be in shape to submit for production next season. My plan after this second draft is done is to lay it aside for a while and get perspective on it, in the interim doing the play that I told Dorothy and you the idea of in Cap d'Ail. I will tell you this much in strict confidence—don't tell a soul!—about my new opus; It is a trilogy—not in the Dynamo sense, this is a totally different idea, a real trilogy with the same characters in all three plays. This means I have written the first draft of three full plays since last fall—quite a job. The first draft I wrote out in a technique of "Desire" naturalism, to get a foundation, but that isn't enough to get all I want out of it so I am now blossoming out from that as a basis into a sort of modified combination of the methods of The Great God Brown and Strange Interlude. I think that will do the trick. I have already been through half the first play that way and the method seems really to belong. So now you know more about it than anyone else does.

Life here continues very pleasant. It is especially beautiful just now when spring is burgeoning on us. I wish you and Dorothy were still on this side so you could get a glimpse of it.

The Bugatti is grand! I shatter the echoes of Touraine with it. Haven't tried for any grand speeds yet, the motor is too young, but have made eighty.

All affectionate best to you both! We think of you often and wish you were over here. Give my kindest to Teddy and Stella and Ian when you see them—also my love to your mother. I will bet she is some excited over Dorothy's glad tidings!

As ever, Saxe
Gene

12. See letter 58, n. 103.
13. *Mourning Becomes Electra.*

75. *To Saxe Commins from Eugene O'Neill.* ALS 1 p.

[early June 1930]

Dear Saxe:

Here y'are. Only too glad to. Just returned from Paris—saw Kamerny Theatre[14] in "All God's Chillun" & "Desire Under Elms." Damned interesting & imaginative! Met Tairoff and the bunch. Fine bunch. Like them extremely. God, if we only had their group spirit and love of the theatre—imaginative love—somewhere in our theatre! Think I will go to Moscow now before I return to States—next winter sometime maybe.

All best!

Gene

76. *To Saxe Commins from Carlotta Monterey O'Neill.* ALS 4 pp.
On stationery headed: Le Plessis / Saint-Antoine du Rocher / (Indre-et-Loire)

Sunday. *July 27th '30*

Saxe dear,

I haven't written for ages because I have had no time to attend to any personal desires as I have been manageress and entertainer for a small hotel! At least so it has seemed for the past seven weeks. But now we are alone again & I am up to my ears in household books & personal mail.—But——I think of you & Dorothy & the Babe so often & say a "Jehovah bless you" in my heart of hearts.

Gene & I had heard nothing re Liveright selling out.[15] We had Mr. Liveright to luncheon with us one day in Paris at the Hotel du Rhin & he drank mineral water & was very prunes & prisms! As I had only met him once before in my life & that had been in N.Y. & he was steeped in liquor & his conversation the vulgarest it had ever been my misfortune to hear (!)—this

14. A Russian theatre company that aimed for a fusion of drama, music, dance, and decor in stylized productions; it was founded by Alexander Tairov in rebellion against the naturalism of Constantin Stanislavski's Moscow Art Theatre.

15. In spite of publishing a good many books that fared well, including such best sellers as Anita Loos's *Gentlemen Prefer Blondes* and Dreiser's *An American Tragedy,* Liveright was chronically short of cash from high living and playing the stock market. Eventually, after he kept selling shares in the company to Arthur H. Pell, his head bookkeeper, Pell owned a majority of the stock and took control. Liveright, at loose ends, hung around his former business place until one day Pell said in a loud voice, for all to hear, "Horace, I don't think you'd better come in any more. It doesn't look well for business." Within a few months Liveright was dead of pneumonia at age forty-six.

Paris episode caused me much merriment. So many people only show Gene their white & holy selves!—

Darlings (this letter is for Dorothy too—of course) I am enclosing a wee cheque for some little thing for the Babe. I wish to God I could send a lot— but I've just treated my own 5 ft. 6 in. baby & my mother to a summer holiday so I am little low.—But with it goes my dearest love & all the blessings of the Infinite.—Gene is enclosing a wee cheque for the Babe also with his dearest love & blessings.—

Life goes on.—Gene & I celebrated our first wedding anniversary with happy hearts & a feeling of having, at last, *arrived*. His work is magnificent, his health excellent. His only complaint that we have no sunshine! We have nothing but grey days—an awful lot of rain—& only now & then really sunshine—. But later we'll try to get away & seek real warmth.—

Nathan & Miss Gish[16] were here. Dr. Geo. Draper[17] & Dr. Alvin Barach[18]—(I adore Dr. Draper!)—And others that don't matter, —with now & then a N.Y. newspaper man thrown in[19] to prove we are normal, healthy, human people. —And so it goes.—

Eventually we are planning to return to America & live in the region of Virginia. *Far* enough to keep "people" from dropping in & *near* enough so that our *friends* can come to us!—

If I don't write as often as you feel that I should do not think it is because I do not think of you—I have many duties & the days fly—.

With our dearest love always,
Carlotta

16. Actress Lillian Gish.

17. A pioneer of psychosomatic medicine, brother of the noted monologist Ruth Draper, and a gifted raconteur.

18. Dr. Alvan L. Barach, an outstanding diagnostician who had treated O'Neill for "nerves" in New York in 1927.

19. Ward Morehouse, drama critic of the New York *Sun;* Richard Watts, Jr., movie critic of the New York *Herald Tribune;* Don Skene, a sportswriter for the *Herald Tribune;* and John Byram of the New York *Times* had all visited that summer.

77. *To Saxe Commins from Eugene and
Carlotta Monterey O'Neill.* WIRE 1 p.
At head of wire: FA13 StAntoineduRocher 12 1445

[September 13, 1930]

LCD Saxe Commins
One Gramercy Park NY
Congratulations[20] Love

Gene and Carlotta

78. *To Saxe and Dorothy Commins from Eugene O'Neill.* ACS 1 p.

[postmarked
November 12, 1930]

Dear Saxe & Dorothy:
Here is the Spanish Bugatti! We are having a grand vacation in Spain.
Hope the heiress is "in the pink."
From here we go to Gibraltar and Morocco.

Love from both!
Gene

79. *To Saxe Commins from Carlotta Monterey O'Neill.* ALS 2 pp.
On stationery headed: CMO'N

Nov. 29th 1930

Saxe dearest,
This has been such a strange year of ups & downs—but a beautiful year
in that Frances came to us.—Her photographs are really awfully good—&
what a nice "Fatty" she is! Dear Dorothy looks so lovely.—
Enclosed, my dear, you'll find the wee cheque. It is for some wee thing
for Frances for Christmas.—I regret I can't send more—but I have so many
babes, this year, young & old that I am a little troubled about my family—
But do know that to you & Dorothy and the Babe I send dearest love &
prayers for health & peace & joy—

Always yours,
Carlotta

Gene sends love too—he will write soon.

20. Frances Ellen Commins was born on Sept. 12, 1930.

80. *To Saxe Commins from Carlotta Monterey O'Neill.* ALS 3 pp.
On stationery headed: Le Plessis / Saint-Antoine du Rocher /
(Indre-et-Loire)

Jan. 2nd 1931

Saxe dear.—

I meant to answer your charming letter & then your second came to Gene re your having left your job.[21] From your letters you sounded *so* miserable there & the man in question being a little far from the straight & narrow— it sounds to me as if you've done a wise thing.—Anyway I'm *sure* your Soul will sing it's Freedom!—

A friend came over for the holidays, from London, & brought an especially fat germ with her.—On Christmas Eve I passed out & for two days knew not & cared not—then came to to learn Gene was going to bed.—I began to drag myself about to nurse both of us & now we're both better. Nothing serious in anyway whatsoever—but the physical & mental lassitude that hangs on for days after these grippe colds is annoying. But, fortunately, Gene has been able to read and smoke all during his attack so he had some relaxation. In a week or ten days we are going to Paris for a change & for some business & to have the play[22] typed. We know a man who will come to the hotel & type it under our noses!—

Each day we loathe the French more—their avariciousness & pettiness. We will be more than happy to return to our own country where we feel we belong. Not New York—but in a part conducive to health & contentment.—

I am so happy to know that Dorothy & Frances are getting strong. What a complete household you now have.—

Our dearest love to you & Dorothy & the Babe.— May this New Year bring you & yours new joys & peace.—

Jehovah keep you—
Carlotta

Gene sends his best—he is sitting before the fire going over his play!—Oh— *that play*—we'll be so glad to be rid of it—.

21. Commins had left Covici-Friede.
22. *Mourning Becomes Electra.*

81. To Saxe Commins from Eugene O'Neill. TLS 2 pp.

Hotel du Rhin,
Paris, France
January 24th 1931

Mr. Saxe Commins,
1 Rutherford Place
New York City

Dear Saxe:

I was tickled to death to learn by your letter of the 4th that you have landed with Liveright. Your work there ought to be very congenial, as I know you will like all the bunch there. I know how you must have felt at the other place. One of those lads is a crook—as you know. I have reason to know!—and I judge the other by the company he keeps. It was fine of Manuel[23] to use his influence with Liveright's in your behalf. Manuel, as I have always said since I first met him, is one rare person. His success with "Coronet" has pleased me more than anything I know of in a very long time.

Yes, there is something that you can do for me at Liveright's—and thus save a lazy man a letter. Alexander King has written to me—a very hectic sort of note—, in which he tells me he is dying of cancer of the kidneys, but he hopes to live long enough to finish the illustrations for "Lazarus Laughed."[24] Well, somehow I suppose I ought to be awfully sorry, but something in the tone of the letter makes me believe that Alex has heard how down I am on his last illustrations for "Anna Christie" and that he is giving me a little sob story to work on my sympathies. People with cancer usually do not go writing letters about it to men they hardly know. Or if they do, they shouldn't.

At any rate, I want you to tell Pell I do not want King doing any more illustrations—and I especially don't want him doing "Lazarus Laughed."

The O'Neill family has been having a run of hard luck. Carlotta is in the American hospital resting up after a bad attack of grippe and I have had it too, and I am here at the hotel getting most of my play typed and trying to rewrite a couple of acts that need it. I am anxious to get the damn thing off my chest now and hope within another month or so this will be done.

Much love from us both to you and Dorothy and Frances. Good luck in the new job,

As ever,
Gene

23. Arthur Pell, now heading Liveright, employed Saxe when Manuel Komroff retired from editorial work to concentrate on his own writings.

24. Far from being in declining health, King went on to become the author of best-selling books and a national celebrity on television. He died of a heart attack, aged sixty-six, in 1965.

---

82. *To Saxe Commins from Eugene O'Neill.* TLS 1 p.

> Hotel du Rhin,
> Paris, France
> Feb. 4th 1931

Dear Saxe:

This is just a line or two in answer to yours about the brochure.[25] I would suggest that you add to the German representation Gerhardt Hauptmann[26] and Schnitzler.[27] As you have probably noticed in two interviews with them which were published in New York Sunday papers lately, they had very nice things to say about me and they would probably be willing to repeat these for the brochure. I would add to Russia Tairov, the director of Kamerny, who has done nearly all my plays in Russia and whom I met in Paris last year when he was doing All God's Children and Desire Under the Elms at the Pigalle. I am sure he will be only too glad to do it and if you can get Dantchenko[28] too and perhaps Stanislavsky,[29] you will have these three most famous men in the Russian theatre. You might land Meyerhold[30] too, but I don't know about that.

I can't provide the statement by Lenormand and I would not want to ask him for it personally, especially as I know he is very busy and in a state of heeby-jibbies with rehearsals for his new play going on. If you want anything from Checkslovakia, I think you can get something from the Capeks.[31]

I think the photostatic reproduction of a manuscript page is a very good idea. See Harry[32] about this. He has my note book in his safe for use in the plagiarism business. Perhaps a page from the note book would be more of a curiosity than just the page of script. Only be sure it applies to an old idea.

Carlotta is out of the hospital and feels much better. I myself feel rotten and "washed-up." I have decided to go to the Canary Islands instead of Sicily

---

25. As a promotional feature, Liveright was planning to issue a brochure of short pieces on O'Neill by noted American and foreign writers.

26. Gerhart Hauptmann (1862–1946), German novelist, poet, and dramatist.

27. Arthur Schnitzler (1862–1931), Austrian dramatist and novelist.

28. Vladimir Nemirovich-Danchenko, famous Russian director and cofounder of the Moscow Art Theatre.

29. Constantin Stanislavsky, Russian actor, director, producer, and cofounder of the Moscow Art Theatre.

30. Vsevolod Emilievich Meyerhold, Russian director and producer who led the revolt against naturalism in the Russian theatre.

31. Karel (1890–1938) and Josef (1887–1945) Capek, Czech brothers and playwrights.

32. Harry Weinberger.

in order to be sure and get some hot sun. I have had the trilogy typed and I'll do what I hope will be my final going over to it there.

Carlotta joins me in all best to you and Dorothy and Francis,

As ever,
Gene

Mr. Saxe Commins
61 West 48th Street
New York City

---

83. *To Eugene O'Neill from Saxe Commins.* TL(cc) 1 p.

February 4th, 1931

Dear Gene:

I make haste to put you at ease about Alexander King. Mr. Smith and Mr. Pell tell me that there is no reason for paying any attention to his sob story. We are under no contractual obligations to Mr. King and we have no thought of letting him do any illustrations for us. His pulling the story of dying with cancer is an out and out fraud. Only the other day he was in the office and there was no sign of any decline, unfortunately. He has been known to pull that sort of thing before. Just ignore him.

By the time this letter reaches you Manuel[33] will be in Paris and will probably have gotten in touch with you. He has all sorts of messages from us to you and Carlotta. I am very happy to say that his new book, Two Thieves, is going over.

By now you must have received my letter regarding the brochure. Perhaps there is a reply on the way. So far I have had enthusiastic responses from Brooks Atkinson and Lewis Mumford.[34] There has been no time for European replies. May we count on the photostatic copy of a manuscript page of yours?

I was awfully sorry to hear of Carlotta's illness. Dorothy and I will write to her in a day or so. Meanwhile give her our love.

Everything is flourishing at 1 Rutherford Place and I am very happy on my job.

Devotedly,

Mr. Eugene O'Neill
Le Plessis,
Saint Antoine du Rocher,
Indre et Loire, France

33. Manuel Komroff.
34. A critic on a wide range of cultural matters.

---

84. To Saxe Commins from Carlotta Monterey O'Neill. TLS 2 pp.

Hotel du Rhin,
Paris, France
Feb. 6th 1931

Dear Saxe:

Thank you so much for your letter of January 22nd received this morning. I can't tell you how pleased I am to know that you are happy in your new job. What with being congenial in your work and having your baby at home life ought to run along very smoothly for you.

We are going back to Plessis tomorrow and hope to sail on the 25th from Lisbon for the Canary Islands. Gene is really looking remarkably well considering he has had the grippe and has been in Paris for a month, but I feel that the sea and the sun will put him in high spirits.

In your letter you mention certain gossip as to whether or not I am to have a baby.[35] This seems to me a very personal topic and I had no idea that people in New York had so little to do that my physical condition could cause them so much upset. Gene and I were pestered to death by reporters even from the Associated Press, sending telegrams and writing letters and even going to the trouble to call at Plessis to discover if we expected an addition to the family. Gene correctly ignored their question and treated them with utter contempt. If you feel that this should be affirmed or denied, you can tell them that it is not true. If they feel they should know more about our affairs tell them that Gene is all for a baby and I am all against! I think Gene has enough trouble at the present time paying ten thousand dollars a year alimony and supporting three children without my adding any more to his responsibilities. I do not want to sound snooty, but it is only since I have met Gene and married him that I have come in contact with so much personal criticism as to my private life, how much rent we were paying, how many servants we had, whether we had one or more automobiles, etc., etc., etc. Even Kenneth,[36] who is one of the most loyal friends Gene has, went to a great deal of trouble going about denying that we live in a château or had so many servants or cars or what not. Just why he put himself out to this extent I do not know. I don't see whose business it is and particularly as I pay one-half of all the bills I don't think it is any of their business. I often wonder what will happen when we return to America, because I am not as sweet-dispositioned as Gene or as patient and if any of these old friends who knew the former Mrs. O'Neill began asking me ques-

35. Syndicated Broadway columnist Walter Winchell had erroneously reported on Sept. 8, 1930, that "The Eugene O'Neills (Carlotta Monterey) are so thrilled!" The rumor that the O'Neills were to have a child persisted for months.

36. Kenneth Macgowan. See letter 66, n. 114.

tions, I am sure they will receive the reply that they might not expect. Dear Saxe, I am not cross with you at all, but I do wish you would not pay attention to gossip and if they continue to annoy you simply tell them you consider it none of their business or if you don't like being that rude tell them *I* consider it is none of their business!

I am so delighted to hear about the baby and I am sure that Dorothy is very happy. But do tell her not to give up her music entirely because I feel that when Frances grows up she will enjoy hearing her mother play so very much.

I will drop you a line from the Islands. With love from Gene and always from me to the entire family,

Carlotta

Pardon typing but I have a bad wrist!—[37]

Again I must say how content I am that you are happy in your job— —because you are a dear!—

Thanks for Frances's snap—she is so pretty.—

---

85. *To Eugene O'Neill from Saxe Commins.* TL(cc) 1 p.

February 20th, 1931

Mr. Eugene O'Neill,
Le Plessis,
Saint Antoine du Rocher,
Indre et Loire, France

Dear Gene:

I hope this letter will be forwarded to you to the Canary Islands. If, however, it waits for you at Plessis, it will be no serious delay. Letters are going out to everyone you mention and we hope to get responses as soon as possible. I shall write to Lenormand and the Capeks. I shall also get in touch with Harry Weinberger and use the material he has in the safe. Trust me to pick out a page that refers to an old idea.

Naturally, I am crazy to see the new script. The newspapers here are keeping its title and its theme a dark secret. All the publicity so far given out by The Guild intensifies the mystery of the trilogy. There has been some allusion to the fact that it will take three nights to play.

Perhaps you managed to see Manuel before leaving for the Canary Islands. I depended on him to convey all the news. It is good to learn that Carlotta is feeling much better. I had a marvelous letter from her yesterday and I shall write to her over the week-end. All love from Dorothy, Frances and me.

Devotedly,

37. This sentence and all that follows are handwritten.

86. *To Saxe Commins from Eugene O'Neill.* TLS 2 pp.

Hotel du Rhin,
Paris, France
April 7th 1931

Dear Saxe:

Much gratitude to you for your long letter about the case.[38] It is all a lot of nonsense, but I hope it will soon be settled. But I don't want to go into that in this letter.

This is to tell you that I am sending scripts of the trilogy to the Guild and to George Jean Nathan by this same mail. I have no extra script to send you, but what I want you to do is call up Nathan after giving him time to read it and when he tells you he is quite through with it get the script he has. I am writing him to give it to you. Also I want you to call round and get it and meet him. I have told him all about you and I know you will both like meeting each other.

Of course, I want everything about the script to be kept dark. I do not know who at Liveright's ought to read it—I mean whom you could trust to keep his mouth shut. Now that Liveright is gone I do not know how things are there. But you can use your own judgment on this and impress upon whoever it is the need for secrecy. You might also let Ben De Casseres read it, telling him to keep it under his hat. And after you have done all this you can give the script to Madden to send to Washington for copyright. Of course, I will have new scripts made and will send another to Liveright in due time. Let me know what you think after you have read it.

I won't go into any of our news because I think we will be seeing you and Dorothy before long. I can't tell you definitely yet, but we might hit New York the latter part of May or in June. This is, of course, strictly under your hat. I don't want my former "frau" to know I am in New York until I have been there and gone.

Thank you very much for sending me the O'Casey letter.[39] It was damned fine of him to write that. I am going to write him and tell him how pleased I was. I admire his work very much.

I enjoyed the sun and the swimming at the Canaries but a vacation is still due me, because I worked there nearly all the time. I feel pretty fagged out now that this trilogy is off my chest.

I forgot to mention in previous letters that you might get something for the brochure from Thomas Mann—the noble prize winner of a year ago. I

38. The *Strange Interlude* plagiarism suit had gone to trial in March; the verdict was not rendered until late April. See letter 58, n. 103.

39. Irish playwright Sean O'Casey had written an extremely laudatory letter about O'Neill for the Liveright promotional brochure.

saw some things he wrote about "All God's Children" in an interview once and it sounded very fine.

Love from us both to you and Dorothy. See you before very long, I hope.

As ever,
Gene

Mr. Saxe Commins
One Rutherford Place
New York City

P.S. Will you phone Ben and tell him I won't bother answering his letter now because I hope to see him very soon. Tell him to keep this quiet. Remember that none of the Guild crowd know that I am coming back yet. I don't want them to for a while.
(Nathan's address
The Royalton
44 W. 44th St.)[40]

---

87. *To Eugene O'Neill from Saxe Commins.* TL(cc) 2 pp.

April 15, 1931

Dear Gene,

Before arranging to see George Jean Nathan, I want to get a letter off to you in response to yours of this morning, dated Hotel du Rhin April 7th. Needless to assure you, I shall carry out your instructions to the minutest detail. No one will know from me what your plans are; they will be kept strictly under my hat. Until you send the official, publication script to the house, I will be the only one here who will have seen the original. After reading it and writing to you, I'll turn it over to Ben and then give it to Madden for copyright.

I can't assure you too strongly that I will make it my chief function to watch over your script as it goes through the various processes to the complete book. Naturally, everyone in the house has a special interest in doing as much as they have done before for your books. You see, the personnel of the organization remains absolutely as it was, with the exception of Liveright. T. R. Smith is in control of the editorial department. Pete Gross manages production; Julian Messner sales and advertising. Arthur Pell is in charge of management and finance. In no sense is the spirit changed. All our authors of importance are with us and will stay. The negligible ones come and go.

It has become very clear to me during my three months here that matters

40. The parentheses and the material within them are handwritten.

are in much better shape than they have been before. In spite of very bad general business condition, the firm is on a more substantial basis than it has been hitherto. The plans for the future are very ambitious. First of these is that on May 1st we move to new offices at 31 West 47th Street. We must give up the house to the new Radio City project and it will be torn down immediately following our departure. Second, our fall list and the tentative list for next spring are undoubtedly of the highest calibre we've had in a long time.

I don't mean this to sound like an ad, but I should like to convey that prospects are bright and to dispel any anxieties you may have.

That I can look forward to you coming back in May or June is the brightest piece of news that has come this way in years.[41] If you will write me, just as soon as you arrange for your passage, I may be able to help about reserving quarters for you in New York. Or anything else I can possibly do—you have but to command. I'll meet your boat and keep the hounds off the trail. Trust me to stay mum.

Yesterday I called up Harry W. to find out whether a decision had been rendered. The judge is taking his time, and I surmise that he is doing it with a purpose. He gave every indication during the trial that he was disposed to put a stop to that sort of thing once for all. Just as soon as his decision is announced you shall have a cable from me.

All goes very well with Dorothy, Frances and me. Dorothy's little book[42] got off to a fine start. Frances is thriving and I am really very happy on my job. It's a joy to be with people whom one can trust.

Thanks for the tip about Thomas Mann. I wrote him a note, but so far there has been no response. At any rate, I'll dig up his article from the files at the Public Library.

All love to you and Carlotta from the three of us . . .[43]

Saxe describes what happened when he brought the finished script of *Mourn-Becomes Electra* to Liveright to begin production:

> When I brought the completed manuscript of *Mourning Becomes Electra* to the Liveright offices in 1931, there was a general dismay over the title. The then editor-in-chief, Thomas R. Smith, looked at the sheaf of papers, concentrated on the title page, played for a while with the long black ribbon on his spectacles, cleared his throat as a preliminary

41. The O'Neills returned to the United States by boat, landing at New York on May 17, 1931.
42. *Making an Orchestra*, published by Macmillan.
43. The carbon of the letter ends at this point.

to uttering a shattering profundity, shook his white-thatched head and exploded the word "meaningless" with an implied exclamation mark at the end of it. As on cue, the editorial assistants and the publicity director embellished the verdict with even stronger adjectives, both commercial and semantic.

Not until patient explanations were offered that the verb in the title was a synonym for "suits" rather than the active word for coming into being, were they relieved of their perplexity. Even then they grudgingly admitted that it made some sense, but not enough to identify such an exploitable property. They insisted, as publishers habitually do, that a book title must smite the beholder in the eye, whether it applies to the contents or not, and must, above all, be easily remembered.

The Liveright firm, as everyone knew but would not openly admit, was teetering on the brink of insolvency and it was hoped that the publication of the new O'Neill play would postpone the disaster for a while.

Fighting for that postponement with every stratagem at his command was an accountant, the new owner of the Liveright publishing company, Arthur Pell. . . .

Pell counted heavily on the sale of 100,000 copies of *Mourning Becomes Electra* and not without reason or precedent. If this could be accomplished, the plus would replace the minus. . . . *Strange Interlude* had been one of the most phenomenal commercial successes in the history of modern play publishing. Approximately 110,000 copies, in the trade edition alone, had been sold, a figure no play by anyone but Shakespeare had attained until then. *Mourning Becomes Electra* became Pell's hope of coming out of financial mourning known by its mournful color as in the black. His subordinates merely hoped that the play would produce a lighter shade of red.

---

88. *To Eugene O'Neill from Saxe Commins.* TL(cc) 1 p.

July 20, 1931

Dear Gene:

After many delays the paper-bound proofs of "Mourning" go off to you today.[44] You will notice that I have transferred the proof marks made by the printer and such queries as he asks. To save time, I will not read proof on it until you will have incorporated all your changes.

I have put the original manuscript, the printer's master proofs and a set

44. O'Neill's plays sometimes appeared in book form before or at about the same time they were first produced on stage. *Mourning Becomes Electra* was published on Nov. 2, 1931; it had its stage premiere on Oct. 26, 1931.

of duplicate proofs in the safe. I am taking it for granted that you have a copy of the manuscript for purposes of comparison with the proof.

All love to you and Carlotta from the three of us.

Devotedly,

Mr. Eugene O'Neill
North Port
Long Island[45]
SC:PKK

———————

89. To Eugene O'Neill from Saxe Commins. TL(cc) 1 p.

July 21, 1931

Dear Gene:

The Literary Guild has expressed an interest in "Mourning," and I wonder if you would give your consent to letting them see a set of galleys. It goes without saying that Carl Van Doren and the other members of the committee will be pledged to secrecy, and will in no way divulge the story or the structure of the play.

As you know, the Guild always brings out its edition simultaneously with the trade edition, and therefore they would have to have the time between now and production for consideration and, if accepted, for distribution.

I am very anxious to get your permission to give the galleys to the Guild under the conditions I outlined, but I shall do nothing until I hear from you. May I hope to have a letter by return mail?

Devotedly,

Mr. Eugene O'Neill
North Port
Long Island

P.S. Did you receive the package today?

———————

90. To Saxe Commins from Carlotta Monterey O'Neill. ALS 2 pp.

Saturday Night
[July 25, 1931]

Saxe dear.—

Gene has asked me to ask you if it is possible (!) for him to have from 6 to a dozen copies of those "books" of "Electra"—(like the one you sent him) for souvenirs?

Also—he asks how many will have been published—?

45. After a brief stay at the Hotel Madison in New York, the O'Neills had in mid-June rented a seaside house for the summer.

You ought to keep one for yourself & we'll have Gene write in it for Frances!—

I must phone to Dorothy tomorrow about her Concert.—

You're *such* a nice family & I'm so fond of you!—

Our love always—
Carlotta

---

91. *To Carlotta Monterey O'Neill from Saxe Commins.* TL(cc) 1 p.

July 27th, 1931

Dear Carlotta:

No trouble at all to get out a dozen bound sets of proofs of "Mourning." But I wonder if you want the version which Gene has in his possession now, or one which will contain all the revisions. If it is the one that Gene has, I shall order them at once.

So far as proofs in my possession go—I have, in the safe, one master set, one duplicate set and there is the set I mailed Gene. If your query about how many will have been published refers to the first edition, I cannot answer it because we have not yet decided how many copies there will be in the first printing.

I cannot tell you how deeply touched I was by your thoughtfulness in calling Dorothy to wish her good luck for her concert tomorrow night. Just like you to think of such things in your usual generous way.

With all our love,
Always,

Mrs. Eugene O'Neill
North Port
Long Island

---

92. *To Eugene O'Neill from Saxe Commins.* TL(cc) 1 p.

July 30, 1931

Dear Gene:

The enclosed correspondence is self-explanatory. Have you a photograph which shows you at work, and would you be willing to submit it for this purpose?

Work is going forward on the revisions very satisfactorily. When may I expect "The Hunted?"[46]

All best,

Mr. Eugene O'Neill
Beacon Farm
Northport, L.I.

46. The second part of *Mourning Becomes Electra.*

93. To Saxe Commins from Eugene O'Neill. ALS 2 pp.

Northport, L.I.
[early August 1931]

Dear Saxe:

I've finished revising the bound galleys of the last two plays. I'm afraid I've done a hell of a lot of rewriting, especially in the last play, which means a job on resetting. But remember I warned youse Liveright guys you better, in your own interest, let me do my dirty work on a script before you printed! The rewriting seemed to me imperative to clear up and intensify parts of the plays.

I hope all my revisions are plainly indicated—also that the printers can reset without unbinding or maltreating. I'd like to have this handwriting-revised copy back in good condition as soon as you have finished with it—for Carlotta.

Before you send me the reprinted galleys for further minor looking over will you do a *thorough* proof reading job on them? I need this help. In three plays there are bound to occur even now plenty of slip-ups on my part which I'm too close to see. (stage directions, grammar, punctuation, etc.)

I want the firm to explain to the Guild when they submit galleys that I have still to do another polishing on them.

Granted production date Oct. 25th what is *latest* date I can get these next new galleys back to you—and what date page proofs—providing there are only minor corrections to make? I'd like to know this definitely as soon as possible so I can plan ahead on time.

All best!
Gene

94. To Eugene O'Neill from Saxe Commins. TL(cc) 1 p.

August 5, 1931

Dear Gene:

This is to answer your question about the galleys and page proofs, if we assume that production date will be October 25th.

I expect to return the revised galleys next week. If you can send them back to us by the 5th of September, it will give us until the 12th to get them into pages. Then, if you return them to us by the 20th, we can have the book plated and on press by the 25th of September, giving us until the 5th for printing and the balance of time for binding and delivery to the house. Do I make the situation clear, and does a full month give you ample time with the galleys?

As soon as the revised proofs come back, I will telephone you and arrange to work with you on them.

Love to Carlotta and you.

Mr. Eugene O'Neill
Beacon Farm
Northport, L.I.
SC:PKK

O'Neill had galleys (2nd) from Aug 12, to Oct 5 (First 2 plays)
    ”   ”   ”   (3rd play)   ”   ” to Oct[47]

---

95. *To Eugene O'Neill from Saxe Commins.* TL(cc) 1 p.

August 6th, 1931

Dear Gene:

In order to keep your bound copy of proofs exactly as you turned them over to me, I have transcribed your corrections most carefully to the master set. This is now in the hands of the printer, and I expect to have the revised proofs of the three plays by Tuesday or Wednesday. I shall write or 'phone you when they arrive. Meanwhile, the corrected manuscript for the first play, and the corrected bound galleys are being kept in Arthur Pell's safe.

All best.

Mr. Eugene O'Neill
Beacon Farm
Northport, L.I.

---

96. *To Frances Commins from Eugene O'Neill.*[48]

To Miss Frances Commins—

pretty heavy reading for you, my dear, at your age and in this hot weather, but never mind, you might as well take your gloom early and get that over so that later we can all say "Joy becomes Frances!" (I feel a certain responsi-

47. These marginal notes are penciled in on the carbon.
48. This inscription appears on a bound copy of the uncorrected proofs of *Mourning Becomes Electra.*

bility about your future because if you had had the bad taste to be a boy your misguided parents would have called you Eugene!)

Love to you!
Eugene O'Neill
August 1931

Saxe's memoir continues:

To my surprise I was summoned one day into the president's office and there I listened to a speech about my value to the company, my devotion to the work and other words of praise as fulsome as they were bewildering. I understood neither the meaning nor the motives of this citation. At its end Pell told me that I had richly earned a rise in pay, but, unfortunately, he could not give it to me. To do so would create ill-feeling among the men who had had their salaries slashed. But there was a way around the impasse: he could prove his appreciation by suggesting something of immensely greater value to me in the long run and with only a minor condition attached: that I must not under any circumstances mention it to my fellow-employees. These preliminaries out of the way, he came to the point: I was to be given the rare privilege and profitable opportunity to purchase fifty shares of Liveright non-voting stock at a token figure.

Pell was now in his element; he could talk in numbers. What he said was, in substance, that based on the earnings of the company over a long period of years, the stock he was about to sell to me was conservatively valued at $25 a share. In lieu of a rise in salary he was prepared to extend the rare privilege to me of purchasing one hundred shares at less than half their worth, or at $1200. If one hundred shares were too many for my purse, I could exercise the option of acquiring fifty for $600 and thereby become a part owner and thus be rewarded for my industry beyond the call of duty. Best of all, he concluded, no one would have to know about it.

I was neither impressed, flattered nor tempted. Such an offer was neither good or bad in my eyes for the simple reason of ignorance; I knew nothing whatever about stocks and read rows of figures showing profits and losses as I would the hieroglyphics on an obelisk. But far more important and decisive than this consideration was the simple if unfortunate fact that I did not have $600, or even $60, in my possession. In all candor I had to declare my insolvency and when I did so I was told that it would be highly profitable for me to borrow the sum, even if it meant the payment of interest. That counsel alone, Mr. Pell made it evident, was worth far more to me than a mere rise in pay, which, after all, was not to be compared with the glories of a nominal partnership in the business. And on this pious note the audience came to an end and I returned to my desk.

When I went to Northport the following day, O'Neill and I set to work on the galley proofs of *Mourning Becomes Electra*. Carlotta remained in the background and came forward only when we stopped work as the severely gracious hostess in her fastidiously kept home. She prepared our food, since the O'Neills were without servants at the time, waited on us after we had finished our labors over the proofs and joined us only at dinner and afterwards for talk and parlor games.

On the afternoon of the second day of my visit I jokingly said to Gene that I came close to being a stockholder in the house that published his books, but the mile I missed by, measured in money, was $600. He pressed me for more details and I explained the offer, omitting any mention of how much the publication of *Mourning Becomes Electra* meant to the survival of the Liveright company. This reticence was not so much discretion as it was lack of certainty about the danger signals; it would do more damage to shake O'Neill's confidence than to offer mine while the storm was gathering. Perhaps it would pass. Certainly it would add to his anxiety on the eve of production and publication to learn that the work on which he was engaged so long might be jeopardized. So the matter was dropped.

At dinner that night Gene told Carlotta that I had been offered stock in the company and added that it would be an excellent idea, especially for him, if I would purchase it, since it would be to his interest if I, as a part owner, would be able to represent and protect him. Carlotta agreed in her firmly positive way, adding that men had no sense in such matters; they should do such things and not talk about them. Literary men, she added, were infants and in need of business acumen to protect them in a hostile world. Whereupon Gene proposed that he lend me $600. When I protested on the grounds that, with my salary, the prospect of repaying the loan was remote, Carlotta dismissed my argument with the single word "Nonsense!" When Gene asked me to take it as a protection for his substantial accumulation of royalties on the Liveright books and as a personal favor to him, my misgivings were overcome. Finally I assented but on the condition that I write a note of debt. On a sheet of Carlotta's stationery I scribbled these words:

"I promise to pay on request to Eugene O'Neill the sum of $600," and added the date and my signature.

While we were drinking coffee, Gene excused himself and went upstairs with the note in his hand. In a few moments he returned with a check for $600 made out to me. I tucked it into my wallet, said my thanks and tried to turn the conversation to other matters. No other reference was made to the note during the following days of our work on *Mourning Becomes Electra*.

Back in New York with the corrected galley proofs, I reported to Pell and told him I was now prepared to take up his offer and would purchase fifty shares of stock. I gave him Eugene O'Neill's check for that sum, made out in my name and endorsed on its back by me to the Liveright Company. At first Pell was delighted, but his face fell when he saw how the check was countersigned. Telling me that I knew little about business, as I had been told many times before, he insisted that I should have endorsed it to him, Arthur Pell. This I did by placing his name directly under the first endorsement. Then he accepted the check and subsequently I was given a green-bordered certificate as evidence of my ownership of fifty shares of non-voting, non-dividend stock in the Liveright Company.

Saxe added a postscript to this story. Several years later, when he began to work at Random House, he tried to repay O'Neill.

As soon as I began to earn my salary at Random House, I set aside a portion of it until, little by little, I accumulated enough to discharge my indebtedness. Happily, I sent a check for $600 to Sea Island. It was returned to me, torn into small pieces. A year later I mailed another check for the same amount, only to be told this time that it had been destroyed. The third attempt to repay my debt brought a severe rebuke and the reminder that I had collected O'Neill's full royalties before the Liveright bankruptcy could reduce them by ninety-five per cent. I was admonished never to repeat the performance that was prompted by a bad conscience, which at best was a nuisance and at worst an imposition.

When I saw Gene in New York I persisted in bringing up the subject again, to his great annoyance. Rather than make the debt a kind of compulsive obsession, I decided to drop these persistent efforts to repay the money, but not until I could learn about the note still in Gene's possession. When I mentioned it, he began to laugh, as if it were a great joke and not a matter of the utmost seriousness to me. He then asked me whether I could recall the circumstances under which the note was written so long ago in Northport. I could indeed. I proceeded to reconstruct the scene in detail. Did I also remember that he went upstairs with the note in his hand and came down soon afterward with the check made out to me? I replied that that too was clear in my memory. Well, now he could tell me that the reason why he went upstairs was not so much to write the check as to flush the note down the toilet.

97. To Dorothy Commins from Carlotta Monterey O'Neill. ALS 3 pp.

Beacon Farm—
Newport, L.I.
Aug 14th 1931

Dorothy dear,

Your charming note just here. Also your nice husband is sitting a few yards from me, on the porch, going over scripts.—

As far as I am concerned I am afraid he has had a dull visit. I am *so* tired & *so* nervous I could "scream the house down"!

All this apartment doing—chasing back & forth to town—housekeeping here, having Gene's business acquaintances—Eugene Jr.—& his bride & now Master Shane for two weeks has about finished me. No matter how nice a boy of that age is—it is very difficult to have him about in a very small house. Particularly when he is not your own to correct etc.— And confusion, noise & disorder drive me mad.— I presume I'm just growing old—.

Saxe is too good a guest—one doesn't know he's here.— He's had swims anyway—and got the job done.

I go to town Monday night for a few days to begin to put *some* things in the apt. & see about curtains etc.[49]— From now on it will be very hard work. I think Gene will stop down here most of the time as he doesn't like the heat in town—

Thank God you & Frances are well.—

Am so glad the autograph to Frances pleased you. I suggested it to Gene thinking it would be more charming as the years go by—to her—than to you or Saxe. Baby things always are (to me) the most charming souvenirs.

It is very warm & sticky.—I rather pause now & again & give a thought to Plessis' cool, grey, dripping moods & the quiet of it all—.

Our love always & God bless you—
Carlotta

---

98. To Eugene O'Neill from Saxe Commins. TL(cc) 1 p.

August 18th, 1931

Dear Gene:

I have just learned from the printer that all corrections will have been made and all single-play bound copies will be ready on Thursday night or

49. The O'Neills had rented an eight-room duplex apartment at 1095 Park Avenue in New York for the winter.

Friday morning. They will go forth by mail to you immediately on their arrival. Or perhaps you might prefer if I could give one or two copies to someone who may be going out for a week-end? Unless I hear from you I shall send them by mail.

Needless to tell you what the two days at Northport meant to me.

All devotion,

Mr. Eugene O'Neill
Beacon Farm
Northport, L.I.
SC:PKK

---

99. *To Eugene O'Neill from Saxe Commins.* TL(cc) 1 p.

August 19th, 1931

Dear Gene:

T. R. Smith suggests that we print a little slip stating the following:

Twelve copies of uncorrected first proofs, set from the original manuscript of "Mourning Becomes Electra" by Eugene O'Neill, have been bound for distribution among his friends. The published version of the trilogy contains the final revisions made from these proofs by Mr. O'Neill.

Horace Liveright, Inc.
August 1931

His idea is that one of these slips should accompany each of the twelve copies of the bound, uncorrected first proofs. In the event that some of these have gone out, he suggests that you mail a slip to your friends who have received the first galleys.

If you approve of the suggestion and if you have any corrections to make in the text of this little statement, will you please communicate them to me? This matter has great bibliographical importance.

Always,

Mr. Eugene O'Neill
Beacon Farm
Northport, L.I.
SC:PKK

100. To Eugene O'Neill from Saxe Commins. TL(cc) 1 p.

August 25, 1931

Dear Gene:

I have gone over the proofs very carefully for typographical slips and I found several minor ones, which stand corrected now on the printer's set. There are a few queries which I shall take up with you when you come to town again.

I am really very sorry about the marked up covers of the bound proofs. But that can be easily corrected on your sets, merely by having new wrappers put on them.

All devotion,

Mr. Eugene O'Neill
Northport, L.I.

101. To Eugene O'Neill from Saxe Commins. TL(cc) 1 p.

August 31, 1931

Dear Gene:

In going over the question of a jacket for "Mourning" with Julian Messner, it occurred to me that we might use one of Robert Edmond Jones's sketches[50] for this purpose. We want to convey the period and the spirit of the plays in a cover design printed on a jacket uniform with those we used on your other books. I thought that perhaps a sketch of the pillared front of the house with a few figures in the foreground, such as Mr. Jones surely must have made, would serve admirably.

Do you think we could get Mr. Jones's consent to use such a sketch?

Devotedly,

Mr. Eugene O'Neill
Beacon Farm
Northport, L.I.

50. Jones was designing the sets and costumes for *Mourning Becomes Electra.*

---

102. To Eugene O'Neill from Saxe Commins. TL(cc) 1 p.

October 17th, 1931

Dear Gene:

Here are three complete sets of the working notes. In my hurry to get them off to you, I have not compared them with the original but I think you will find them accurate line for line and word for word. If there are any mistakes or corrections, they can be made when we compare this script with your written notes. Please notice that I have numbered the items throughout from one to thirty-eight.

The fourth carbon, a blurred one, is being held here in my desk for our printer when ready. I believe Mr. Sisk[51] has the facilities for making copies for his purposes.

The presses are rolling steadily now with the sheets for "M.B.E.". I believe we have a letter perfect job.

All best,

Mr. Eugene O'Neill
1095 Park Avenue
New York City

---

103. To Eugene O'Neill from Saxe Commins. TL(cc) 1 p.

November 10th
1931

Dear Gene:

T.R. Smith gives me the following information on the subject of copyrights:

No matter in whose name the copyright for "Thirst"[52] was taken out, it has a life of twenty-eight years, renewable at the end of that time for twenty-eight more. Even if the Badger firm is defunct, the copyright can be renewed in your name in 1942.

All rights to "Tomorrow" were in the possession of The Seven Arts Magazine[53] until they went out of business. That is to say, the story was copyrighted with all other material appearing in the same issue. But no one, under any circumstances, can use it without involving a suit for very large damages for having violated your commonlaw rights of possession. A pub-

51. Robert Sisk, publicity director for the Theatre Guild.
52. *Thirst and Other One-Act Plays,* O'Neill's first book, published in 1914 by Richard G. Badger's Gorham Press in Boston, financed by the author's father.
53. See letter 69, n. 123.

lisher who would undertake to bring out "Tomorrow" in any form without your permission, could be put out of business.

I hope you and Carlotta have a marvelous trip[54] and I need not tell you how much I appreciate the beautiful inscription in my copy of "Electra."

Always devotedly,

Mr. Eugene O'Neill
1095 Park Avenue
New York City

---

104. To Eugene O'Neill from Saxe Commins. TL(cc) 1 p.

January 29th, 1932

Dear Gene:

The enclosed is one of those things that I do not like to dismiss on my own authority. We always do our best to get a book into braille without any thought of recompense. I imagine you feel the same way about it. So, may we have your permission to give ours?

Always,

Mr. Eugene O'Neill
1095 Park Avenue
New York City
SC:PKK
Enc: 1

---

105. To Eugene O'Neill from Saxe Commins. TL(cc) 1 p.

March 25th, 1932

Dear Gene:

The suggestion has been made that a very short, perhaps two- or three-paragraph Foreword to the Black and Gold Edition of "Strange Interlude" would help immensely.

Would you be good enough to provide us with such a Foreword?[55]

All best,

Mr. Eugene O'Neill
1095 Park Avenue
New York City
SC:PKK

54. The O'Neills were to vacation in Sea Island, an exclusive resort off the Georgia coast.
55. O'Neill apparently refused this request, as no such foreword appears in the book.

---

106. To Saxe Commins from Carlotta Monterey O'Neill. ALS 1 p.
(On stationery headed: 1095 Park Avenue)

Saturday
[April 2nd 1932]

Saxe dear—

Will you please see to the enclosed.—

Do hope all goes well with you. Have been nursing Gene for ten days with grippe—& Blemie[56] is in the hospital with gastric catarrh—(cold in his middle). —My daughter is here but returns to school Tuesday—We *hope* to go away soon for a couple of weeks—Georgia—.[57]

Love as always
Carlotta

---

107. To Saxe Commins from Eugene O'Neill. ALS 2 pp.
On stationery headed: Sea Island Beach / Georgia

May 22nd 1932

Dear Saxe:

Your letter was misaddressed and didn't reach me till today. There's no "Atlanta" about it—only the above.

About that jack: Don't be a nut! I'll be "uneasy" if you think of paying it before 1942. Otherwise uneasiness on that score won't visit me. Forget it, Saxe! I tore up your meticulously businesslike note long ago. No such things exist between you & me. And I really owe that money to you for your services as Doctor Commins in Rochester long ago. So, in fact, in short, and finally, go to hell with your damned nonsense! I'm your friend, ain't I? That used to mean that what's mine is your'n—and I'm old-fashioned.

It's rotten about your having to take a cut—but I suppose it's on the cards these days. Wait until this income tax the great minds at Wash. are contriving takes its cut at me next year—and we can go out with tin cups together! However, I'll have this home down here—and it's a peach!—paid for—and there are plenty of free fish, schrimp, & oysters around.[58]

56. While living at Le Plessis, the couple had bought a Dalmatian, an exceptionally bright dog named Silverdene Emblem (nicknamed "Blemie"), whom both of them loved with a wholehearted affection they never seemed to have felt for their children. They always in fact talked of Blemie as their "child," as the only one who appreciated what was done for him.

57. Sea Island.

58. The O'Neills had bought land in Sea Island and had built "Casa Genotta." They moved in early in July 1932, staying in temporary quarters until the house was ready.

Carlotta is now in N.Y. doing the final packing. She is going to call you up. I know. If she hasn't by the time you get this, beat her to it. She's working herself to death to get it over and get back here, I'm afraid. Longest time we've been separated. I miss her like hell!

I feel fine again—sea & sun—New York is bum stuff for me. Hard at work on my new one[59]—good start in 1st draft—it looks like a real one, this play.

Thanks for the snap of your child. The depression is going right over her head, I should say from appearances! Give her my love. And Dorothy. I'll try to listen in on her last broadcasts after our radio gets here.[60]

And all blessings be on her and the anxiously awaited one![61] Dorothy is a grand, brave human being and you are a lucky guy!

All love to the three-four of you!

As ever,

Gene

------

108. To Eugene O'Neill from Saxe Commins. TL(cc) 1 p.

June 16, 1932

Dear Gene:

We have it on unofficial but very reliable authority that the Board of Education of New York City has approved "Representative Plays,"[62] effective January 1st, 1933. Official announcement will be made in the fall term. That, of course, merely postpones the sales of this volume for six months. Meanwhile we are presenting it to boards of education throughout the country, and so far the response has been unanimously favorable, although no official action has been taken; it is too early.

By now, you must be fairly established in your new house. May you and Carlotta have great joy there. My love to you both.

Always,

Mr. Eugene O'Neill
Sea Beach Island
Georgia

59. "Without Ending of Days," subsequently retitled *Days Without End.*

60. Dorothy Commins was participating in a series of radio broadcasts devoted to the history of piano music.

61. Saxe and Dorothy Commins were expecting their second child.

62. *Representative Plays by Eugene O'Neill,* published by Liveright in 1932, which included *Marco Millions, The Emperor Jones, "Anna Christie," Where the Cross Is Made,* and *The Moon of the Caribbees.*

109. *To Saxe Commins from Eugene and Carlotta Monterey O'Neill.* WIRE 1 p.

[July 1, 1932]

QA809 1—SeaIslandBeach Ga 1 738P
Saxe Commins—
1 Rutherford Pl NYK—
Congratulations and our dearest love to you and Dorothy & baby—[63]

Gene & Carlotta

110. *To Saxe and Dorothy Commins from Carlotta Monterey O'Neill.* ALS 3 pp.

Sea Island Beach—
Georgia
[July 9, 1932]

Dearest Dorothy & Saxe,

I have thought of you incessantly—but days have gone by leaving me so fatigued that letter writing has been out of the question.— You have a son!—— My admiration & respect for you both is boundless. Your extraordinary courage shames me.— To wish you well sounds a feeble thing—I wish you all the happiness & success that you deserve.—

Our house is, at last, on the completed side. Eugene Jr., & wife & Shane have been here since the first— & are leaving Friday—Then I will try to arrange the final touches.—We love our *home*. It is the first time Gene has *built* a home & he takes great pride in it. My ideas have been fairly well carried out & I, too, am pleased. Gene's study is very comfy & really unique.—

It is almost as difficult to get things done here as in the French Provinces.— And no one hurries! The chauffeur leaves the first & the cook I brought from N.Y. A couple & a little coloured cook whom I will train will have to do it all.— It is amazing the garden we already have—considering it was a sand dune. Later will take some snaps & send them to you.—

Gene sends love—with mine—& Jehovah guard the four of you now.

Bless you—
Carlotta

Saturday

63. Eugene David Commins was born on July 1, 1932. He was named for O'Neill, who was his godfather.

111. *To Eugene David Commins from Carlotta Monterey O'Neill.* ALS 2pp.

> Sea Island Beach—
> *Georgia*
> *July 10th 1932*

Dearest Babe,

This to welcome you & wish you all the most beautiful things in the world—. May every new day be more interesting to you than the last & bring you greater beauty, wisdom & joy.—

Always love & honour your dear parents for they are brave & dear & good—God keep you always—is the wish of Eugene & Carlotta.

The enclosed is for you—to purchase some wee thing that will add to your comfort—

112. *To Saxe Commins from Carlotta Monterey O'Neill.* ALS 1 p.

> Monday—
> [July 11, 1932]

Saxe dear.—

Gene imagined that the quotation "Without Endings of Days" was from the Old Testament. Those (supposedly) in the know say "no"!—Do you know anything of this—or any person well up in Biblical lore who could tell us—— ——?

> Our love
> Carlotta

113. *To Saxe Commins from Carlotta Monterey O'Neill.* ALS 2 pp.

> Casa Genotta,
> Sea Island Beach,
> *Georgia*
> [postmarked July 18, 1932]

Saxe dear.—

Thanks so much for your charming letter. Regarding "Without Endings of Days" Gene is completely up a tree! He saw it as a quotation & (foolishly) did not write it down. He says now it *may* be in "Jew Suss"[64]—But chuck it, Saxe, he'll have to figure out some way to say *where* he got it—

Of course little Frances is hurt—you must make it up to her for not being *the* baby any more!

Eugene Jr., & wife & Shane have gone North—I am busy getting things in order,— & hope the painter will really finish this week & all workmen will be out of the house.—

God—how I've worked on this house—but it is worth it— & I *think* Gene is pleased—you know he never *says* very much!——

Dorothy is too *amazing*—I can *work* but I have no talent for child birth or children—. It's the being Jewish that gives her that magnificent understanding & knowledge.

My dearest love to my four Commins'.—

Carlotta

It has been hot—but we have a grand breeze from the sea today going thro' the house.—

Gene sends love.

---

114. To Carlotta Monterey O'Neill from Saxe Commins. TL(cc) 1 p.

July 28th, 1932

Dear Carlotta,

Our bookkeeper tells me that the sales figures will not be available until next week. That means you shall have them as of June 30th immediately after they are recorded.

On a further hunt for the quotation, I looked through the Shakespeare and Milton Concordances and could find no trace of it. In "Samson Agonistes" there appears, "without all hope of day"—that is the closest I have come to it so far.[65]

Dorothy's first recital in the series was a great success. She played Beethoven's "Pathetique"—movements 1 and 2. Tuesday, August 9th—2:45— Schumann.

Gene David is flourishing like a green bay tree.

All love,

P.S. Since dictating the above, a Southern girl, Gladys Baker by name,

64. Novel by German Lion Feuchtwanger (1884–1958), published in German in 1925 and translated into English in 1926. Reference may be to a dramatic adaptation of Feuchtwanger's novel by Ashley Dukes and published in 1929 as *Jew Süss*. The American translation of the novel was called *Power*.

65. Sheaffer, *O'Neill: Son and Artist*, p. 402, speculates that the title was actually suggested by a letter from Robert Edmond Jones.

who represents the House Beautiful and Home and Field, asked me to suggest an interview. She wants to do a piece on your new house. I promised to submit her request. She is highly recommended by George J. Nathan and Mencken. If you care to have this interview, just say the word in your next letter and I'll tell her so—or no.

Mrs. Eugene O'Neill
Sea Beach Island
Georgia

---

115. *To Saxe Commins from Carlotta Monterey O'Neill.* ALS 2 pp.

> Sea Island Beach—
> Georgia
> [postmarked July 21,
> 1932]

Saxe dear—
Thanks so much for your letter.
Will look for the sales figures later—
Don't bother any more about "Without Endings of Days"— it may have been in the Elsie books or the Police Gazette!
So glad the Babes are flourishing—with such parents they should conquer the world!
No interviews for Southern *or* Northern girls—on *any* subject.— We are nearly driven mad by people who *mean* well! Only this morning I've put a huge sign at our gate—"Private—no admittance"! (This is no time to discuss new houses!!)
Entre-nous—isn't Komroff's book *terrible?*[66] At least, I thought so, —he cannot write of passion or vice—he knows nothing about it—except from books——.
Love to the parents & the Babes—

> Carlotta

Saturday

66. *A New York Tempest* (New York: Coward-McCann, 1932).

116. To Saxe Commins from Carlotta Monterey O'Neill. ALS 2 pp.

Wednesday
[August 3, 1932]

Saxe dear,—

Thank you so much for your nice letter.

No—we have no radio here. We are in the Wilds!—

Gene says that in "W.E.D." to change the *"which"* to *"that"* where ever the "something which laughs" occurs.——

And when you finish typing give scripts to Madden with the exception of one to Cerf—& please explain to the latter that the play is much too long now—& Gene expects to cut from 20 minutes to half an hour out of it during rehearsals. —Therefore Gene thinks it would be foolish to get out bound galleys—, for the start of rehearsals. Please find out from Cerf what the dead line would be—the latest date before opening—that it is necessary to have the corrected galleys for him to be able to publish on the production date.—

That's all today—
As always—
Carlotta

---

117. To Eugene O'Neill from Saxe Commins. TL(cc) 1 p.

August 3rd, 1932

Dear Gene:

In order to provide you with an absolutely accurate account of books sold and royalties as of June 30th, this delay was necessary. The accompanying statements are absolute duplicates of what will be submitted to Dick[67] in due course of time. These figures are accurate in every detail.

So much for business. All goes well with us. The kids are flourishing and Dorothy is immensely happy with the enthusiastic response she has had on her new series. Even I am feeling a little better after a short siege of illness.

All love to the two of you from the four of us.

Yours,

Mr. Eugene O'Neill
Sea Beach Island
Georgia

67. Richard Madden, O'Neill's agent.

118. *To Saxe Commins from Eugene O'Neill.* TLS 1 p.

> Sea Island Beach,
> Georgia
> [August 1932]

Dear Saxe:

Thanks for the statement. I really needed it in order to do some planning for the future—won't need any of the money until it is due, though.

But I want hereby to emit a howl through you to the firm that I have been meaning to emit every time I got each of the last three statements. And that is in reference to the returned copies business for which I am docked. This is a new developement since Liveright got out. I was never docked while he was in charge of things—and I will be damned if I like it, or if I can see any justice in passing this on to the author—or, which is more to the point, if I believe that it is permissable under my contract. This idea of having copies of Dynamo sent back at this late date is too ridiculous! Believe me, if they can get by with this under my present contract, it is not going to be renewed that way, if I have to find another publisher!

Also I cannot see where they arrive at their present "Dynamo" figures. It requires a lot of explaining—that unearned balance of 114.53 on the trade and 96.25 on the limited edition! It has [a] balance 12/31/31 of 90.90 on the trade sheet but I can find no mention in the statement ending on that date for any unearned balance but 21.00.

I don't like all this monkey business, Saxe, and I want you to tell them so. Horace had his faults but none of these things ever came up in his time. And I object most emphatically, and doubt if it is permitted under my contract, to be handed a bill against royalties—if that is what it is—at this particular time (or any time!) for two hundred and fifty bucks or so. I don't count in the Black and Gold advance for manifestly that only applies on the future sale of that particular "Strange Interlude" volume and is in no sense deductible from general royalties. What I object to is the injustice of penalizing the author for mistakes in judgment he did not make, or for agreements with booksellers to which he was not a party. Certainly I think my books can be sold in sufficient quantities at this time without giving booksellers a turn-back permit. They ought to be able to judge how many they can sell. I'm not an unknown quantity.

Perhaps I am all wrong in my deductions as to how this thing is worked out between publisher and bookseller—but I know I am not wrong in believing that it is a matter of business between them and should not be carried back to the author.

Well, That's that! How's my young namesake? Grand, I hope! Tell him all he has to do to have a grand youth is not to have one like mine! It was great news to hear that Dorothy came through so well. Carlotta and I kept wondering as the days went on just when it was going to happen. But I had a sure inner hunch that Dorothy would be fine. There wouldn't be what little justice there is in life, otherwise. Much love to her and to you and to God's Chillun and kiss them both for me, and give my namesake an extra one, meaning no partiality against the young lady, but because he sort of starts off under a handicap and needs a break!

Suppose it's no good inviting you down here—but if anything turns up that you can make it anytime, why come a-running! I'm working well. Think this will turn out to be a real one.

Love from us both!
Gene

————

119. *To Saxe Commins from Carlotta Monterey O'Neill.* ALS 2 pp.

Casa Genotta—
Sea Island Beach,
Georgia
[Summer 1932]

Dear Saxe,

That woman, Gladys Baker, wrote to Lillian Gish about an interview with Gene & also "doing" the house—so I wrote her (Baker) this morning & that ends that.——

A woman named Rita Mathias(?) is translating "Electra" into German; —since she started this (Gene gave her the job & some money on account of a long hard luck story) things have developed in which she has become very important & demanding "rights" & God knows what-not——. Gene has *insisted* he read her translation before he O.K.'s it—as he is afraid she will add a "trifle" here & there to appeal to German taste (& her own rather coarse ideas)— &, as he doesn't know five words of German he asks you do *you* know anyone who can be relied upon to read this & tell us is it O.K.?— All this entre-nous—(destroy this letter) but I know you understand.

Love to all my
Commins's!—
Carlotta

Thursday
She has only sent the first play to date. Gene is afraid she'll change his New England woman into passionate Jewish women!—

120. *To Saxe Commins from Carlotta Monterey O'Neill.* ALS 3 pp.

> Casa Genotta,
> Sea Island Beach,
> *Georgia*
> [August 6, 1932]

Saxe dearest,

Thank you so much for the translation notes. —As I expected it is *not* right (another mess Master James Light is responsible for!)——and Gene is going to have a lot of trouble about it—. (All this entre-nous)—Gene will write you in a few days or *I* will & tell you what to do with the 'script—in the meantime hang on to it, please. Also, Gene wants to know what you consider a fair price for the going over it your cousin(?)[68] did. (Please see that you answer this question *properly* & be more business like in future for now you have four in your family!)—Yes, I *will* mind my own business!—

The Talkie[69] criticisms arrived—you were a dear to send them—Am afraid they haven't got it over. Thalberg shouldn't have put his wife in it for one thing—business before relations!—

It has been very hot— & I'm trying to paint all the iron work in the house as this sea air rusts & mildews everything— We have over 4000 books in the house, & these & clothes & shoes & every thing has to be gone over continually.—

Gene working hard & swimming & fishing when the mood takes him. He seems to get a real inner joy out of his *home* & I am delighted because I've slaved over it & still do.—

Has this false spurt of prosperity hit your business at all?—

People are fools.——

More soon again dear Saxe. With our dearest all to "you all"—

> *Carlotta*

Saturday—

68. Mrs. Michaela Welch, whom Saxe had gotten to look over the German translation of *Mourning Becomes Electra*.

69. Reviews of the movie version of *Strange Interlude*. Irving Thalberg, the production head of M-G-M, cast his wife Norma Shearer as Nina Leeds, with Clark Gable playing her lover, Edmund Darrell. The film was neither a critical nor a commercial success.

———————

121. To Saxe Commins from Carlotta Monterey O'Neill. ALS 6 pp.

Casa Genotta,
Sea Island Beach,
Georgia
[September 1932]

Saxe dear,

Thank you so much for your nice letter & for that charming photograph of the angel child Frances! She makes me smile every time I look at the photograph—*What* an angel gazing Heaven ward—the cat that swallowed the canary! The imp—I'll wager she was plotting some devilment at that very moment!

Send us a copy of "More Merry-Go-Round"[70] please so we can see what is why!—

The summer is over—the sun hot but nights cool & we need a blanket—I shall be glad to be able to wear a few clothes again.

Just hold the manuscript until you hear to the contrary.—

Enclosed is a very small cheque—If you *won't* be business like you make it *very* difficult for us to ask for favours at your hands!—Remember there are always *two* sides to every argument—! But with this small amount send your cousin some fruit, flowers or what you think she'd prefer.—

Saxe, where do you get the style of paper you have written to me on? Just single white sheets & envelopes with the address on each.—Is it expensive? I'd like to get some for my business & house letters. With just—

Casa Genotta
Sea Island Beach
Georgia

on the paper & on the envelopes.—Just like yours. —If you could order some for me—(as you order yours) I'd be grateful & send you a cheque. —But, for God's sake, remember this is *business*.

Could you ever come down to see us do you think?

I have developed into a first class housemaid, painter, gardner & Jack of all trades— & never have a moment—am useful anyway—so that counts for some thing.—

Sunday—

I was interrupted yesterday.—

To-day is blowy, grey & blustery. I took Blemie for a walk on the deserted beach & sang Ave Marias at the top of my voice!—

70. A best-selling gossipy account of goings-on in Washington, D.C., by Robert S. Allen and Drew Pearson, published by Liveright in 1932.

I get lonely now & again so have to have some out let—as long as it's singing Ave Marias all will be well!——

Gene is working on *two* plays![71]—— ——I am furious about the Matthias translation etc. I *begged* Gene not to let her do it— Every time Gene has followed J. L.'s[72] advice it has cost him money & heart ache. —I think this has been a good lesson to him —But Gene is as stubborn as Frances at times particularly when he *knows* some of his so-called friends have let him in for something. He hates to admit it. —About personal things I don't mind—but when it touches his work I am furious & justly so—as I give him my entire existence, thought & energy to make things & conditions so as to help his working hours & keep him as well & happy as I can.— And these idiots hurt all that. ——Oh—well. ——Life goes on.—

Dearest love to you & Dorothy & the Babes—from us both—

Bless you—
Carlotta

What is said of Sin. Lewis's new book?[73]— Didn't you think Komroff's book bad (?)—it was neither fish, flesh nor fowl—. Am rereading Gautier—*delightful.*

P.S. Gene has asked me to ask you if you can send him the dates of the publications of *Shaw's earlier* plays—*before & around* 1907.——

---

122. *To Eugene O'Neill from Saxe Commins.* TL(cc) 1 p.

September 20th
1932

Dear Gene:

The enclosed bibliography of Shaw is, I hope, what you want. Since Brentano's publish all of Shaw, this is as accurate as anything we could get in this country.

I shall write at greater length the first moment I get. Meanwhile, all best.

Yours,

SC:pkk
Enc:
Mr. Eugene O'Neill
Sea Island Beach
Georgia

71. *Days Without End* and *Ah, Wilderness!*
72. Jimmy Light.
73. *Ann Vickers* (Garden City, N.Y.: Doubleday, Doran, 1933).

---

123. To Saxe Commins from Eugene O'Neill. ALS 2 pp.

Sea Island Beach,
Ga.
Oct. 7th 1932

Dear Saxe:

What is the big idea in Liveright holding up my royalties? The contract reads "during Sept.," as I remember, they hold off until the last day of Sept. and then they hold off some more! I don't like such stuff a damn bit! It only makes trouble for me holding off people I've promised to pay with that cash. And there's no reason for it—unless they are going broke? (Are they?) They could very well put my money aside in advance. It gets me sore. If I were an author who kicks all the time, you bet there would be no delay!

I note by your wire the Book League deal[74] is through and await your letter with great interest. Hope you get more out of them than was indicated in your other letter.

All best, Saxe! Please convey my kick to Pell, will you? If Madden doesn't receive those royalties next Monday, as Pell promised, I am going to be sore as hell!

This in haste,
Gene

---

124. To Eugene O'Neill from Saxe Commins. TL(cc) 1 p.

ROUGH DRAFT

October 7th
1932

Dear Gene:

As I wired you yesterday, the contract with the Book of the Month Club was consummated.

During the negotiations, the Book of the Month Club was insistent upon the inclusion of MOURNING BECOMES ELECTRA, saying that the entire proposition hinged upon having this play. We acceded to this and managed to raise the price from ten cents to twelve cents per copy on the first edition of 50,000. This makes your share of it above 9000— This will be sent to you on Jan. 5, 1933 as requested by you.

74. Liveright was planning to publish a volume of selected O'Neill plays in Dec. 1932; the Book-of-the-Month Club had expressed an interest in publishing a special edition.

They will choose ten plays from the following list:

MOURNING BECOMES ELECTRA	HAIRY APE
	STRANGE INTERLUDE
GREAT GOD BROWN	MOON OF THE CARIBBEES
BEYOND THE HORIZON	ALL GOD'S CHILLUN GOT
EMPEROR JONES	WINGS
ANNA CHRISTIE	MARCO MILLIONS
DESIRE UNDER THE ELMS	LAZARUS LAUGHED

Your condition that GOLD, THE FIRST MAN, WELDED, DYNAMO and THE FOUNTAIN should be omitted was observed. They agree to pay the twenty-five cents per copy of additional printings and that the retail price of the additional issue will not be less than $4.00 per copy. They also agree that this agreement is only for two years, dating from December 1st, 1932, which is the tentative publication date of the Book of the Month Club volume.[75]

Because we carried on the negotiations directly with you, we have found no opportunity to inform Dick Madden. Do you want to write him on this subject or shall we tell him how the whole thing came about?

We are all very happy about the conclusion of this contract since it means a new distribution of your plays and a new means of keeping you before the public.

With all best,

---

125. *To Saxe Commins from Carlotta Monterey O'Neill.* ALS 6 pp. On stationery headed: Casa Genotta / Sea Island Beach / Georgia

Wednesday
[October 12, 1932]

Bless your dear heart—you're just infant enough to play with Frances!!— Enclosed is your cheque.

Have just finished typing a long wire to you from Gene. If they don't stop dragging Nathan in with Gene it will do him (Gene) much more harm than good.—I should think they could get other opinions which would be much more valuable from all points of view.—[76]

Well—Fischer-Verlag[77] now have the face to say they had *not* read the

75. Saxe here crossed out: "Paragraph to be written by Arthur Pell stating the income tax situation in regard to O'Neill portion."

76. Apparently, critic and editor George Jean Nathan had been suggested as the person who would choose which O'Neill plays would be included in the Book-of-the-Month Club edition.

77. German publishing house.

translation of "Electra" (had taken Reinhardt's[78] playreader's word!) & upon doing so (reading it) agree with the criticism sent—that it could be improved! Matthias even agrees!!!!! And she was threatening a law suit a few weeks back! (Oh—God such people). ——It is to be rehashed & Gene insists it be sent back (I saw to this) for further examination. I am curious to see *what* they'll do.—Of course they were full of alibis—! Just a lot of crooks & liars! And one is helpless. Fischer-Verlag *should* do all they can for Gene's work—but there you are.— We'll see what happens now.—We have a radio! —Has Dorothy any set time, hour or station—as to her Concerts?—

I am trying to get leaks repaired in our house—all this drives me mad.—Touraine was the Champs Elysées compared to this place.—We have houses all 'round us—but it's the devil to get anything done *properly*. These Southerners are so lazy & so slack. Their eyes *don't see* the things that are wrong because they *don't want to see!*—There are so many things I want to do outside of the house & garden—but the endless supervision of that & *manual labour* gives me no time.— Perhaps—some day!——

Did I thank you for the envelopes? —I meant to. Could you get me 100 envelopes the size & quality that you use at Liveright's for contracts etc.—& send them to me? They don't have to be stamped. —But I have to have some of the larger size than these I've just rec'd. Either send them *C.O.D.* or let me know how much they are.—*Please*—I hate to bother you with these silly errands but I know you don't mind. You *see* how we all impose upon you? It is really disgusting.—

Do you really think you can come to us later. I *do* hope so.—

Gene seems more content than I've ever seen him. Of course he has his worrisome days re work, responsibilities & income tax.—But we are all worried crazy these days afraid of *tomorrow*—! A damn stupid state of mind—for we become blind to *today's* blessings & no matter *what* comes—we always get thro' some how.—

We, who are blessed with love, should sing praises to Jehovah & go about with warm hearts.—

Carlotta

Have you ever read "O Mon Goye" by Sarah Levy? A *most* fascinating book—translated from the french & *stupidly* called "Beloved"— (Simon & Schuster). It is of a Jewess in love with a Christian— —It held me—
Love to Dorothy & the Babes.—

78. Max Reinhardt, director of Berlin's Deutsches Theatre, founder and director of the annual Salzburg Festival, and Europe's leading director and theatrical producer.

126. *To Saxe Commins from Eugene O'Neill.* ALS 3 pp.

[ca. October 12, 1932]

Dear Saxe:

This in haste to supplement my wire. I object to Nathan in this instance because when a volume including as many plays as this is put out it will stand in everyone's mind as representing the whole significant trend of my work—and, between us, I don't like leaving such a choice to Nathan. In spite of my friendship for him and my respect for his judgment along many lines, I by no means believe, or have ever believed, that he is any infallible critic of my work or has a comprehensive understanding of its inner spiritual, as opposed to its material outer dramaturgical, trends. He has too many (frankly confessed by him) blind spots. He is too Latin-rationalistic-sceptic-sentimental in the influences that have moulded his critical viewpoint. He is antipathetic to all plays with a religious feeling (he liked "Brown"[79] for its other aspects), all plays involving any tinge of social revolution. He liked "The Fountain," "Gold"! —he despised "Lazarus," totally misunderstood what I was driving at in "Dynamo," thought "Hairy Ape" was radical propaganda and disliked it for that, considered "Desire"[80] imitation Strindberg. I will say nothing about the many Nathan conceptions of life he has read into my plays and praised to my irritated amusement.

Don't misunderstand this as any panning of Nathan or any lack of gratitude for all the fights he has made for me. I'm only saying things about his criticism that I've often said in my arguments with him.

And on practical grounds I think in a case of this kind its always a mistake to do the obvious thing that everyone accepts without interest as predetermined. Nathan is the obvious thing here. It's poor business, it has no imagination, no drama to it. The only comments on his choice and his foreword will be: "Of course. Old stuff." And I think its bad policy from Liveright's as well as my end to always have Nathan as sponsor. If he were the only prominent critic who appreciated my works—but there are plenty of others—Krutch,[81] Young,[82] Atkinson, Gabriel,[83] W. P. Eaton,[84] etc., etc., etc.

My suggestion is to let *me* select *ten* plays. In a couple of sentences of foreword—no more—I would say my selection was based on my own good judgment and what the best criticism all over the world had said about either productions or the printed play. Then I would suggest that the Book Month

79. *The Great God Brown* (1926).
80. *Desire Under the Elms* (1924).
81. Joseph Wood Krutch, drama critic of *The Nation*.
82. Stark Young, drama critic of the *New Republic*.
83. Gilbert Gabriel, drama critic of the New York *American*.
84. Walter Pritchard Eaton, drama critic of the New York *Herald-Tribune*.

ask one prominent American critic to do a *short* appreciation of a single play—
ten critics for the ten plays—such appreciations to include a dire panning of
the rest of my work by comparison, if the critic felt that way about it. I
append a list of my selections of plays and possible critics for each play. This,
of course, is tentative. By looking up your press records & old jackets you
could probably add greatly to this list of alternatives of critics for each play.
Let every critic appreciate his pet play as *the* best, that's the idea. Broun,[85]
for example, and Woolcott[86] would probably say kind words about "Jones" or
"Glencairn" if they were allowed to add that all my work since then has
been trash! You get the idea? Difference of opinion, clash, argument ensuing,
fresh interest and angles from the public and press standpoint—with my
choice of ten plays as the background.

If this thing is worth doing, it's worth doing well. Trouble is with any
organization like the Book M. too lazy to take trouble—do the obvious—and
loose out.

Or if B. of M. won't do this then I suggest choice of plays to be made
from consensus opinion of one poet (Robinson or Jeffers, say) one novelist
(Dreiser or Lewis) one historian (Beard[87] or Adams[88]) one dramatic critic
(Krutch or Atkinson or Young or—endless list of possibilities) & one psy-
chologist (White[89] or Jeliffe[90] or—another endless list) & one publisher (?).
And Nathan to do foreword.

The above second suggestion is just dashed-off suggestion—may have nothing to it. What I'm after in this suggestion is to get away as far as possible in
the choice matter from arbitrary choice by one dramatic critic whose opinion
is already well known followed by foreword by same critic. Sabe? The list
of plays to be submitted to parties to have all long plays on it except ones I
barred. Of course, its doubtful if you could find one person in each class who
had read or seen the plays! But some other scheme along these lines might
be thought out. The good points about such a consensus scheme is that noone
but the boobs would regard such a selection as having any real artistic authority! Whereas it would be interesting & comment-provoking.

But I suppose this is all useless talk. The contract is signed, isn't it?—and

85. Heywood Broun, critic and formerly drama reviewer for the New York *Tribune*.
86. Alexander Woollcott, critic who at different times was the drama reviewer for
the New York *Times*, the New York *Sun*, *Vanity Fair*, and the New York *World*.
87. Charles A. Beard (1874–1948), whose four-volume *Rise of American Civilization*
was then appearing.
88. James Truslow Adams (1878–1949), also a widely read American historian.
89. Dr. William Alanson White (1870–1937), superintendent of St. Elizabeths
Hospital in Washington, D.C. from 1903 until 1937, cofounder of the *Psychoanalytic
Review*, and one of Freud's earliest supporters in the United States.
90. Dr. Smith Ely Jelliffe (1866–1945), managing editor of the *Journal of Nervous
and Mental Disease* and cofounder of the *Psychoanalytic Review*.

that's that—and the B.M. will do the obvious thing, entailing the least amounts of effort, thought & imagination.

As ever,
Gene

6   M.M.—Atkinson or John Macy[91] or Gabriel
9   S.I.—Nathan or Littel[92] or Krutch or
10 Electra—Krutch or Young or Mason Brown[93]
2   Em.J—Broun or Wolcott or Eaton
3   H.A.—Young or Gabriel or Eaton
1   Glencairn—Woolcott or Anderson[94] or Broun
8   Lazarus L.—Mumford or De Casseres or Krutch
5   Desire—Barrett C[95] or Krutch or Gabriel
4   All God's C.—Lewisohn[96] or Nathan or Krutch or
7   Great God B.—Nathan or Krutch or
Chron.   select critics who are also authors of books
order   by preference—give them credit for that
           authorship under their article—
Plays to be printed in chronological order

---

127. *To Saxe Commins from Carlotta Monterey O'Neill.* ALS 2 pp. On stationery headed: Casa Genotta / Sea Island Beach / Georgia

Friday
[October 14, 1932]

Dear Saxe.—

The telephone girl just told me that you were trying to get us on the phone this morning.—We have left orders that if our phone number is given anyone we'll have the phone taken out!! So *no one* can get us without the number. We don't want people phoning.—because Gene will *not* talk over the phone & I don't want to. Hence you're not being able to get us.—The number is 638 if you should need us—but don't call unless really necessary because Gene

91. Critic who at one time was a drama reviewer for the New York *World* and who, from 1905 to 1932, was married to Anne Sullivan, Helen Keller's teacher-companion.

92. Robert Littell, former drama critic of the New York *Post*, the *New Republic*, and *Theatre Arts*.

93. John Mason Brown, drama critic of the New York *Post*.

94. John Anderson, drama critic of the New York *Journal*.

95. Barrett Clark, critic and author of *Eugene O'Neill* (1926), the first book-length study of O'Neill, which subsequently went through four revised editions (1929, 1933, 1936, 1947).

96. Ludwig Lewisohn, former drama critic of the *Nation*.

loathes going to the phone.—I know you're fussed over this B. M. Club business—don't be! Life is too short.—

Love as always—
Carlotta

---

128. *To Saxe Commins from Eugene O'Neill.* ALS 1 p.
On stationery headed: Le Plessis / Saint-Antoine du Rocher /
(Indre-et-Loire)

Sea Island Beach
Ga.
Oct. 20, 1932

Dear Saxe:

"In choosing the nine plays of full length or over which would best represent my work, I have been guided not only by my own preferences but by
the consensus of critical opinion, foreign as well as American, on either the
published plays or productions of them in the theatre.

The plays are given here in the chronological order in which they were
written."

How about this, Saxe? Will do? If they want to set down dates under
titles, I give them herewith—more meticulously accurate than in the L.[97]
volumes, I think. I think it would be good idea if they used these dates.

Jones — 1920
Ape — 1921
All God's C. — 1923
Desire — 1924
Marco — (1923–'24–'25)
Brown — 1925
Lazarus — (1925–'26)
Interlude — (1926–'27)
Electra — (1929–'31)

As ever,
Gene

97. Liveright. Eventually, when *Nine Plays* was published in Dec. 1932, it included
the titles O'Neill had chosen, along with an introduction by Joseph Wood Krutch.

129. To Eugene O'Neill from Saxe Commins. TL(cc) 1 p.

Nov. 10th, 1932

Dear Gene:

The enclosed inquiry from Bradley is one that you may want to answer yourself. It concerns translation rights of MOURNING BECOMES ELECTRA and, as you probably know, he is considered the best agent in France. Do you want to drop me a note on this and have me write Bradley or do you want to do it yourself?

We are waiting for your approval of the jacket proof and also for your O.K. on the letter which I wrote concerning terms of our edition of the NINE PLAYS.

Schirmer's promise Dorothy that the conductor's stand goes forth this week. I hope it will suit your needs.[98]

All best,

Mr. Eugene O'Neill
Sea Island Beach
Georgia
SC:pkk

---

130. To Saxe Commins from Carlotta Monterey O'Neill. ALS 8 pp.
On stationery headed: Casa Genotta / Sea Island Beach / Georgia

Nov. 19th 1932

Saxe dearest,

Thanks so much for your dear letter. I felt "Camille" would be just as you describe it. I like Lillian[99] & she has *charming* qualities. But—she has no more passion, desire or understanding of what a woman of "Camille's" life or feelings were than our Blemie!—I got so furious at her attempt at it that Gene thought me a little—*critical!* (?) But, "render unto Caesar the things that are Caesar's"! And so it goes——

The music rack arrived & it is *grand!*—— A thousand thanks—*please* tell me if I am in your financial debt—otherwise you make it impossible for me to wear you down with commissions!—

98. O'Neill customarily wrote in large notebooks which Saxe supplied to him. He wanted the conductor's stand so he could spread his manuscript out while he worked on it.

99. Lillian Gish, who had opened on Broadway on Nov. 1, 1932, in the title role of a new stage adaptation of Dumas's classic co-adapted, directed, and designed by Robert Edmond Jones. It lasted only fifteen performances.

I am busy from morning until night.

I *loathe* being poor.— It keeps one from doing those wee things one formerly got so much pleasure out of.——

Shane has been playing up at school—Is *lazier* than the devil— & backward in every thing. The Head Master wrote to Gene—. I refused to let Gene be worried & wrote the Head Master & gave him "what for" for coddling the boys & gave Shane hell— & then wrote Weinberger to get hold of Shane's Mother & tell her to discipline her own son.——We're going to have trouble with these offspring— but (knowing how Gene takes all this) will try to be the buffer between them.— When Eugene Jr., was down here this summer he *refused* to return to N.Y. in anything but a *compartment!!* So I bought it— I went to N.Y. in a section!— Gene gets *crazy* but *won't* say anything! But one day he'll just say "no more"! And then what a blow up there'll be.—The "Professor" is really amusing, —but Gene says he hope's to God he'll get sat all over in Germany & maybe he'll come home a human being![100]— (All this entre-nous)—Gene's play[101] is finer than any thing he's ever attempted—a spiritual thing—. No one will get half he's putting into it. He works sometimes from 9/30 in the morning until 6/30 P.M. I make him good soups & junkets etc.—& he has a tray in his study.— Only last night he was marvelling at being able to do so much more than formerly—harder stuff— & feeling fit!—

I have been rereading Gautier's "Travels"—marvellous,— dear old "Les Miserables" "Notre Dame." —Also "Josephus" by Feuchtwanger & "The Sleepwalkers" from the German—. I have never worked so hard in my life— & feel years older— but I *am* some good to Gene so what the hell!——

Am anxious to see what your cousin thinks of this new version of "Electra."[102] We *may* be able to get to N. Y. before Christmas for a few days for you to type (can you?) the first draft of the new play.[103]— It will *not* be ready until next Season.

As to the times—damn politicians & crooks in all countries!—what an age to live in—. And life used to be so pleasant—at moments.—

Love to dear Dorothy & the Babes——& God bless you & yours—

Carlotta

---

100. After graduating from Yale in June 1932, Eugene, Jr., had received a fellowship to begin postgraduate work in classical studies at the University of Freiburg in Germany.

101. *Days Without End.*

102. The German translation. See letter 120, n. 68.

103. *Ah, Wilderness!*

131. To Saxe Commins from Carlotta Monterey O'Neill. ALS 2 pp.
On stationery headed: Casa Genotta/Sea Island / Georgia

Saturday
[December 1932]

Saxe dear,

I wrote to the Book-of-the-Month Club & asked them to send me a copy of Eugene O'Neill's "Nine Plays" of the *last* printing! (I wanted to see if the dedication page[104] was in!) I sent my $4.00 & they promptly sent the "Nine Plays"—but it did *not* have the dedication page in— & now, this morning, I receive the enclosed! —I don't want any book without paying for it— particularly in these times. —But I *did* want to see the dedication page in the volume of the last printing.

Now what can I do?—I don't want to pester them *or you*— they have been most courteous—I want to pay for anything they send me— & there you are!

The play is ready to be typed—. Shall I send it or keep until you come down—?

Our dearest love to you & yours,
Carlotta

132. To Saxe Commins from Carlotta Monterey O'Neill. ALS 2 pp.
On stationery headed: Casa Genotta / Sea Island / Georgia

Tuesday 3 P. M.
[December 1932]

Saxe dear,

Have typed you a wire & sent it off—Enclosed is a cheque for your expense account to us (& return) & if it doesn't cover *everything* I beg of you to be business like & let me know.—[105]

Please Ask Madden if he has a copy of the agreement signed March 2nd (?) 1932 signed by Pell in which Gene's "contract & all rights owned by Liveright are *cancelled*," in case of bankruptcy etc.—? This paper should be handed over to Weinberger to tell Madden——

104. O'Neill's dedication of *Mourning Becomes Electra* to Carlotta, a lengthy one, in which he said: "In memory of the interminable days of rain in which you bravely suffered in silence that this trilogy might be born. . . . In short, days in which you collaborated, as only deep love can, in the writing of this trilogy of the damned!"

105. Saxe was planning to visit the O'Neills, and they had insisted on paying for his trip.

If there is a "first" of "Interlude" do grab it for me—I have the Ltd., but some one stole my "first!" I'll pay for it, of course.—Our phone number is *Sea Island 638*—Keep this on you as they are forbidden to give it to *anyone!*—

All news when we see you—thank God you are coming—I regret that Dorothy can't come too—Perhaps later?—

Dearest love to you both from us—

Carlotta—

---

133. *To Saxe and Dorothy Commins from Carlotta Monterey O'Neill.* ALS 4 pp.
On stationery headed: Casa Genotta / Sea Island Beach / Georgia

Wednesday
[ca. December 21,
1932]

Dearest Saxe & Dorothy,—

Your letters just here—& no more beautiful Xmas present have I ever rec'd. Bless you & yours always.—I have had two wee objects I wanted to send you for ages but was afraid you would think them presents which they are *not!* I had hoped Dorothy would keep her programes in hers—& you would use yours—as wee objects of affection from me! It's sweet to have friends who *understand.*

I am having a happy Xmas getting my little orphans stuffed with candy & fruits & arranging a Christmas dinner for the family of our half starved gardner— He pays for rent, clothes & food (for 4) on $37.50 a month!! Gene gets cross because I don't buy myself a present. But this is so much more fun—. I wish I could teach Gene's kids to think of *others* a bit—but I'm learning (at last!) to mind my own business in that direction. They have Mothers!——

Will you, someday, send me a copy of your book "When Goats & Chickens Ran on Park Ave." Gene also—asks me to ask you to send to him (& *charge* to him) 6 of the Black & Gold "Strange Interlude"—.

We have all got to prove what we're made of now.—I don't mind being poor but I *do* want to meet my obligations & help Gene meet his that are unjustly heavy. —Things can't get better for a year—really better—& the strain will, at times—be a burden. But, I tell Gene we must *never* loose sight of the blessings God has bestowed upon us—we must, at least, keep richness in our *souls.*—

Bless you both & the dear babes. —Keep well & keep love in your hearts.—

Carlotta

Eugene and Saxe at Brook Farm in Ridgefield, Connecticut, 1923

Saxe, Paris, 1928

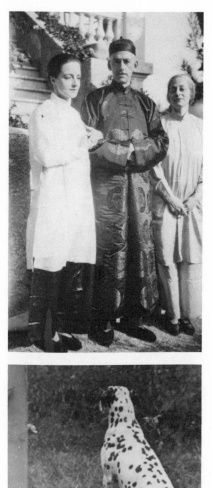

Carlotta, Eugene, and Dorothy
Commins in Chinese dress in
front of Villa Les Mimosas,
Cap-d'Ail, 1929

The O'Neill's dalmation, Silverdene
Emblem, known as Blemie

Saxe and Eugene in the garden at Casa Genotta

Casa Genotta,
the O'Neill's home in
Sea Island, Georgia

Eugene on the beach at Sea Island,
Georgia, in the thirties

Eugene, 1933

To Dorothy & Saxe —
Dearest love
1933.   Carlotta

Carlotta, 1933

*Eugene at Tao House, Contra Costa
County, California, 1941*

134. To Saxe Commins from Carlotta Monterey O'Neill. ALS 2 pp.
On stationery headed: Casa Genotta / Sea Island Beach / Georgia

Dec. 27th '32

Saxe dear,

I wouldn't have wanted the damned old book only I thought it was *your* version![106] We both liked the "9 Plays" so very much—also Krutch's "say so"— & all. —It *should* sell if any one *wants* Gene's plays today & can afford to buy them.—

As to the corrected proofs of "Interlude"—They *were* to have been mine. Did you give them to Gene? I can't (& Gene can't) remember if we took them & put them in the safe deposit in N. Y.—The only *marked* thing of "Interlude" anyone can honestly possess is Philip Moeller[107] who has the one used in rehearsals that Gene made corrections & what not on. —Please let me know *what* you have belonging to Gene (at the office) so we can straighten this out.——

Dearest love from us both—
Carlotta

Congratulations on your wedding anniversary! God, & we're all getting on—.

---

135. To Carlotta Monterey O'Neill from Saxe Commins. TL(cc) 1 p.

December 30th, 1932

Dear Carlotta:

Certainly the enclosed report speaks for itself. It makes me immensely happy, not only because it is favorable, but because one of Gene's plays[108] will at last be presented to a foreign audience in a manner that does him justice. I believe that the suggestion that you try to get the name of the man who really did the work a very excellent one. In the future it is he who should get first call on the translation of Gene's work into German. In this case it seems to me a rank injustice that Matthias should get all the credit.

As to the proofs of INTERLUDE. The book was done long before my coming to Liveright, and I never handled it. I am sure, however, that the rumor which emanated from the Phoenix Book Shop is entirely false, and that the proofs locked away in your vault are the only authentic ones.

106. Possibly Horace Kallen's *Individualism: An American Way of Life* (New York: Liveright, 1933). See letter 138.
107. Director of the original production of *Strange Interlude* (1928).
108. *Mourning Becomes Electra.*

I do know, however, that I issued strict orders on ELECTRA and that the proofs which bear my marks in red ink in the margins, are all securely put away in our safe. These are the proofs upon which Gene and I worked in Northport. They do not have a single mark of Gene's.

The other day I had a call from the Book of the Month Club asking me how I liked their volume of the NINE PLAYS. Inquiry revealed that they had not yet sent Gene a copy. I forthwith asked them to do so and I am sure it must be in your possession by now.

This is the last letter that I shall write you during the year 1932. May all those I write during 1933 be happy in their tidings and carry an ever-growing and more profound love from the four of us.

Mrs. Eugene O'Neill
Sea Island Beach
Georgia
SC; pkk

EVENTFUL YEARS

1933 – 1939

136. *To Saxe Commins from Carlotta Monterey O'Neill.* ALS 2 pp.
On stationery headed: Casa Genotta / Sea Island Beach / Georgia

Jan. 1st 1933

Saxe dear,

A thousand thanks for your New Year's wishes— This is my first letter of
1933.——

Rec'd the "Electra" report & am, naturally, *delighted.* (Gene hasn't read it
yet!)—— But he thinks Mathias's husband must have done it!——

I am sending you—under separate cover—the first & only draft of a play
Gene has done.[1] He wants 3 *carbon* copies & the first (?) copy. —This is a
kind of play Gene has never before done—(it is charming!) & must be the
deadest of *dead secrets*—it may be done some day under another name. So
nary a breath—Weinberger has been here for two days to talk over "business"
(he knows nothing of *this* play!)—& leaves tomorrow.

Let us hope this 1933 gives us a better chance against the odds!——

Dearest love to you four—

Carlotta

1. *Ah, Wilderness!*

---

137. To Saxe Commins from Eugene O'Neill. ALS 2 pp.

Sea Island, Ga.
Jan. 3rd 1933

Dear Saxe:

Just to add a word or two to what Carlotta has written you re "Ah, Wilderness!" The subtitle[2] really indicates in exactly what spirit this simple, sentimental comedy—with undertones, oh yes, with undertones!—was written, and the nostalgia for our old lost simplicity and contentment—and youth!—it expresses. I woke up one morning with this play fully in mind—never had had even a hint of an idea about it before—title and all. Immediately laid aside "Without Endings of Days," on which I was laboring and started writing this. It simply gushed out of me. Wrote the whole damned thing in the month of Sept. Evidently my unconscious had been rebelling for a long time against creation in the medium of the modern, involved, complicated, warped & self-poisoned psyche and demanded a counter-statement of simplicity and the peace that tragedy troubles but does not poison. The people in the play are of the class which I get least credit for knowing but which I really know better than any other—my whole background of New London childhood, boyhood, young manhood—the nearest approach to home I ever knew—relatives, friends of family, etc. all being just this class of people.

And, of course, there is the intention in the play to portray the startling difference between what we Americans felt about life, love, honor, morals, etc. and what we are conscious of feeling today.

I got immense satisfaction out of writing this play—and I feel a great affection for it—so great that I don't know whether I'll ever subject it to the humiliation of production or publication. For me it has the sweet charm of a dream of lost youth, a wistfulness of regret, a poignantly melancholy memory of dead things and people—but a smiling memory as of those who live still, being not sadly dead.

If you know what I mean—

Not that any of the people in this play are portraits of real people. Rather they are each portraits of many people.

Secrecy in this case, Saxe, above all others! Don't let a soul know a damned thing—even that you have it! You will appreciate why.

"Without Endings of Days," on which I have sweated blood, has reached a third draft—and there it seems likely to stop forever unfinished. It has run itself into all sorts of blind alleys and exhausted me mentally & physically to the point where I've had bad nervous indigestion—a new one for me! I am thoroughly disgusted with it. See no way out and think I will junk the

2. "A comedy of recollection."

damned thing—see what it looks like a year or two years from now—and after a rest now start something else. I have plenty of other ideas, God knows. The whole experience with this opus has been very discouraging. I've worked so damned hard on it and given so much intense thought & energy—with such confusing results! But I suppose that's all in the game.

I'm enclosing a check with which I want you to get something as a gift for my translator-supervisor from me.[3] You will know what she would like. I would not insult her by attempting to pay her for her kindness but I would like to show my grateful appreciation some way. Please express my immense gratitude to her when you write! She has been a peach about this and I will never forget her kindness! Would she like a complete set of my books, duly inscribed & autographed, do you think? If so, send them to me from Liveright. Charge to me, give me her name & I will do the rest.

Carlotta joins in love to you, Dorothy & the kids.

As ever,
Gene

---

138. *To Saxe Commins from Carlotta Monterey O'Neill.* ALS 4 pp.
On stationery headed: Casa Genotta / Sea Island Beach / Georgia

Jan. 9th 1933

Thanks for your letter—dearest Saxe—.

I am not surprised that Gruenberg's[4] behaviour towards you has been as it has.—His whole public insistence of being unappreciated & misunderstood & left to starve is a bit thick & very undignified to say the least. If he can use you for any thing he'll turn up again!!—

We could hear nothing much over the radio—but what I could hear sounded like a *play with music*—not grand opera!

I was so unhappy not to see my little dedication page (in the "Nine Plays") before "Electra."

Am glad Mr. Kallen (?) was decent enough to thank you in his preface.—Gene likes the book & would *like* to be able to say so publicly—but you know he has had to make it a *rule* to say nothing for *any* writer or *any* publisher on account of past unpleasantness.

3. Mrs. Michaela Welch. See letter 120, n. 68.
4. Louis Gruenberg's operatic version of *The Emperor Jones* had premiered at the Metropolitan Opera on Jan. 7, 1933, with Lawrence Tibbett in the title role. Most reviewers praised O'Neill's play more than Gruenberg's adaptation.

You might say this if you think wise to Mr. Kallen—Gene wanted to praise Lee Simonson's book[5] too but couldn't. Friede[6] sent the filthiest novel (saying if E.O'N. wrote a novel *that* would be the kind he would write—*this* on the jacket!—) & will ask for an opinion later. I threw the novel away & won't even reply to the request when it arrives. I think the book was called "Bright Summer" or some such & was *anonymous!*[7] And so it goes.——

We are in the throes of income tax findings! (I feel as if a large black bird was hovering over the house casting it's gloom)——

I like Feuchtwanger's "Josephus"[8]—didn't you?

Gene is shelving the play he worked six months on[9] & beginning another!!

Have you a "magnifier" to read Gene's script with? You'll need it.——

Dear love to the Four!

Carlotta

---

139. To Saxe Commins from Eugene O'Neill. ALS 2 pp.

Sea Island, Ga.
Jan. [12,] 1933

Dear Saxe:

I've inscribed all the books—with the main inscription in Electra, of course—and they will go off to Mrs. Welch at once. I remember her well now from all you used to say about her. Up to your letter, I hadn't placed her as David's[10] sister of Manila.

Thanks for what you say of "Ah, Wilderness!" I have been doubtful if anyone would feel in it what I felt. You see, it's such a simple little play, no shooting after great tragic drama, and its whole importance and reality depend on its conveying a mood of memory in exactly the right illuminating blend of wistful grin and lump in the throat—the old tears-and-laughter stuff on exactly the right delicately caressing note.

But did you laugh? That's what I want to know! To me it's full of comedy—but that may be a perverted sense on my part. The dinner, for example. How I remember the dinners in New London! I feel I've caught them. And

5. *The Stage is Set* (New York: Harcourt, Brace, 1932), by Lee Simonson, set designer and member of the board of the Theatre Guild.

6. Publisher Donald Friede of Covici-Friede.

7. This title could not be identified.

8. The first volume of a trilogy—*Josephus* (1923; Eng. trans., 1932), *The Jew of Rome* (1935; Eng. trans., 1935), and *Josephus and the Emperor* (1942, first published in English).

9. *Days Without End.*

10. David Hochstein, the distinguished American violinist who was killed in the First World War.

do you like Pa & Ma and all the rest? Fine people, all of them, to me. Lovable! I hope they will seem so to others. And it's truth! There were innumerable such people in these U.S. There still are, except life has carried us out of their orbit, we no longer see or know them, our gaze is concentrated either above or below them. But if America ever pulls out of its present mess back to something approaching its old integrity and uniqueness, I think it will be owing to the fundamental simple homely decency of such folk, no matter how much corrupting, disintegrating influences have spoiled it since the War. I mean I believe its still there as a basis to build a new American faith upon.

All best!

Gene

----

140. *To Saxe Commins from Carlotta Monterey O'Neill.* ALS 2 pp.
On stationery headed: Casa Genotta / Sea Island Beach / Georgia

Jan. 15th 1933

Saxe dear,

Thanks for your very sweet note.— Don't hurry with typing "Ah, Wilderness," as Gene is hard at work on another *serious* play.[11]—

Tell me (& I'll never mention it again, I promise!) *why* did they *not* put the dedication page before "Electra" in the "Nine Plays"? I am very upset about it!—

Gruenberg is a fool!—And a little big for his hat!

What happened re that note I sent you about publishing Gene's plays in a cheap edition abroad that I sent you to answer & Gene said 'twas O.K. with him if it were with you?

After three wet, grey, cold days the sun shines & my garden looks so green— Gene & I so often say—"Gosh, if Saxe were only here"!—

Bless you

Carlotta

Love to that *amazing* Dorothy & the two sweet devils!—

11. Discouraged with the way *Days Without End* was shaping up, O'Neill began working on "The Life of Bessie Bowen," a new title for "It Cannot Be Mad," the play he envisioned as the final panel of the *Dynamo* trilogy. After a short while he shelved "Bowen" to resume work on *Days;* several years later he returned to "Bowen" as part of a multi-play cycle, one that he never realized.

141. To Saxe Commins from Eugene O'Neill. ALS 1 p.

> Sea Island, Ga.
> Jan. 20th 1933

Dear Saxe:

Much gratitude for your second letter on "Ah, Wilderness." I wanted your reaction on the comedy end. That's where I feel uncertain—the question of the laughter in it which I don't attempt to gain by the usual easy route of being superior to the period and spoofing at it without attempting to understand it or see its contrasting virtues. And, of course, that marks untried ground for me—hence, my doubts.

Here's something important which I wish you would take up with Liveright. Carlotta has called to my attention—I hadn't looked through them carefully—that in both the Book of M. and Liveright editions of the Nine Plays the dedication page to her of "Electra" was omitted. I rise to ask, and I am damned sore about it, who took it upon themselves to do this without consulting me? That page is as much an integral part of the published play as the cast of characters and I certainly demand that it be put back in all future copies of this edition to be printed. What the hell was the big idea, anyway? The page was all there already set up for the regular edition and one page more certainly wouldn't add to the size of the book. Will you please get after the printer or whoever is responsible, Saxe. I tell you I feel so strongly about this that I never would have agreed to the Book of M. volume at all if there was any question of leaving this page out.

I had a fine letter of thanks from Micaela. I'm so pleased the books pleased her!

As ever, love from us to Dorothy, you & the kids.

> Gene

---

142. To Saxe Commins from Carlotta Monterey O'Neill. ALS 2 pp.
On stationery headed: Casa Genotta / Sea Island Beach / Georgia

> *Jan. 21st '33*

Saxe dear.

Thanks so much for your nice letter.—

I showed Gene (last night) the "Nine Plays" (he really hadn't looked at them) & he was furious. I knew he'd be!—But it's all too late now & nothing can be done—but, they had no business leaving out *anything* without asking Gene! —So that's that.—

Am so glad you are enjoying "Ah, Wilderness" it's a dear play—really—.
And means *so* much to Gene! He *adored* doing it. Of course that's only the
first draft you have.— Thanks so much for the photostats—I think them very
successful. How much were they, please?—

Must get to my labours now—

Love to you, Dorothy & the Babes—

> Always—
> Carlotta

---

143. *To Saxe Commins from Carlotta Monterey O'Neill.* WIRE 1 p.

QA396 8 XC—SeaIslandBeach Ga 27 109P   [January 27, 1933]

Saxe Commins—

   1 Rutherford Pl NYK—

Please have Wilderness bound before returning it Love—

> Carlotta

---

144. *To Saxe Commins from Carlotta Monterey O'Neill.* ALS 2 pp.
On stationery headed: Casa Genotta / Sea Island Beach / Georgia

Jan. 27th 1933

Saxe dear.—

Enclosed please [find] cheque for $4.55—is that for the 12 prints as well as
the "black positive"——?

Little Miss Commins is a darling.—She would make a grand add for health
foods—& her pants are too chic!—You have reason to be proud.—

Life goes on but, I think, *underneath* keeps us all a little fearful.—

Gene says it's time for another flood & I'm about ready to agree.—

Three very close friends of mine have died in the last six months from
"stroke"—it's beginning to make *me* afraid.—

Gene fussing over work—the world in general & life.—But, on the whole,
has a calm, "put" self that is gratifying to me.—Am busy every day & every
hour.—

Our dearest love always to you four—

> *Carlotta*

145. To Saxe Commins from Carlotta Monterey O'Neill. WIRE 1 p.

QA626 8–SeaIslandBeach Ga 1 407P   [February 1, 1933]
Saxe Commins–
    1 Rutherford Pl NYK–
Manuscript arrived Thank you Love to the family–

                                                    Carlotta

146. To Saxe Commins from Eugene O'Neill. ALS 1 p.

                                                    Sea Island,
                                                    Ga.
                                                    Feb. 4th 1933
Dear Saxe:
    The script is fine. You did a grand job. I enclose check for your labors–
but it is no adequate expression of my gratitude for the pains you took!
    I was aware of most of the confusion you detected. Meant to go back and
fix them up and then forgot to.
    Love from us both to all of you!

                                                    As ever,
                                                    Gene

147. To Carlotta Monterey O'Neill from Saxe Commins. TL(cc) 2 pp.

                                                    Thursday
                                                    February 16, 1933
Dear Carlotta,
    The best possible response to the enclosed letter of Sanborn[12] is to tell all
the facts as I know them. They are the facts that I told Sanborn himself
when he came in to cross-examine me, for what reason and by whose authority I have no way of guessing. But there is nothing to conceal.
    A month or so ago an agent for rare literary items, Hauser, by name, came
to me with a batch of proofs of Mourning Becomes Electra. He was considering purchasing them and wanted to establish their authenticity first. A first
glance showed no marks in Gene's handwriting or in mine. I could not tell

12. Ralph Sanborn, a book collector, collaborated with theatre historian Barrett H.
Clark on *A Bibliography of the Works of Eugene O'Neill,* published in 1931 by Random House. Evidently he was operating as a literary sleuth in 1933.

right away whether they were the printer's set belonging to the very first version—of which twelve sets were pulled and bound—or the printer's set of the second version. But they were obviously the printer's set, i.e., the proofs which he keeps as a record directly the type comes out of the linotype machine. To find out which version they belonged to, I asked Hauser to come to my house that night, so that I could compare the proofs in his possession with Frances' bound set. Comparison established that they were. I asked him how he came by them and he told me the following story:

A boy in the employ of our printer, Van Rees Press, knew that all such printer's proofs are thrown into a huge rubbish bag six months after a book is published. He guessed that O'Neill proofs would have a value, and when these were thrown away, he emptied the bag and fished out the set. He kept them at home for almost a year, and, being hard up, he tried to dispose of them to Hauser for $100.

Early the next morning, I got Van Rees on the phone and delivered an ultimatum, saying that those proofs had to be in my hands by noon, if they had to buy them back or steal them. At noon promptly a messenger boy brought the proofs in and in the presence of almost every member of the staff I tore them into a thousand pieces. Hauser and the boy afterwards told me that Van Rees, in their turn, had issued an ultimatum that the proofs had to be returned by eleven o'clock—and they were.

I never wrote you anything about it because I saw no reason for bringing up a subject and bothering you after it was satisfactorily disposed of. It was one of those things over which we had no control. It never occurred to the Van Rees people that anyone would go through their rubbish bags, which they assumed were immediately thrown into the fire. The boy who took it was not entirely culpable either, for he looked upon it as an article found after it was thrown away.

That is the accurate story of that set of proofs. It is what I told Sanborn. Why he suddenly appoints himself stool-pigeon extraordinary, as if a great crime had been committed, is beyond my understanding. Sometimes an excess of zeal leads one to do such things. In my ethic, it's unpardonable.

As to T.R.'s[13] reasons for selling his bound set of the first proofs, I cannot explain any better than you did yourself. The best and most charitable interpretation is "anyone has a perfect right to sell a gift book . . . In these hard times, some natures are easily tempted—" I wouldn't part with my gifts because they represent an emotion that is beyond money. Others may feel differently about it. That's their affair. You are right.

Now for something more agreeable. The Book of the Month Club finds a great demand for the Nine Plays and they are printing a new edition of

13. T. R. Smith, chief editor at Liveright's.

10,000 copies. This on the basis of 25 cents per copy, according to the contract.

The dedication will be inserted. Josephy[14] has been given his orders in this matter and he is submitting proofs to Pete Gross,[15] which I shall see when ready.

I hate to make my letters so entirely business. But today I must let you infer that all goes well with the four of us. But you must believe, not infer, our everlasting love . . .[16]

---

148. To Saxe Commins from Carlotta Monterey O'Neill. ALS 4 pp.
On stationery headed: Casa Genotta / Sea Island / Georgia

Feb. 18th 1933

Dearest Saxe,—

Thanks so much for your letter. Sanborn *is* a damnable pest—I grant you that.——But—he knows where to find most things of Gene's & is an absolute crank on the subject.—But [he] has given years to study to it & is a *Collector*—you know what *that* means! These things happen & what the hell!———

Forget it———. I just wanted to know if he knew what he was talking about.—

We are so pleased about the extra 10,000 copies of the "Nine Plays" & the dedication going in!———

Well———we had a burglar in our house last night! The village chief of Police just left—& oh—dear, we might have been murdered in our beds!—As our bedroom doors were wide open—& Gene & Blemie (!) & I sleep right thro' it. The fountain & the sea make so much noise that one can hear nothing upstairs of what is happening downstairs! A screen was cut—window pane cut out & opened & a small clock & bottle of home made wine taken—but everything rummaged thro' looking for money! I never have a cent in the house—so the devil got nothing. But it makes one feel so uncomfortable.—

I will *lock* my bedroom door in future!— And so it goes.— I am sure it was some one who worked on the house in construction or one who worked on the landscape gardening.—

No more today—I am dying with a headache from the excitement.

Dearest love to you—dear Dorothy & the babes—

Always—
Carlotta

14. Presumably a Book-of-the-Month Club employee.
15. A Liveright employee.
16. The carbon ends here.

149. To Saxe Commins from Carlotta Monterey O'Neill. ALS 8 pp.
On stationery headed: Casa Genotta / Sea Island / Georgia

Feb. 26th 1933

Thank you, Saxe dear, for your charming letter.—

Don't do *too* much—because, after all, you *are* just a human being.—That's where you & I & a few others go astray—we try to carry the world. No good— my child.—The world always has been— & always will be—a place of greed & stupidity— Look thro' your histories—no matter *what* form of government is in power—the leaders always loose their sense of equilibrium & yearn to be gods! This is just a repeat!—And, as long as we can meet our rent & food bills we're jolly lucky——. (Says she, who is getting grey haired thinking about it all!)—

No one (but you & Dorothy) has read "Ah, Wilderness."—Gene is back working on "Endings of Days" & is making many changes which—at the moment—seem to please him.—

As to the burglar—we're not isolated really—except on the beach side which is very dark at night.—

But I insist we each lock our bedroom doors at night. I don't think he'll (the *burglar*) return—As ours is the largest house here I presume they thought they would find money strewn all over the place! —*What* an idea!

I am looking forward with such pleasure to receiving "The Sinner"[17]— Yes—I too like warm-blooded, alive—decisive & honest human beings. Oh— Saxe dear, look about you—Listen to the conversation of these poor struggling, white livered, non-functioning creatures. —All struggling for the front page— & not getting there, shriek that they are misunderstood!—Their feeble sex efforts—their disgusting "explanations"—. Who cares!? Our men are feeble & our women worse.—When one meets a womanly-woman these days one gasps with surprise & joy—Oh—well—Christ tried to help & look what He got!——

Live as best we may—look ourselves in the eye—squarely & truthfully—& we can't go far wrong.

Now—at Christmas time Barrett Clark wrote me that he had purchased a Columbia-Kolster—(Viva-tonal) gramaphone (phonograph?) for *about* $40.00 & that it was marvellous. It was *electric*. As our Victor Orthophonic was a hand winder we'd got in France—I thought I'd get one for Gene for Christmas. B. Clark ordered it for me & it's *lousy*. No earthly good. I am sure it was made ages ago—& the parts ("pick up") are rotten—Now we must have a

17. A novel by I. J. Singer, translated by Maurice Samuel and published by Live-right in 1933. *The Sinner* was later adapted for the Yiddish stage under the title of *Yoshe Kalb*.

decent machine. I think the *Victor* is best & the tone of the *Orthophonic* was marvellous for symphonic music—That's what we want most—*tone* for Beethoven—Bach etc. symphonic things.—

Enclosed is a letter I rec'd—Now I'm afraid these bargains are *no good* machines on hand.—

Do you know any one you can trust in this game? I will pay up to $125.00. I do *not* want a radio combination. The Columbia-Kolster I bought at Christmas came from the Elaine Music Co.—150 East 42nd St.—(I had never heard of it)—

Now—someday when time permits will you try to find out something about all this for me? Don't you let them sell you a *good* machine & *send me* an old wreck! How can one avoid this? Now—look what I ask you to do for me!

I have been interrupted so many times in writing this that God alone knows what I've said & meant to say! Can you make head or tail of it?—

Dearest love to Dorothy & the Babes—from us always—

Carlotta

---

150. To Saxe Commins from Carlotta Monterey O'Neill. ALS 6 pp.
On stationery headed: Casa Genotta / Sea Island / Georgia

March 7th 1933

Well—Saxe dear—what a life!

I have 35¢ & no chance of getting more.—We are to have "script"[18] down here. I'm glad it's come to this.—*Maybe* something will be done now to insure more security for our hard earned cash in the banks. And *maybe* some of the crookedness will come to light (& be punished?) of those who pose as the foundation of our financial system.—It's all so mad—& yet not new at all. But history seems to teach nothing at all—to any Nation or people.—

How *can* Dorothy get time to go about listening to machines?[19] Saxe—she mustn't even attempt to do it.—And—now that I have used my head—I realize you are worked to death in & out of office hours.—What a bungler I am! —And, also, I have only a cheque on my New York bank.—!?

18. With banks failing in all parts of the country and depositors worried about their savings, newly elected President Franklin D. Roosevelt on March 5, 1933, ordered all banks closed for four days from Monday, March 6, 1933, to Thursday, March 9, 1933, while his financial advisers worked on a plan for reviving the banking system. During the bank holiday, people resorted to script, barter, and credit to get through the emergency.

19. Dorothy Commins was attempting to find a suitable phonograph for the O'Neills. See letter 149.

I am delighted that you find such happiness in your babes. I missed my child's baby years (after fifteen months) completely—.[20] But now get a great comfort in recognizing a nature that is far superior to mine. She has a terrific sense of justice, fairness, loyalty, & a divine sense of humour & *insists* upon *laughing* which will give her & those about her a great "lift" in hours of trouble.—She *appreciates* Gene's kindness to her & my generosity—which pleases me no end—(because it shows good manners—which is nothing else, really, but thinking of the other fellow!)—. So life isn't so bad.—I *do* know families where children not only take everything for granted—but scream for more & never even stop to think how jolly lucky they are. But we all are *as we are,* and God give us the courage & the strength to do the best we can.——

Gene is now going to *rewrite* the whole of "Without Ending of Days!" Such patience & labour.—

I have a feeling that Hitler will accomplish something in Germany—order & a new & sound commencement of new life.—Of course I know *nothing* about it! ——But I have German Bonds!!!!

Dearest Saxe, we have about hit bottom—so don't give way to black despair.—Things will recreate themselves along sounder lines & in five years you will have forgotten all this.—This is the *first* time, since 1929, that *I* have felt any "prosperity around the corner"[21]——.

Our dearest love to you—Dorothy & the Babes.—

Carlotta

---

151. To Saxe Commins from Carlotta Monterey O'Neill. ALS 4 pp. On stationery headed: Casa Genotta / Sea Island / Georgia

March 10th '33

Dear Saxe—

Gruenberg is a conceited ass— & he will never have the privilege of working with Gene again. Tell him so—if it will give you any pleasure!—! I presume he thinks no one ever thought of "Jones" until his mediocre score was added to it— He even got his best effects (in music) from Gene's tom-tom idea.— And so it goes!——But he is a nasty type of man,—licking boots when in need—arrogant when a bit of adulation comes his way—& whining when he doesn't get the "plums" of good things—. *He gets his deserts!*

---

20. When her child Cynthia Jane, whose father Melvin C. Chapman was Carlotta's second husband, was less than two, Carlotta had turned her over to her mother in California and returned to the Broadway stage.

21. For several years, once the Depression began, members of the Republican administration kept predicting that "prosperity is just around the corner."

Entre-nous—is there any danger of Gene *not* getting his money (when it is due) from Liveright?[22] Don't worry about us.— We get on—, by stint & dint, manage to pay the demands of the former wife & children & keep Eugene Jr., in Germany.— We worry——who doesn't—(Outside the Boulton family!) But I feel Mr. Roosevelt will pull things 'round a bit &, at least, let us build our houses on rock foundations.—

Do you know *Kuprin's* works? I think him so marvellous. Did you ever read "Gambrinus"—?[23]

I hadn't even 35¢ (when the "holiday" came) to pay for eggs! But now have a bit of *real* money to carry us on—.

It really is the bottom I think—they can't keep us good humans down—can they?

No more now—I have been working all day. I am house maid—personal maid, under gardener,—secretary,—nurse & what not! It's good for me—I haven't time to think.—My hands are ruined but what does that matter if Gene is at peace & comfy.—

Dearest love to you & Dorothy & the Babes—

Our love—
Carlotta

———

152. To Dorothy Commins from Carlotta Monterey O'Neill. ALS 2 pp.
On stationery headed: Casa Genotta / Sea Island / Georgia

March 17th 1933

Dorothy dearest,

I am in the dust at your feet—forgive me.—

We *have* "alternating" current. And from your survey I feel every confidence in your *Victor* (I—too—have always thought them the *best*).—I don't think the "case" matters a blow if the *works* are good—as it sits upstairs & is (no matter what cloak it has) a mechanical music machine!

I enclose a cheque for $150.00 to cover all incidental expenses. —& will it be so put in condition & so *carefully* packed—that all I have to do is to put a plug in the wall & sweet music will come out!———

I can never tell you how very much I appreciate your kindness in taking all this trouble.—

22. In spite of Arthur Pell's salary-slashing and other bone-cutting economies, the Liveright firm was in financial trouble because of the Depression.

23. Aleksandr Ivanovich Kuprin (1870–1938), Russian novelist and short-story writer, whose most famous work was his novel *The Pit* (Eng. trans., 1909). "Gambrinus" is one of his most famous stories.

Am hastening this to catch today's post.—
Dearest love to you & Saxe & the Babes.

Carlotta

Gene up to his ears in work—has now struck the "medium" he likes— & is
rewriting for the 5*th* time!!!!
For God's sake tell me if I haven't sent money enough.—

As conditions worsened at Liveright, Saxe, as always, was looking out for
O'Neill's interests.

In 1933 as . . . [the] depression was approaching its nadir, our salaries
were cut in half and from all sides creditors were clamoring for some sort
of settlement from Pell. There was only the question of how long it
would be postponed.

As O'Neill's editor I was very concerned about the large sums of
money due O'Neill in royalties from *Mourning Becomes Electra* and his
other plays. Worry impelled me to call a meeting of the principal stock-
holders and to place an ultimatum before them. Either a certified check
covering all of O'Neill's royalties would be given to me within twenty-
four hours or I would announce on the book page of the *New York
Times* that O'Neill had decided to transfer his publishing program to
any one of the five leading publishers of the country.

It was a staggering threat which . . . could be carried out, for I had a
virtual power of attorney in O'Neill's behalf and had been authorized
specifically to exercise my own judgment, as his editor and in the protection of his royalties.

Late that afternoon a certified check for the full amount due O'Neill
was on my desk. The reason for the alacrity with which they submitted
to my seeming blackmailing threat was that an announcement of
O'Neill's intention to change publishers would precipitate bankruptcy
proceedings among the many creditors. . . .

With the check safely in my possession, I took the train for Sea Island,
Georgia, where Gene and Carlotta had established themselves in manorial style in Casa Genotta, a large home, architecturally Spanish, near
the Atlantic shore, its name compounded from the given names of its
owners to sound somewhat Iberian. On my arrival I merely turned over
the check to Gene, saying as little as possible about the circumstances
under which it had been obtained.

My visit was brief but pleasant. Gene brought a football and we spent
many hours on the hard crusted beach throwing it back and forth. We
swam often, I near the surf and he far out of sight in the ocean. We

went for long walks along the shore, reminiscing about the old times and old struggles and a now romantically recalled poverty. Our companion on these walks was Blemie, a Dalmatian of aristocratic canine lineage, idolized and pampered by Carlotta and protected by Gene. Blemie's food was shipped from New York after consultation with animal dieticians. Special steel instruments were made for scaling tartar from his teeth. He slept in a made-to-order bed in the upstairs hallway. Sheets on this bed were changed at frequent intervals and a monogrammed blanket was provided for his comfort.

When I walked alone on the beach with him, it gave me a perverse pleasure to see him stick his aristocratic nose in the debris washed up by the sea or the offal of less privileged dogs. . . .

From the isolation of Casa Genotta on Sea Island, with all its opulence, I returned to New York and its anxieties over little more than survival. On my arrival it was all too evident that the Liveright creditors were organizing to deliver the coup de grace. The blow came with suddenness and a fierce bitterness in April 1933, when Van Rees, the printer who staggered under a load of $280,000 due him, Herman Chalfonte, the paper supplier, and the Ace Paper Company, constituting the necessary legal triad, filed suit. The sum due authors in unpaid royalties added up to more than $150,000. . . .

It was in this atmosphere of tension, suspicion and conflict that the Liveright bankruptcy proceedings reached their climax. Just before the end came, all employees were given notice of dismissal, salaries were abruptly stopped and the seemingly irrational activities required for giving form to ideas in books came to a dead end. The green-bordered stock certificate I had acquired through the loan from Eugene O'Neill was worthless. A fool and another man's money were quickly parted. Pell had cashed the check for $600 in his own favor, as he had planned to do from the beginning. His personal profit on the transaction was maximal, in brief $600. Finally I realized why he demanded that the check I had brought back from Northport be endorsed in his name.

I consoled myself for my fiscal stupidity with the knowledge that O'Neill had collected all the royalties due him just before the debacle. . . . Unfortunately for all the other authors under the Liveright banner, they were able to realize only five percent of the royalties due them. To a writer, whose earning powers at best are meagre, such a settlement is just short of catastrophe. . . .

Quite as severe was the penalty imposed on the Liveright staff; it was liquidated. T. R. Smith, editor-in-chief, an old man now still believing in the genteel tradition of publishing, was shorn not only of his security, but also of his dignity. Without any financial resources or prospects he could only look ahead to a bleak future; he was unwanted. For a while he subsisted on the sale, item by item, of his library, preponderantly volumes of erotica. All that passion spent, he died in loneliness and abject poverty. Julian Messner established his own publishing company and Leane Zugsmith devoted herself to free-lance writing. Louis Kronenberger, by far the ablest member of the group, became drama critic for *Time* and the author of many distinguished books on some of the principal figures of the eighteenth century. It was my good fortune to work with him several years later in another place and in happier circumstances. His many-faceted, sparkling mind earned my admiration—and envy. Aaron Sussman, that anomaly in advertising, an idealist, established his own agency and is now the representative of the world's leading publishers. Albert Gross, Liveright's production manager and the most companionable of men, created a place for himself with the firm of Coward-McCann and continued his interest in Yiddish literature as critic and translator. He died of a heart attack only a few years after the bankruptcy.

My own outlook was somewhat brighter. I profited by the gathering of the ghouls. Virtually every publisher in America hovered over the Liveright corpse, eager to inherit whatever of value remained of the company's assets. The most desirable of these reside in the continuing contracts with established authors and this property, so-called, becomes free under bankruptcy. That is to say, the writer is then at liberty to choose a new affiliation. Existing contracts are abrogated and the author can seek the shelter of a new house.

The most highly coveted "property" at that time and under those circumstances was Eugene O'Neill. Out of generosity and loyalty he made it plain that he would sign no contract without my counsel and consent. Furthermore, he wanted it stipulated in writing that no arrangement to publish his plays could be made unless the agreement included a clause which guaranteed me a job as his editor and a general editor of the company of his choice for the duration of his contract. To this latter condition, I raised an objection on the ground that I might conceivably embarrass him and that he should not under such circumstances be bound to me or I to him. O'Neill saw reason in this precaution and agreed that a literary alliance is, at best, a hazardous venture. He insisted, however, that I remain his editor.

At once, virtually all the publishers in New York began to court me. I went to Sea Island to lay before Gene all the offers that had been made and tried to assay their worth in terms of his advantage. My preference was for Bennett Cerf and his company, Random House and the Modern Library. The reason for that choice was that I had known Bennett professionally during the Liveright days and recognized in him the potential of an imaginative, resourceful, adventurous and trustworthy publisher. From my first meeting with his partner, Donald S. Klopfer, I was impressed by his quiet competence, his reliability and good sense. Subsequently, through a quarter of a century of daily association, I was to learn of his many attributes, not the least of which was his complete selflessness.

O'Neill suggested that Bennett fly down to Sea Island to consummate the arrangement and this was done in an atmosphere of mutual trust and friendliness. With the signing of the contract, a separate agreement was drawn up which provided for my employment as a general, working editor for Random House for a three-year trial period and I began my work on July 9, 1933.

---

153. To Saxe Commins from Eugene O'Neill. WIRE 1 p.

[April 18, 1933]

QA438 59 DL XC—SeaIslandBeach Ga 18 107P
Saxe Commins—
    1 Rutherford Pl NYK—
Suggest in case bankruptcy you have confidential consultation with Weinberger before you take boat Stop He will be wiring me for instructions and I wont know what to say Stop Remember Harry is on retainer No extra expense involved and whatever legal steps necessary will have to be taken through him Stop Hope to see you soon Carlotta writing—

Gene

---

154. To Saxe Commins from Eugene O'Neill. WIRE 1 p.

[May 15, 1933]

QA207 26 DL XC—SeaIslandBeach Ga 15 943A
Saxe Commins—
    1 Rutherford Pl NYK—
Have received fine offer Random House Stop Am inclined now give them every consideration Stop Advise you sound them out what they can do for you—

Gene

155. *To Saxe Commins from Carlotta Monterey O'Neill.* ALS 4 pp.
On stationery headed: Casa Genotta / Sea Island / Georgia

Sunday
[May 21, 1933]

Saxe dear,

Gene asks me to return the enclosed & to tell you not to be a damned fool. Wait until you're making good money & you & Dorothy are free from worry—then perhaps! Gene says, anyway, he owes you that for what you did for him in the past—. Now—for myself—your effort to repay this showed up some of Gene's old Provincetown *friends*— & made me smile!—But, seriously, stick it in the bank—'tis a good feeling to know *'tis there!*———

The Coward thing[24]—I feel—will be the best bet—for all "three"—(that means Gene, you & Mr. Gross!)[25]——We'll wait & see what he says re the Contract—& *you* be sure to get a contract—(no matter how charming he is!)—

Gene says the stationery & books "fine"—

The bird book is excellent, please thank those who recommended it to you.—

Also—please tell Mrs. Welch(?) that we are delighted to know she is better.——

Please accept this letter for Gene too. We both took calomel last night & feel rather "the morning after" today.——

I get *dozens* of *gardenias* each day. The house is filled with their beauty & their fragrance—. I do wish you could see them.

I am delighted to know you *like* the play—[26]

Cold bloodedly (as a publisher) what do you think of it?—(Entre-nous).—

An owl or night hawk stole the baby mocking birds from their nest—we're so upset about it.—

It is nice to be able to see you about our home now (in our imagination)— you are part of it— & our life here.[27]

With all love & wishes for future success—

Our best to you and yours,
Carlotta

24. An offer from Coward-McCann publishers.

25. Peter Gross, production manager at Liveright, whom O'Neill was also trying to get his new publisher to hire.

26. *Days Without End.*

27. A reference to Saxe's visit to Sea Island.

---

156. To Saxe Commins from Eugene O'Neill. ALS 2 pp.
On stationery headed: Casa Genotta / Sea Island / Georgia

Wednesday p.m.
[May 24, 1933]

Dear Saxe:

As I am wiring you, since looking over the Coward McCann list which arrived this a.m. I feel more than a bit doubtful about them. You must admit that, judged by their list, they are pretty third rate. I am inclined now to favor Random House as offering a much more fitting background both for your labors and my stuff—class and distinction. And I'd like to string along in Jeffers'[28] company. Coward-McC. seems to me to possess hardly a single writer of first class on their list—and what a crowd of bums they have!

I'm sure Cerf would be willing to give you a better break on permanency—especially if he knew my coming with him depended on it.

But I'll keep an open mind and hear all Coward[29] has to offer judiciously. He arrives this eve.

But that list is a black eye. It's too damned bad I didn't see that sooner. Honest, I thought they had more stuff than that.

Cerf suggests you fly down with him when he comes. How about it? Love to see you again—but you must use your own judgment about it, from the standpoint of your own interests. You know Cerf and I don't. It might help to get your end definitely settled. If you think so, by all means come. But that is absolutely up to you, sabe? You might have another long talk with him first, tell him frankly your misgivings about his present offer to you, let him think you will come with him and help him with me provided— You get me? You can also say for me that one of my greatest desires is to help you get permanently fixed. See his reactions to this.

Has Madden put my contract up to the other publishers' with favorable financial reports?

All best!
Gene

28. Poet Robinson Jeffers, who was published by Random House.
29. Thomas R. Coward of Coward-McCann, who came to plead his case in person.

157. To Saxe Commins from Eugene O'Neill. WIRE 1 p.

[May 24, 1933]

QB263 52 NL XC—SeaIslandBeach Ga 24
Saxe Commins—
  1 Rutherford Pl NYK—
Since looking over Coward third rate list received this morning feel very doubtful if his is right association for me or you Stop Inclined now favour Cerf Stop Am asking him fly down next week He suggests you come with him Do what you think best your interest as regards accompanying him—

Gene

158. To Saxe Commins from Carlotta Monterey O'Neill. ALS 4 pp.
On stationery headed: Casa Genotta / Sea Island / Georgia

Thursday 6/30 P.M.
[May 25, 1933]

Saxe dear,
  Your letter came today by air mail— & Mr. Coward is now packing his bag—preparing to leave, after dinner, on the train to New York.—
  Mr. Coward *is* all that you said—a charming and decent creature. We both like him immensely—But, business is business (a thing you must *try* to grasp in it's full sense!) —& we can make no plans until after Cerf's visit next week.—Then we'll see. Forgive my seemingly abrupt letter last week—but Gene was upset by Madden's many (& not all wise) suggestions.— Saxe—I *beg* of you to try to count on nothing, in business, (or in life) until you've *got* it. People may say "yes"—in conversations as to what *would* or would *not* be a good plan—but those are only *conversations*. Don't forget the terrible times we are going thro'—don't forget Dorothy & Francis & Eugene—don't forget *yourself!* The latter person more important than you realize—for without yourself in good fettle & on a solid footing—you are no good to the others—.
  Your loyalty to friends is a splendid trait—but don't let that take the place of loyalty closer home! And now I'll mind my own business.
  We—in Georgia—love you too, were delighted to have had you with us—& look forward to having you again—
  To-night is the kind of night you'd love—
  God keep you & yours—

Dearest love—
Carlotta

159. To Saxe Commins from Carlotta Monterey O'Neill. ALS 4 pp.
On stationery headed: Casa Genotta / Sea Island / Georgia

Friday Night
[May 26, 1933]

Saxe dear,

Gene asked me to write and tell you that Coward told him that Dreiser was asking a guarantee of $15,000.00 per year! Gene was wondering if this was a thing done in the publishing business. And, for example, supposing Gene asked for a guarantee of $10,000.00 a year.—And it is O.K.—Say the *first* year his royalties amount to $12,000.00 well—all is well. The *second* year they amount to $7,500.00 a year—then the publisher digs down in his pocket & pays $2,500.00 —The *third* year the royalties amount to $17,500.——does the publisher deduct the $2,500.00 he had to pay last year or does Gene (?) get the whole $17,500.00——? Do you know anything about such a business deal & what do you think of it?—

Now—Gene says that Coward told him, that things being as they are, he has a place for you—but, unfortunately, none for Gross now. Gene says this being so he will (when he signs his contract with Coward or Cerf) ask for a 3 yr. contract & an option and a 3 yr. guarantee for a job for you—& then they won't be able to do any thing about you until Gene's option becomes due— but you must get your own contract drawn up—& it's up to you to take it to a *good* lawyer & see that there are no flaws in it & no "trickey bits" to be got round.

Saxe, I beg of you to believe *no one* & be intelligent about work & all business dealings. Everybody is awfully busy these days making a living & everyone has all they can do to pay the rent—so, please, take the world of work seriously & make yourself & family secure in—at least—the knowledge of iron clad contracts. *Don't* think about social position & charm! *That* is an "extra"—just thrown in for good measure!—

Pardon me for making such a mess of all this—Can you make it out?

Love—my child—
Carlotta

top of Page 2

Gene will ask for a 3 yr. contract & option—& a 3 yr. guarantee for a job for you— & then they won't be able to do any thing about you *until Gene's option becomes* due—— and then *we'll see what's* best!——It's too bad about Gross but your family *must* come first in all loyalty—[30]

30. Carlotta wanted this paragraph inserted at the end of the second paragraph of the letter.

---

160. To Saxe Commins from Carlotta Monterey O'Neill. WIRE 1 p.

[May 29, 1933]

QA924 8 XC—SeaIslandBeach Ga 29 710P
Saxe Commins—
  1 Rutherford Pl NYK—
Manuscript arrived All Best Stop Cerf just arrived—

Carlotta

---

161. To Saxe Commins from Carlotta Monterey O'Neill. ALS 4 pp.
On stationery headed: Casa Genotta / Sea Island / Georgia

11 A. M. Tuesday
[May 30, 1933]

Saxe dearest,
    This letter is in strictest confidence.—
    We have talked long & much with Cerf.—He is a *very clever business man.*
And can get away with a lot on account of an exterior of boyish enthusiasm &
a care free manner.—I have had a long talk with Gene—& advised that Cerf
would be a much better person to handle his books than Coward—as he Cerf
knows more tricks of the trade & would always come out ahead of a man like
Coward. Coward is a gentleman & I *much* prefer him as a man—but this is
not a question of a social gathering but cold blooded business!—
    We have just *talked*—on both sides—& Gene has said nothing as to whether
or no. —Madden will hear from us as to contracts & insisted upon data—if, &
when, Gene chooses his man.—Don't think I don't like Cerf—because I do—
But he is a bit like all those N. Y. friends of his—(Dorothy Parker,[31] Woollcott, Ross[32] of the New Yorker,—etc., etc.,) & his humour runs a little to the
vulgar.—But—as I said before, we are only interested in him as far as
publishing goes.—It is unfair to compare him with Coward!—
    He kindly brought us books & is most cheery— & leaves Savannah to-
morrow, very early, in a plane for N. Y.—
    No doubt you will see him— & it will be amusing for you to hear his reac-
tions of us!—
    I have been seedy—but am better today.——

31. Short story and verse writer, drama and literary critic (1893–1967), known for
her amusing, satirical remarks.
32. Harold Ross, editor of the *New Yorker.*

Blanche Knopf[33] asked Cerf—just *what* your relationship to Eugene O'Neill was? *Ha! Ha! Ha!* Life goes on—

> Love as always—
> *Carlotta*

You would have smiled to have heard Cerf trying to pump me as to when Gene's next play would be ready etc.—

Just a little half wit—that was

> *Carlotta!*—

---

162. To Saxe Commins from Carlotta Monterey O'Neill. ALS 2 pp. On stationery headed: Casa Genotta / Sea Island / Georgia.

> [postmarked May 31, 1933]

Saxe dear./

Gene & I nearly had a fit when we saw you had taken the end of the play[34] quite from the wrong angle.

It has *nothing* to do with *Christianity* or *prayer* that brings Elsa back—it is her *great & all consuming love for her husband!* Thro' her love she senses that her husband is in danger & that *love* gives her the strength to *come back* & live for him— We suppose *no one* will understand that tho'—that you didn't!

I asked Cerf to try for a *sapphire blue* for Gene's books. We went all over the colour & binding things.

Pardon haste.—

> All best—
> Carlotta

---

163. To Saxe Commins from Carlotta Monterey O'Neill. ALS 3 pp. On stationery headed: Casa Genotta / Sea Island / Georgia

> *May 31st 1933*

Dear Saxe,

Your letter reached us this morning.—

Mr. Cerf left early to take a bus to Savannah to get a plane there for N. Y.

33. Wife of Alfred A. Knopf, New York publisher.
34. *Days Without End.*

—I feel that, before he left—he felt & understand more perfectly *what* Gene & I were like—because he fell more into our rhythm!—If you know what I mean.—

He spoke understandingly & sympathetically about you. But that means nothing.—Contracts count. Gene told him what you must have— & even I (perhaps I should not have?) spoke to him of you—(as if you were my son!)—and I am certain, with his quick business sense, he knows how you stand with us—at least!—

I pray to God all this will be settled up soon.—

He is to draw up a contract—tell Weinberger *you* are to see that *before* it is sent down here—so that you can send your criticism along.—

Freeman[35] was so pleased that you mentioned him—& Vera[36] fluttered to giggles over your mention of our cuisine!—

Gene & I are both feeling better.—

I want to get this off so no more now.—

Dearest love to you—Dorothy & the Babes—

Carlotta

---

164. *To Saxe Commins from Eugene O'Neill.* ALS 3 pp.
On stationery headed: Casa Genotta / Sea Island / Georgia

June [5?,] 1933

Dear Saxe:

First, I want you to get it absolutely straight about Gross & Coward, that I was declared out of that by Coward himself at the start. The first thing he insisted on in our business talk was that he couldn't possibly find a place for Gross—and he was pretty indefinite about having a place for you unless I went with him. These are the facts!

Now re Coward contra Cerf: I needn't tell you I liked Coward immensely personally—but then, I also liked Cerf. I feel, as far as the personal element goes, association with either could not fail but be pleasant. As business men and business publishers, my reaction was that Cerf must be the more able. He has drive and enthusiasm, coupled with keen shrewdness. Moreover, I felt Coward was trade publisher, pure and simple—but Cerf has more to his publishing than that, a love of beautiful books, an appreciation for good literature, an ambition to keep his firm above the level of the others, to expand only along lines of distinction. That, of course, appealed strongly to me.

35. Herbert Freeman, the O'Neill's factotum, who remained with them till he was drafted in World War II.
36. Vera Massey, the couple's black cook.

As for background for my stuff, there is no comparison. Coward has nothing to offer. Cerf has two unique things—Modern Library and Random House.[37]

So I figure my place is with Cerf—provided a few remaining differences can be ironed out. For one thing I understand the five thousand advance on new plays was to apply only on the first play when I suggested to him I guarantee him three new plays. As applied to three plays it would amount to less advance per play than I would have got from Liveright. So I'm asking five more on first play plus five on each of other two when they are accepted for publication. This may be a blow to him but I think it's fair, don't you? At 20% royalty a sale of ten thousand would pay it off on each book and he can be pretty confident of getting that on each as a minimum. So he can't lose.

I've also kicked against the clause making me pay on over 10% changes. It would be okay if I didn't turn in script until rehearsals were over, but not if publisher wants publication simultaneous with production. That way I have to let script be set up in galleys before I can call it a final version.

There's one clause I wish you'd look over carefully—No. 3. I don't get clearly all that about "retail," "discount," "net price," etc. I mean, you will know if that's all according to Hoyle and means what I want it to mean.

Re Coward contra Cerf again: I felt strongly that Cerf is the better bet for your present and future content—that with him you will have a real chance to do your stuff and a most congenial atmosphere. With Coward, outside of my stuff, you would be confined to a pretty shabby line of trade goods of little interest, it seemed to me. With Cerf you will undoubtedly be called upon to contribute real imagination and judgment of real writing, once you've fitted in there. I hope I'm right in this. Certainly it's my honest opinion, putting myself in your place and figuring out for which firm I'd rather work, considering all angles.

Let me know how you feel, will you? You know exactly what Cerf is offering better than I do.

Coward, for example, as far as I remember, didn't come forward definitely with any offer to tie you up by contract for a term of years. Cerf did. And it seems to me the principal object for you, under your present circumstances, in these unsettled times, is to nail down security for the next few years until this crisis passes—or we all blow up together!

In a word, I don't need to tell you that along with my own interests I've had yours in mind too—and the answer seems "Cerf." I don't want McMillan or Stokes or any of the others—and I know you wouldn't be happy swamped and tied down in a big place.

37. Cerf had originally been a vice-president at Liveright's. When he left in 1925, he purchased for $235,000 Liveright's Modern Library, a list of modestly priced classics, and joined forces with Donald Klopfer in publishing the Modern Library and founding Random House.

I enclose check for paper, covers, etc.

Carlotta joins me in love to you, Dorothy and the kids!

As ever,

Gene

P. S. My namesake seems to have all the fat I lack! He better trade me some! Frances is grand! They sure are fine kids!

---

165. *To Eugene O'Neill from Saxe Commins*. WIRE(copy) 1 p. [Yale]

6/9/33

Eugene O'Neill

Casa Genotta

Sea Island Beach, Georgia

Have just recovered all galleys from Liveright

Will hold them here Letter follows

Saxe

---

166. *To Saxe Commins from Carlotta Monterey O'Neill.*
On stationery headed: Casa Genotta / Sea Island / Georgia

Saturday—

[June 10, 1933]

Saxe dear,

So—at last—the bankruptcy is a fact. —Nothing lasts forever—even Mr. Pell's sleight of hand work!

I typed a long letter to Coward yesterday—that I regretted—but there can be no social leanings where business is concerned—Blemie must eat!——

Please send me, (as soon as the contract is signed & you are at work) some of the enclosed—as we don't autograph books—we sell them!—

I told Cerf of these papers & he started to chat about "of course there are some exceptions" —I answered there were damned few— & we would use our own discretion in the case! —Gene says we'll never need see Cerf—at all— that all will be as it was at Liveright's—that *you* will attend to all Gene's work & do all the writing back & forth. Cerf is inclined (in fact he asked me to call him Bennett when I'd known him two hours!) to use every one's Christian name & invite them to parties & invite himself to things. All this in good heartedness, mark you, but it must be nipped in the bud, so to speak. —You can—by a frank remark at the beginning—save us all unpleasantness later on. — And I merely mention this now as it is *how one starts at the beginning*—that the habit is formed! I know you understand.—We want no parties or dinners of "introduction" to celebrate Gene's going to Random House—Gene isn't that kind of an author!—A word to the wise—I know you understand.—

We had three hot days—but a rainstorm at 8 this A.M. washed everything off & it is just nice summer weather now. Did I tell you I'd taken a place in the Adirondacks (on a lake) for Aug. & Sept.— more housekeeping! But we must get away from here for a bit.

Don't mention to Cerf ever when or not we are to be in town—unless we say to!

Gene now (having reread *"Ah — Wilderness"* & thinking it a "lousy Owen Davis opus"[38]) is discontented with all his work.—But I can nurse him out of that—

Dearest love to you & the "3"
Carlotta

I sincerely hope that you do *not* keep my letters!

---

167. To Saxe Commins from Eugene O'Neill. ALS 1 p.
On stationery headed: Casa Genotta / Sea Island / Georgia

June 15th 1933

Dear Saxe:

I am sending you under separate cover, registered, the typed script of "Ah, Wilderness" which I have just finished cutting & revising. Will you start in at once retyping—(original & three copies, as before)? This is a rush order! I want this final script here for Nathan to read. He arrives on the 24th. So it will be a great favor if you'll get it out at your very earliest convenience— without breaking your back on it.

I think all changes I have made are clear—and a big improvement. It was a bit repetitious and cluttered up.

All best!
Gene

P.S. Have copies bound same as old ones

38. One of the most prolific authors in American stage history, Owen Davis (1874–1956) began with sensational, old-fashioned melodrama but eventually graduated to writing more restrained fare, including both comedy and drama. Adopting a grim, O'Neill-like tone, he won the 1923 Pulitzer Prize with his *Icebound.*

168. To Eugene O'Neill from Bennett Cerf and Saxe Commins.
WIRE(copy) 1 p. [Columbia]

6/16/33

Eugene O'Neill
Sea Island
Georgia

Several papers have called asking about your publishing plans We have refused all statements Nevertheless Times printed note this morning hinting
that you were coming with us Man who wrote note has apologized but that
does not help We would like to make definite announcement and end all
gossip if OK with you Will you wire collect and tell us what you think

Bennett and Saxe

Charge to Modern Library

---

169. To Saxe Commins from Eugene O'Neill. WIRE 1 p.

[June 18, 1933]

QA782 34 NL XC—SeaIslandBeach Ga 18
Saxe Commins—
1 Rutherford Pl NYK—
Nathan not leaving for here until twenty third Please see that he gets number one copy new script of Wilderness at forty four West Forty Fourth Street
so he can read same on boat—

Gene

---

170. To Saxe Commins from Carlotta Monterey O'Neill. WIRE 1 p.

[June 27, 1933]

QA642 7XC—SeaIslandBeach Ga 27 300P
Saxe Commins—
1 Rutherford Pl NYK—
Manuscripts arrived Beautifully done Many thanks Writing—

Carlotta

171. To Saxe Commins from Carlotta Monterey O'Neill. WIRE 1 p.

[July 5, 1933]

QA972 49 NL XC—SeaIslandBeach Ga 5
Saxe Commins—
    1 Rutherford Pl NYK—
Want to send you script of Days Without End Stop Which is best to send
it to Rutherford Place or care of Random House Stop Will try to send so it
will reach you Monday Stop In same mail will be long letter All best Please
wire reply—

                                                    Carlotta

172. To Saxe Commins from Carlotta Monterey O'Neill. WIRE 1 p.

[July 6, 1933]

QB50 15 XC—SeaIslandBeach Ga 6 1110A
Saxe Commins—
    1 Rutherford Pl NYK—
Have sent script first class mail special delivery Should reach you Saturday
morning All best—

                                                    Carlotta

173. To Saxe Commins from Carlotta Monterey O'Neill. ALS 4 pp.
On stationery headed: Casa Genotta / Sea Island / Georgia

                                            Wednesday & hot!
                                            [late June 1933]

Saxe dear.—
    Even this Liveright mess can't go on forever! So cheerio!— Buck up!—
    Things like the enclosed (please return to me!) make the O'Neill's wish
they had never heard of this gentleman (!?!) Gruenberg. I hope Mrs.
A. Wertheim[39] doesn't ask any more favours for her little musicians—& I
hope somebody puts Gruenberg in his place. But he can't be insulted—his
skin's too thick.
    Enough of him—may Hitler catch him!——

39. Mrs. Alma Wertheim, whose husband Maurice was an investment banker and a
member of the Theatre Guild's board of managers.

I rec'd a charming letter from Mr. Coward—I *do* like that man.—I know exactly how you feel about hanging around waiting—it drives me mad.—

I am so glad Dorothy is giving radio Concerts again—I hope I'll be able to catch her someday—but the static is terrible now with our hot weather.—

The 'script was *perfect,* as always. Gene is now going to call the play "Days Without End" which *I* like so much better— Does that sound familiar to you? It does to me.—It seems to have been in a prayer I used to say!—

Gene went deep sea fishing yesterday & caught great mackeral—amber jack & what not. Small sharks!—He came home black & dead.—

Oh—also in the play there will be no "priest," just a *good* man— a religious man who has his God!— So all that Catholicism thing will be got round.—

Expect Elsa & Terence[40] down for a week—then Nathan[41] & Shane—& that ends it for this summer. We're taking a house up North in the Adirondaks (on a lake) for Aug. & Sept.—

No more news—

Love from us to "you all"
Carlotta

The personnel are always asking how you are!—

---

174. To Saxe Commins from Eugene O'Neill. ALS 2 pp.

Casa Genotta,
Sea Island, Ga.
July 1933

Dear Saxe:

I am mailing you under two separate covers, registered, 1st a new last long hand act I have written for "Days Without End," and 2nd the other three typed acts which I have cut and revised. Please wire me when you receive these as I shall be anxious until I know they are safely in your hands. Will you go ahead with them and retype the whole play accordingly? This need not be a particularly rush job but if you can get it done by the 20th of the month, so much the better. I want to give time for Nathan and the Guild members who are in U. S. to read it before we come to New York, on the 27th or thereabouts.

Here's the scheme for the new scripts: Get ordinary typewriting paper that will make four carbon copies (five, if possible. The last one Madden will have to send Copyright Office need not be much good). When finished, de-

40. Elsa and Terence Holliday, who ran a bookstore in New York City.
41. George Jean Nathan.

liver the No 1 to Nathan the others to Madden. (Nathan's copy he will hold for me). As for binding—and this is important—all copies except No 1 to be bound like "Ah, Wilderness," but with No 1 I would like some loose-leaf binding arrangement. Can't you get a loose-leaf cover for typewriting size paper and then have holes cut in No 1 to correspond? Anyway, I leave this to you, knowing you can dope out the best thing better than I can.

Of course, keep the original scripts I'm sending with you until we come up.

On going over "Days Without End" I found I did not like the old last act at all. Elsa's death and the final suicide seemed to me unconvincing, out of character, no solution, not inevitable, simply a dramatic evasive easy way out. In the present end I find some inspiration and a bit of exaltation and mysticism—moreover it seems so humanly true to John and Elsa's souls.

Boyd becomes Baird throughout, as you will note—to avoid obvious Irish-Catholic connotations. Also he ceases to be a Servant of God and goes back to his status in my first draft of the play—first impression being right in this case!—and becomes an old fashioned country doctor of the old general practitioner type, with a deep religiousness added. Thus we get away from all the Christian or Catholic priest confusion and still preserve all values—without much change too, for most of his dialogue was written in first draft when he was a doctor as now.

Note particularly the new scheme for Scenes—a subtitle for each section, no more Acts or Scenes. I think this is good. It will prepare reader or theatre audience for the "different" quality of the play.

For the rest, I think you will find the other general revising tightens up the play and points it better.

I'm sorry about the delay in the Cerf contract but I did feel it needed a bit of clearing up and emphasizing. But that's all spilt milk now. I sure hope you are going to like the job there. I'm sure you will, once you feel "put."

Nathan liked "Ah, Wilderness" enormously—thinks it is one of the best things I've done! How "Days W. E." will strike him, I dunno. It concerns itself so much with currents he doesn't feel.

If it's all right by you, I'll give you a check for all this typing stuff when I see you in N.Y. in three weeks.

Carlotta is fine. We both enjoyed Nathan's visit. He is a grand company and friend.

Love to Dorothy, you & the kids from us both!

As ever,
Gene

P.S. The "Ah, Wilderness" scripts are fine!

Am sending only *one* package—please wire me when you have rec'd it—
CMO'NEILL[42]

42. This line is written in Carlotta's handwriting at the bottom of the second page of O'Neill's letter.

175. *To Saxe Commins from Carlotta Monterey O'Neill.* ALS 4 pp.
On stationery headed: Casa Genotta / Sea Island / Georgia

July 7th 1933

Dear Saxe—

What good news to hear how well & happy Dorothy & the babes are.—The change will do them worlds of good.—The whole arrangement sounds perfect.—Yes—I, too, think the country is the only place to *live*——.[43]

Thank you for the information re "sales" of books.—

A professor named Sophus Keith Winther has written a critical study of Gene's work[44]— & it is the only book (*I* have ever seen) that seems to say anything. This man knows every word in Gene's plays. (Gene says better than *he* does!)—& my God—how he has worked on this thing.

Winther is at the University of Washington (Seattle—Wash.) & Gene met him for an hour or so at Sisk's[45] office, in the Guild, at Sisk's desire, when we were living in N. Y.—Gene was struck by the man then.

When we come to N. Y. we will bring the work along—it is *excellent*——.

I have just finished typing a long letter from Gene to Winther.—re it's publication etc.——I have to type a long letter to Cerf now.——

Freeman has gone on his two weeks holiday & Vera is chauffing & all that along with regular duties. I had him go now so he would be here while we are away—

I *dread* packing & going to N. Y. —We'll only be there a few days going North—but, if Gene allows production we'll be a long time there for rehearsals.—Don't you think "Days Without End" is greatly improved? Gene changed *Boyd* to *Baird* to get away from a Catholic name!—

No more now—Our loves to you & yours,

Carlotta

43. Saxe and Dorothy Commins had rented a house in Riverdale, N.Y., for the summer.
44. *Eugene O'Neill: A Critical Study,* later published by Random House in 1934. Prof. Winther and his wife Eline became good friends of O'Neill and Carlotta.
45. Robert Sisk, the publicist for the Theatre Guild.

176. To Saxe Commins from Carlotta Monterey O'Neill. ALS 2 pp.
On stationery headed: Hotel Schenley / Pittsburgh, Pa.

[September 27, 1933]

Saxe dear/
    A line because I know you are anxious.
    We went to the matinee today.[46] What *hell!* I was sick with nerves.
    The house was full & they laughed a great deal.—I think the public will resent Gene's writing this type of play!— Entre-nous Cohan[47] is very "draggy" in parts—but in total a good performance.—
    Gene still busy cutting—(but *not* for the published book)—to get the time down.—
    We are both beyond the place where our criticism can mean anything.
    Love to you & Dorothy from us both—

Carlotta

Wednesday Night.
I will get the tickets to you in time for the performance—

177. To Saxe Commins from Eugene O'Neill. ACS 1 p.

Oct. 17, 1933

Dear Saxe:
    Much gratitude for the birthday wire!

All best!
Gene

178. To Saxe Commins from Carlotta Monterey O'Neill.
TLS 1 p. [Columbia]
On stationery headed: Casa Genotta / Sea Island / Georgia

April 20th 1934

Dear Saxe,
    Gene asks me to send you the enclosure with a few suggested changes.
    Gene is following the doctor's orders as to a complete rest cure[48]—hence

    46. Of *Ah, Wilderness!* O'Neill was usually against out-of-town tryouts of his plays, but the Theatre Guild won his permission to do so this time, to learn the audience's response to the play, since this is so important to a comedy.
    47. George M. Cohan, who played Nat Miller in *Ah, Wilderness!*
    48. After struggling to get *Days Without End* into shape for production, O'Neill

my writing this note. He has had me write to Weinberger, Madden, and Langner[49] as to the necessity of resting and not being annoyed by the usual outside world. He loathes discussing such things (which are purely personal) and so do I but it is necessary to say that the Press this time was *not* making up a story. Gene is resting, eating, playing, and doing only what he wishes to do—for months to come—there is to be no work.

There is nothing seriously wrong but there *would* be if he did not take precautions now.

When you do the other prefaces send them along—if you wish—and Gene will go over them.[50] I think that would be the happiest thing for all concerned.

Love to you and Dorothy.
Carlotta

---

179. To Carlotta Monterey O'Neill from Saxe Commins.
TL(cc) 1 p. [Columbia]

Mrs. Eugene O'Neill,   April 26, 1934
Casa Genotta,
Sea Island, Georgia

Dear Carlotta:

I have been so overwhelmed with work that I have not been able to get at the introductions, or even be courteous enough to answer your last note. I hope the enclosed will be satisfactory to Gene. The others will follow in rapid succession.

All goes well here and I hope that both of you are able to bask in the good old Sea Island sunshine. I was glad to see that D.W.E. won such enthusiastic response in Dublin.[51]

---

was exhausted and dispirited by the harsh reception accorded it by critics and audiences when it opened on Jan. 8, 1934, on Broadway. It lasted for only fifty-seven performances. O'Neill's doctor warned him, before he left New York after the opening to return to Sea Island, that he was "teetering on the verge of a nervous collapse" and must rest indefinitely or risk what O'Neill described as "a complete bust."

49. Lawrence Langner, producer, director, and member of the managing board of the Theatre Guild, which had produced all of O'Neill's plays since *Strange Interlude* (1928).

50. Early in 1934 Charles Scribner's Sons had obtained permission from Random House to publish a twelve-volume edition of O'Neill's plays. The author was asked to provide a preface for each volume, giving details about each play included. He declined but agreed to Donald Klopfer's suggestion that Commins prepare the forewords and have O'Neill sign them as his own after he saw and approved them.

51. At William Butler Yeats's instigation, *Days Without End* had been successfully

Dorothy and the kids are flourishing and so am I when I get enough time to think about it.

All devotion,

sc; pk

---

180. *To Saxe Commins from Eugene O'Neill.* TLS 2 pp. [Columbia]
On stationery headed: Casa Genotta / Sea Island / Georgia

May the sixth, 1934

Dear Saxe,

Frankly, I feel that you are off on the wrong foot on this stuff for the Scribner edition. I felt this about the previous ones you sent and especially about these last ones. What I mean is, there seems to be a misunderstanding about what I agreed to with Cerf to do for Scribner and what I said I would *not* do—that is, offer any comment or explanation of the plays meaning, etc. All I would agree to do was to stand for a brief write-up of the facts in each case—origin of the idea (in the few cases where this has been put on record by me in Clark's book[52] or publicity—as "Jones," "Electra," for example)—when written and where—when first produced, where and by whom—run in New York (if a substantial one)—if made into Movie, when, where and by whom—in plays with star parts, state who created them in original production—finally, state in what foreign countries produced.

You see what I mean—no comment, no explanation—just facts. It will make it a lot simpler for you. You will find most of these facts in Clark's book. When you can't, simply leave blank space and I will fill in when you send draft to me.

I don't want comments on my work in this sucker edition. I want to save all that stuff for a first appearance in the future.

I'm sorry you've had this extra labour. We should have had a talk on it before I left, but I thought Cerf had explained my stand on this Scribner business.

How about making this an excuse for a visit? You know I'd be glad to pay expenses down and back, as last year. And we'd be glad to have you.

Love from us both to Dorothy, you and the kids.

As ever,
Gene

---

produced at the Abbey Theatre in April 1934, directed by Lennox Robinson and with some of the Abbey's finest actors, including Barry Fitzgerald, in the cast.

52. See letter 126, n. 95. Clark's book included reports of conversations he had with O'Neill about his plays and life.

181. To Eugene O'Neill from Saxe Commins. TL(cc) 1 p. [Columbia]

May 7, 1934

Mr. Eugene O'Neill,
Casa Genotta,
Sea Island, Georgia

Dear Gene:

Here is another installment of forewords. I have been so close to them for the last few days that I am a little foggy about their merit. I tried awfully hard to give variety. But that is explaining and explanations have never been exchanged between us before. There are one or two little things, however, that I must speak of. Chiefly they concern dates. For example, I have "Beyond" in 1918, "Desire" 1924, "The Fountain" 1921, and "Welded" written in 1923 and produced in 1925. This last date is a pure guess. Will you fill in the correct ones? There now remain only three more forewords to do—"Dynamo" and "Diff'rent," "The Straw" and "The First Man," and the nine one-acters.

Everything was going along swimmingly until Friday when Gene took sick and had us scared witless, but now, thank goodness, he is on the mend. I too have recovered from a bum gut, and the outlook is a little brighter now.

Devotedly,

sc; pk

182. To Eugene O'Neill from Saxe Commins. TL(cc) 2 pp. [Columbia]

May 8, 1934

Mr. Eugene O'Neill,
Casa Genotta,
Sea Island, Georgia

Dear Gene:

I am terribly sorry that this misunderstanding had to arise. I would have real reason to reproach myself if you felt that the comments on the plays were false and in any way compromised you. I was extremely careful to make each statement ring true to a conviction which, as you know, amounts to a passion about your work. It is too bad that we did not have the opportunity to talk this matter over more carefully before you left so that I could get a clearer understanding of what you wanted. Bennett, probably thinking that you and I had had such a conversation, simply left the whole matter to me.

My feeling is that anything of yours which appeared in print should get the best that is in me. The Scribner edition will probably get as dignified a format as anything of yours has had in the past. It will remain a printed record of your works even though limited to 750 copies. Although I don't approve of letting it interfere with the Random House definitive edition I still feel that these notes can be improved upon a lot for what will become the standard set under our imprint.[53] My only consideration, as I have said, is that you should not be compromised. If anything I had written had done that, I would be inconsolable. My whole viewpoint is summarized in the notion that no edition of your works can be inconsequential. Whoever prints it has a record of what you have written. That's why I took the liberty of making these notes a little more than a mere factual record.

Naturally, after having sent off last night's batch, I have stopped work on the balance.

Much as I'd love to have a holiday with you and Carlotta, I am afraid it is impossible. First of all, I am swamped with work in the office that must be gotten out to meet a deadline. I have the complete works of Browning, a book on architecture, a book of short stories, a novel, two books of poems and the regular Modern Library list to prepare before Bennett returns from Europe. This means that I must keep my nose constantly in my scripts and proof sheets. Then too, little Gene is not entirely well and I cannot think of leaving Dorothy for a moment.

I hope I have made everything clear.

Love to the two of you from the four of us.

                                                        Devotedly,
sc; pk

---

183. *To Saxe Commins from Carlotta Monterey O'Neill.*
TLS 1 p. [Columbia]
On stationery headed: Casa Genotta / Sea Island / Georgia

                                                        May 11th 1934
Dear Saxe,

Gene asks me to thank you for your letter and to say how disappointed we are that you are unable to come South.

Enclosed you will find corrected proofs and Gene says to just stick to facts. With love from us to you, Dorothy and the youngsters.

                                                        Carlotta

53. Apparently, Random House planned to publish their own large-scale edition of O'Neill's plays. No such edition appeared until 1941, when they issued *Plays of Eugene O'Neill*, a three-volume boxed set that included the same plays as the Scribner's edition.

184. To Eugene O'Neill from Saxe Commins. TL(cc) 1 p. [Columbia]

June 1, 1934

Mr. Eugene O'Neill,
Casa Genotta,
Sea Island, Georgia

Dear Gene:

Here is a new batch of introductions. You will notice that they present the bare facts, gleaned from Barrett Clark's book, from those year books compiled by Burns Mantle[54] and the accumulated issues of "Cast."[55] You will no doubt want to make factual additions.

I was in a fog when I mentioned that the Winther book omitted reference to Wilderness. My first glance was at the last chapter. It didn't occur to me to look elsewhere. Consider that query not asked.

Having bellyached my family illnesses for the last few letters, I beg to announce with great joy that we are all in the pink.

Devotedly,

sc; pk

---

185. To Eugene O'Neill from Saxe Commins. TL(cc) 1 p. [Columbia]

June 13, 1934

Mr. Eugene O'Neill,
Casa Genotta,
Sea Island, Georgia

Dear Gene:

Harry just called me up to tell me about the stolen letters and to ask my advice in the matter of publicizing and advertising the whole mess.[56] Until Carlotta's letter came day before yesterday all I knew about it was that I had seen a transcript of two letters in the catalogue of the Chaucer Head Bookshop. Dick had written me a letter and he said he was frightfully upset about it all. Beyond that I knew nothing until Harry gave me the facts today. He asked

54. For many years Mantle edited an annual *Best Plays and Yearbook of the Drama in America.*

55. *The Cast,* a weekly magazine which for fifty-five years (1899–1954) published the complete programs of the leading New York theaters.

56. Some letters O'Neill had written to Richard Madden had shown up in a dealer's catalogue.

what would be the best medium for reaching booksellers and those who trafficked in stolen or honest scripts and letters. The only place for such advertising or publicity, it seems to me, would be Publishers Weekly, the trade magazine which goes to every bookseller in the country and is read by every publisher and book reviewer. I would suggest that if any advertising is to be done, it be done in Harry Weinberger's name, to give it a legal aspect. From my point of view it is best to have you stand above such a battle. I could get publicity in Publishers Weekly and give it the kind of dignity that ought to go with your name. In view of all the circumstances I don't think it wise to use the daily newspapers, simply because such a scandal would be featured on the literary page and would give an even greater value to those stolen letters which are being held by unscrupulous people who look for scandal to raise the prices of their illegal possessions. In the end, I am afraid, publicity in the newspapers would boomerang on you, especially if it seemed that that publicity emanated from you. My conviction is that the best place, if any, is Publishers Weekly. If the newspapers take it up from there they will quote Publishers Weekly and the whole thing will make a better impression.

Harry said something about instituting suit. On that subject I know absolutely nothing. Personally, I always fear and detest them (lawsuits) because the chances of getting a fair shake are sometimes very slim. If I can help in any way in regard to the Publishers Weekly affair, you have but to call on me. I am terribly sorry all this has happened and upset you when you are trying to find peace.

Always,

---

186. *To Eugene O'Neill from Saxe Commins.* TL(cc) 1 p.

June 21, 1934

Mr. Eugene O'Neill,
Casa Genotta,
Sea Island, Georgia

Dear Gene:

Harry sent me copy for an ad in Publishers Weekly. Accordingly I had Louis Greene, one of the directors, come up this morning and talked over the general situation with him. He took the ad and asked me to write him a letter covering the situation so that they may use it for editorial purposes. Enclosed is a copy of the letter I wrote.[57] The ad will run in the June 30th issue and

57. See the following letter.

it would be best if they managed to run their editorial comment at the same time.[58]

I hope my letter covers the situation to your satisfaction.

Always,

sc; pk

---

187. *To Louis C. Greene from Saxe Commins.*[59] TL(cc) 1 p.

June 21, 1934

Mr. Louis C. Greene,
c/o Publishers Weekly,
62 West 45th Street,
New York City

Dear Louis Greene:

This letter will serve to amplify our this morning's conversation in reference to the question of the unethical and illegal use of Eugene O'Neill's letters. As I told you, a number of dishonorably acquired letters written by Eugene O'Neill have been thrown on the market. They have been reprinted in full in catalogues and have been generally passed around as if they were handbills and not letters of the utmost privacy.

A fine question arises which, perhaps, may be worthy of an editorial in Publishers Weekly. It is this: How far can one go to exploit a letter which is the physical property of the person who sold it, but which contains *confidential business or personal* matter *whose dissemination might tend to* injure the writer? It must be remembered that the writer never gave permission to

---

58. In place of an ad *Publishers Weekly* ran the following "Special Notice," with no editorial comment, on June 30, 1934:

EUGENE O'NEILL herewith gives notice to all whom it may concern, that any and all letters written by him to others are not to be published in any manner, in whole or in part, for advertising or other purposes, in catalogues or elsewhere, nor may these letters be bought or sold by anyone, without his written consent.

Under the law, the writer of a letter has property rights therein and can prevent any publication or sale by the receiver of the letter, and any other person in whose hands they may be. (13 Corpus Juris 963—Rice v. Williams 32 Federal Court 437; Matter of Ryan 115 Misc. N.Y. 472; City of N.Y. v. Lent, 51 Barb. N.Y. 19.)

Anyone buying or selling letters written by Eugene O'Neill, or publishing them in any manner or form, will be held strictly accountable according to law. Harry Weinberger, Attorney for Eugene O'Neill, 70 W. 40th St., New York City.

59. This copy of Saxe's letter to Greene is what he sent to O'Neill for his additions; O'Neill's handwritten insertions are marked by italics in this text. What appear to be other insertions are probably Saxe's.

sell his letters. It is obvious that the sale is illegal and unethical, to say the least, and he actually has redress in law. Naturally he hesitates to resort to law because the attendant publicity only focuses attention on the letters and plays into the hands of the unscrupulous people who want these very letters publicized. It is a racket that deserves exposure. It seems to me that Publishers Weekly should lend its editorial columns to a defense of the writer, famous or obscure, against unscrupulous dealers of personal letters.

For your information, some of the letters which *have been* bartered were taken[60] from the files of *Eugene O'Neill's former agent,* the American Play Company. The others were sold by a few of *his one time* so-called friends.

Cordially,

sc; pk

---

188. *To Eugene O'Neill from Saxe Commins.* TL(cc) 1 p. [Columbia]

July 2, 1934

Mr. Eugene O'Neill,
Casa Genotta
Sea Island, Georgia

Dear Gene:

With these introductions the whole list is completed. You will observe that I have stuck to the barest facts. Should you want to add any on your own account, please do so. You may find that one or two dates are inaccurate, particularly the date on which "The Moon" was written.

You will see that scant space is given to "Dynamo" and "The First Man." Attribute that to my ignorance of the facts. You can decide what is to be added to these.

We have had an urgent call from Mr. Maxwell Perkins[61] for the introductions. Accordingly, I have sent over those which you have already OKd, adding, of course, the data you subjoined in pencil.

All goes well. I am busier than the well-known paperhanger might have been if he suffered the amputation of his remaining arm and was attacked by hornets rather than fleas.

All best,

sc; pk

60. O'Neill's proposed substitution of the word "stolen" here was apparently rejected by Commins.
61. The senior editor at Scribner's.

189. To Eugene O'Neill from Saxe Commins. WIRE(copy) 1 p. [Columbia]

7/6/34

Mr. Eugene O'Neill
Casa Genotta
Sea Island Ga.

Scribner wants a general name for their edition Will you OK Glencairn
Edition as general title Please wire acceptance or rejection or new suggestion

Saxe

190. To Saxe Commins from Eugene O'Neill. WIRE 1 p. [Columbia]

[July 6, 1934]

NAU97 19 DL XC—SeaIslandBeach Ga 6 1045A
Saxe Commins—
    Care Random House 20 East 57 St—
Glencairn absolutely meaningless to ninety nine out of hundred Stop Suggest
Wilderness edition[62] Stop Gave okay to Burns Mantle—[63]

O'Neill

Continuing to heed his doctor's orders, O'Neill did little work during the
spring and summer of 1934, escaping the Georgia heat by spending two
months in the Adirondack mountains of upstate New York. He also spent
time in New York, where he visited with his oldest son, Eugene, Jr., who was
continuing his graduate studies at Yale in preparation for a teaching career.

Returning to Sea Island healthier and twenty pounds heavier, O'Neill
began writing again and, early in 1935, began work on a project that would
occupy him on and off for several years. "A Tale of Possessors Self-
dispossessed" began as a cycle of five plays, soon grew to seven, then to nine,
and eventually to eleven. Of these, only *A Touch of the Poet* and the incom-
plete *More Stately Mansions* survive.

Except for a two-week visit to New York in October, O'Neill worked

62. The volumes were published as "The Wilderness Edition."
63. Reference may be to Mantle's reprinting of *"Anna Christie"* in *A Treasury of
the Theatre,* which he was editing with John Gassner and which was published by
Simon and Schuster in 1935.

steadily on the cycle in Sea Island throughout 1935. He completed the first draft of *A Touch of the Poet* in early spring 1936 and continued to map out the rest of the cycle. The O'Neills remained in Sea Island through another hot summer, where they were visited by Professor Sophus K. Winther and his wife. Winther, a professor at the University of Washington, had written a critical book on O'Neill that had impressed the latter and had led to an extensive correspondence between the two couples. When the Winthers saw how worn the O'Neills were by the heat, they suggested an exploratory visit to the scenic beauty and bracing climate of the Northwest. Both O'Neills responded warmly to the suggestion, and they arrived in Seattle on November 3, 1936, renting a house for three months on secluded Magnolia Bluff near Puget Sound. There, their privacy was shattered when, on November 12th, O'Neill learned he had been awarded the Nobel Prize for Literature.

After remaining in Seattle for two months, the O'Neills moved on to San Francisco where, on December 26, 1936, he had an appendectomy and suffered major complications that kept him in the hospital for two months. Upon his release, he was again warned by his doctors to refrain from work for a year. In the spring of 1937 they rented a house in Contra Costa County, near Lafayette. At the same time they bought 160 acres of land on a ridge of the Las Trampas Hills above Danville and began to build their permanent home there.

---

191. To Saxe and Dorothy Commins from Eugene O'Neill. WIRE 1 p.

[November 15, 1936]

EAU66 10 NM—Seattle Wash 15
Mr and [Mrs] Saxe Commins—
    1361 Madison Ave NYK—
A million thanks to you both for your congratulations Love—

                                                                    Gene

192. *To Saxe Commins from Eugene O'Neill.* ALS 1 p.

Lafayette,
Contra Costa Co.
Cal.
June 1937

Dear Saxe:

Query: Can you dig up for me any English translations of Bakounine, Kropotkin[64]—or any book of Emma's—which gives as clear picture of the structure & workings of society if this Anarchists Utopia came to be? Are such books or pamphlets still published in England, perhaps—if none are here?

The same query as to Syndicalism? Can anything be obtained on that?

No, I'm not thinking of hitting the convert trail! But it has occurred to me that I might have one of my characters in the Cycle[65] dope out for himself an ideal society which would be similar to Anarchism or Syndicalism.[66]

If you can be of help on this, a million thanks! I haven't started to work again yet, and may not for some time, but I am feeling better and my brain is beginning to do a little thinking about work, at least.

Carlotta joins in love to you & Dorothy & the kids.

As ever,
Gene

193. *To Saxe Commins from Eugene O'Neill.* TLS 1 p.
On stationery headed: Lafayette / Contra Costa County / California

July 24th 1937

Dear Saxe,

I am looking forward to receiving the library of Anarchist-Syndicalist literature—and let's hope we don't both get pinched for conspiring to pollute the mails with seditious propaganda!

64. Mikhail Bakunin (1814–1876) and Peter Kropotkin (1842–1921), Russian aristocrats and leading anarchists of their time. Bakunin's writings included *God and the State* (Eng. trans., 1893), Kropotkin's *Fields, Factories, and Workshops* (1899).
65. "A Tale of Possessors Self-dispossessed."
66. A movement which, like Anarchism, favored the overthrow of the existing order and a reorganization of society. Syndicalists stressed the function of productive labor and regarded the trade union as the essential unit of production and of government. In the United States, the Industrial Workers of the World (IWW), which flourished prior to World War I and figured prominently in one scene of O'Neill's *The Hairy Ape* (1922), was the chief syndicalist organization.

A million thanks for the trouble you have taken! Let me know as soon as you know how much I owe you.

No news on this end, either—except that they are starting the foundation of our new home. A beautiful spot! You will love it.

I am beginning to flirt with work again—notes, but no more. Am going carefully and taking no foolish risks. Won't really start on the job for some time to come.

Love from us to you, Dorothy, and the kids.

Gene

---

194. To Saxe Commins from Carlotta Monterey O'Neill.
TLS 1 p. [Columbia]
On stationery headed: Lafayette / Contra Costa County / California

August 24th 1937

Dear Saxe,

Maybe Jehovah is really watching over you. Or a really on-the-job lawyer! Now you are free from a world of worries and won't have to call your house Mortgage Manor as Gene says we'll have to call ours!! All the building trades are trying to get a general strike on out here. So there you are. They find fourteen dollars a day not enough for plasterers! And so life goes. In a way I envy you. But I feel *we* must have a home and in the country. For city life kills Gene.

At the moment I am on the hop for there are a thousand things to see to. So excuse short letter.

Our love always,
Carlotta

P.S. That awful woman Mrs William Brown Meloney wired Gene to ask him to sit to a Mrs Jacobs for a portrait in a book—with *others*—to be published by Scribners Sons. Do you know of this opus?

P.S. Gene says to suggest to Bennett and Donald that a several volume collection of best works by Nobel Prize Winners should certainly be a fine bet. Each winner, of course, to be represented by one piece of writing. The one for which he, or she, probably got the prize. If the Pulitzer Prize Book was a success, the above should sell a million.

195. To Dorothy Commins from Carlotta Monterey O'Neill. * ALS
On stationery headed: Lafayette / Contra Costa County / California

[postmarked
October 24, 1937]

Dearest Dorothy—

Thank you so much for your note & your programe.[67] Congratulations!
Saxe had already sent us your programe & I was amazed at the labour of it.
How *do* you manage to do all that & be a wife & mother?————For God's sake
don't work too hard.—The old body turns, you know, if we don't let up—
now & again.

I have seen Gene's break-up— &, even I nearly went to the dust heap!—

Life is so God awful these days that the worry is what kills. Responsibility.
The ghastly feeling of *in*security. This last Stock Market crash actually laid
me low. Building a home, at this time, is no joke. Plasterers demanding
$13.00 a day—for 6 hours work!— This man Bridges[68] ought to be deported—
or shot!— It is the Labour Agitator who keeps the Racket going. The workers
are trapped— &, of course, will suffer like hell this Winter for all people will
stop building, etc. —At least, out here. One simply can *not* pay what they are
demanding. And they are so damned impudent. —I don't know *why* I should
write all this to you. —Maybe, indirectly, because I am glad you didn't take
on the responsibilities of a *house*. You would have been *swamped* with responsibilities. Taxes, *upkeep*, and God knows what.— And commuting, in
Winter, is no fun!

The bright side of life for me is that Gene is feeling so much better.—And
that we sold our Sea Island home. Here we have a splendid climate, no
negroes, sand flies, hookworms or mosquitoes. All of which I dislike—in
quantity. Also, we have friends here—people we can talk with. And Gene
adores the football. California has a grand team. (This letter is for Saxe, too,
hence the football news!)

As I sit here & write I can't help but wish that you were here. Lovely
sun,—fresh breeze, beautiful rolling hills enclosing a long valley, with Mt.
Diablo at the end. The garden is so lovely. Our view (from the new house)
is even more lovely than this.—

I hope Saxe's tummy is better. Can't he rest more & work a little less?—He

67. Dorothy Commins was presenting a piano recital on Nov. 16, 1937, at the New
York Times Auditorium.
68. Harry Bridges, radical leader of West Coast longshoremen. Roosevelt's secretary
of labor, Frances Perkins, was criticized by congressional leaders for not calling for
Bridges' deportation.

looked so well when we saw him here. I do hope he'll have to come West next Spring.—

We will think of you on the 16th of November & wish you *great* success.—

With our dearest love to you both— & the youngsters—

As always
Carlotta

---

196. To Dorothy Commins from Carlotta Monterey O'Neill. WIRE 1 p.

FA157 AI75CC 3M 18 SC
   Berkley Calif
Mrs Dorothy Berliner Commins
   DLR16 1361 Madison Ave NYK
We are both thinking of you and wishing you great success in your concert tonight Love to all

Carlotta

---

197. To Saxe Commins from Eugene O'Neill. TLS 1 p.
On stationery headed: Tao House / Danville / Contra Costa
County / California

July 10th 1938

Dear Saxe,

Just a line to tell you the books arrived. They are a grand job from every standpoint. Random House has got them out beautifully. Both Oates and O'Neill[69] have certainly done something that needed doing, is worth doing, and does them proud. I know I am tremendously pleased at Eugene's part in it.

Thanks for your information on the Flexner gal. I don't give much of a damn about her Left Wing bias. That always discounts itself. But I did want to be certain that her book was to be published, and that she wasn't trying the old gag of using names and permissions to persuade a publisher.[70]

69. At Saxe's suggestion Random House had published *The Complete Greek Drama,* a two-volume set coedited by Prof. J. Whitney Oates of Princeton and Eugene O'Neill, Jr., then a professor of classics at Yale.

70. *American Playwrights, 1918–1938,* by Eleanor Flexner, which was published by Simon and Schuster in 1938 and contained a sixty-seven-page chapter on O'Neill's works viewed from a left-wing perspective.

I'm feeling fine now, working hard and well, and making excellent progress on the Cycle. But, of course, it's still a long hard row to the end.

Can't you wangle a job for Random House on the Coast—like last time—so you can visit us on our ranch?[71]

Carlotta joins me in love to you,

As ever,
Gene

---

198. *To Saxe Commins from Carlotta Monterey O'Neill.* ACS

7/26/39

Dear Saxe—

Thought this would amuse you![72]

We are harvesting the wheat & digging a well—you can imagine the noise.—You know how dry California is in the summer & our springs are running low. Hence the well—pray God we'll hit water—The "witch" said we would! ?!

Please send us six "Nine Plays"[73] (charging same to Gene's account)—

Hope all goes well with you & yours— & try to keep the mad world out of your heart— But I presume it really effects us all.

Our love to you all—
Carlotta

Eugene Jr. & bride are due![74]

71. In Nov. 1937 the O'Neills had moved into their newly built house, which they named "Tao House." The Chinese word *tao* means "the right way of life."

72. This message is written on the back of post-card size photograph of O'Neill at his player piano, which he called "Rosie" and which was one of his most cherished possessions. The photograph is reproduced on p. 475 of Louis Sheaffer's *O'Neill: Son and Artist*.

73. Random House had reissued *Nine Plays by Eugene O'Neill* (originally published by Liveright's in 1932) in 1936, calling it the "Nobel Prize Edition."

74. Eugene, Jr.'s first wife had divorced him in 1937; he had remarried almost immediately, but that marriage had ended within a year, and he was now married for a third time.

199. To Saxe Commins from Eugene O'Neill. TLS 2 pp.
On stationery headed: Tao House / Danville / Contra Costa
County / California

October the 31st 1939

Dear Saxe,

I'm enclosing the letter from the League of American Writers to you.[75] It will be a great favor if you will handle this for me. Simply call up this Jerome Brooks and tell him I've written you that I've already made arrangements for the distribution of all my original scripts and cannot comply with their request.

Reason for wishing this on you is that I have no use for this League. Between us, it strikes me as a phony—one of those Communistic inspired organizations which use sucker names for a fake front. I have ignored requests that I join it. Perhaps I'm wrong about them, but statements of aims and purposes they've sent me have a very fishy smell, and I should hate to be so dumb that I could ever be kidded into aiding and abetting something which, if it had the power, would promptly ban everything I've written, take all I've got, and then send me to a local Siberia or shoot me! There is a lot too much of idiotic enemy-kissing abroad in our land, no? What inside dope have you got on this League, if any? In confidence, of course.

The Krutch book[76] hasn't arrived yet, I shall be damned glad to have it. But I couldn't make any comment—if you mean for publication—in spite of my admiration for his stuff. I never have on any of Nathan's books, as you know, and it would look very peculiar—and be a lousy trick—if, after all these years, I started commenting on a dramatic critic's work and chose a book by Krutch!

By all means, write us a real letter when you get the time and tell us all about you and Dorothy and the kids. Also, I'll be amused to hear anything you have heard about how the Comrades—particularly the Jewish Comrades!—work the old dialectical racket so that they can bless the Stalin-Hitler sweetheart act[77] as being all for the best. It must have been terribly upsetting. But I have implicit faith that the Comrades here are moronic enough to add it up so they can still attend the same old church as true believers!

75. On Oct. 24, 1939, Jerome E. Brooks of the League of American Writers had written to Saxe asking him to intercede with O'Neill on behalf of the league's manuscript sale "for the benefit of exiled writers in Europe and America."

76. _The American Drama Since 1918_ by Joseph Wood Krutch, recently published by Random House and including a sixty-page chapter on O'Neill.

77. The Hitler-Stalin nonaggression pact of Aug. 1939, which paved the way for Nazi Germany's attack on Poland and the start of World War II.

A very, very amusing world, isn't it? And yet when you laugh it leaves a taste of vomit in your mouth.

I wish we could see you. There's a hell of a lot I'd like to talk about. Not my pessimism on world affairs. I guess you hear enough of that. About the work I've been doing. But it's too long a subject for letters. So I'll just have to say I have been working hard.

Love from us to you, Dorothy and the kids,

As ever,
Gene

DECLINING YEARS

1940 – 1953

After *The Iceman Cometh*, written in 1939, and *Long Day's Journey into Night* (1940), O'Neill managed, despite the increasing tremor of his hands, to complete two more plays, both of them among his greatest achievements, the full-length *A Moon for the Misbegotten*, a kind of sequel to *Journey*, and *Hughie*, a long one-acter that is virtually a monologue. Thereafter as his health deteriorated, all he could accomplish was fragmentary revising and polishing. Plagued by ill health much of the time and worried over the war raging around the world, he could take no comfort from matters closer to home, including the lives of his children. The academic career of his elder son, once so promising, had begun to fade; his other son, Shane, was drifting, and, worst of all in O'Neill's eyes, his daughter Oona had married Charlie Chaplin, thrice her age, whose marital and amorous history had inspired as much publicity as his comic genius.

As living at Tao House became less and less comfortable due to wartime conditions—it was difficult to get adequate domestic help or transportation from their isolated mountainside home—the couple moved to a hotel in San Francisco, and after the war they returned to New York for a production of *The Iceman Cometh*.

The last of O'Neill's works to be seen on Broadway during his lifetime, *The Iceman*, staged in 1946, failed in general to impress the critics as it deserved, partly because of an inadequate performance in the central role. The following season the Theatre Guild also produced *A Moon for the Misbegotten* but withdrew it during its out-of-town tryout when, on top of rows with censors in a couple of cities, the Guild brass became dissatisfied with the *Moon* principals.

Paralleling the decline in O'Neill's theatrical fortunes, relations between him and Carlotta deteriorated at times into scenes that could have been written by Strindberg. While in New York they were estranged for months, a period that found him hospitalized with a fractured shoulder from an accident. After their reconciliation they settled in Marblehead, near Boston, where again, several years later, they underwent a separation, and once more Eugene was hospitalized with broken bones. This time his friends hoped for a permanent separation, but he, apparently feeling that they were "welded" together to use the title of his most Strindbergian work, returned to his wife. Peace came to him at last, through death, in 1953.

---

200. *To Saxe Commins from Eugene O'Neill.* ALS 1 p.
On stationery headed: Tao House / Danville / Contra Costa
County / California

[December 1939–
January 1940]

Dear Saxe:

Be sure and come!! Seeing you again would be worth more than an ocean of medicine to both of us semi-invalids in Tao House!

Will you thank Bennett for me for his letter re the Bond Drive stuff I sent. Was it ever auctioned off?

Love to you, Dorothy
& the kids
Gene

---

201. *To Dorothy Commins from Carlotta Monterey O'Neill.* ALS 3 pp.
On stationery headed: Tao House / Danville / Contra Costa
County / California

Saturday—
Jan. 20th, 1940

Dorothy, my dear,—

Your Saxe arrived nine hours late—& we were so happy to have him here.[1] My, how well he looks. Last night he had a bit of sniffles—so I gave him rock & rye (enough to knock him out!) & aspirin & soda.—This morning he is better—but I'm keeping an eye on him!—

1. During Saxe's stay at Tao House he typed the newly revised and completed script of *The Iceman Cometh* for O'Neill and returned to New York with it to be deposited for safekeeping at Random House. Only Bennett Cerf and George Jean Nathan

Dorothy, what *lovely* handkerchieves. I never saw the dark ones before & think them extremely smart.—A thousand thanks—altho' you were naughty to be so extravagant on me.—

The years are going by—our children becoming real citizens in this mad, bad world.—But you look so beautiful. (Saxe showed us the photograph he had of you & the children.) I love your white hair. I wish mine would get *white*. I just have salt & pepper hair. I loathe it.—

Gene is better this winter than I have ever known him. He is ageing—but gently and serenely so. And has qualities that few of the outside world dream of.—Speaking of ageing—I feel, at least, 110 years old! But manage to get about & do my job. Poor old Blemie, now *twelve,* is full of rheumatism. And on foggy & damp days groans & moans & sets up a great to-do. Gene & I spoil him no end—but always say he is the only one of our children who has not disillusioned us— & seemed always conscious (& *grateful*) of our effort to do all we could for his welfare & happiness!!

I hope you will be able to come to us some day, with Saxe. I would love having you here. But not in January—but later when the spring has brought out the blossoms.

Gene joins me in love to you—and, again, I thank you for the very beautiful handkerchieves.—

As always—
Carlotta

---

202. *To Saxe Commins from Carlotta Monterey O'Neill.* ALS 2 pp.
On stationery headed: Tao House / Danville / Contra Costa
County / California

6 P.M.—
Saturday—
[February 24, 1940]

Saxie dear,——

Gene and I (& Blemie!) have just come back from walking to the gate.— Spring in the air—the hills like green velvet after a light rain, blossoms everywhere & Blemie chasing imaginary rabbits!—

As Gene & I walked back, hand in hand, we spoke of you & wished that you were here with us!—

We rec'd Bennett's wire saying he had been moved by "T.I.C." —& that

---

were allowed to read it, as O'Neill felt the times were not right for such a nihilistic play to be produced and because he was unwilling to undergo the strain of rehearsals and a New York production.

George Jean had "it" now. I said to Gene,—"I knew Bennett would like it." Gene replied, "That doesn't mean anything. That is just a publisher's wire. He says that to all the playwrights whose plays he publishes"!! Isn't that Gene all over?!

This is not a real letter—just a greeting from Tao House.

As always—
Carlotta

———

203. *To Saxe Commins from Carlotta Monterey O'Neill and Eugene O'Neill.* ALS 4 pp.
On stationery headed: Tao House / Danville / Contra Costa County / California

[Spring? 1940]

Dearest Saxe/——

Have just rec'd your letter & am furious with that small time Sal!² Gene & I both wish Dorothy had thought quickly & told Miss Sal that she Dorothy regrets deeply(!) she couldn't have her but Grandma & Aunt Sue are arriving for an indefinite stay. If Dorothy has already said "yes" I presume it is too late for *this* visit. But, for God's sake, (& your own) talk while she's there so she'll know there will be no more such hospitality.

I have just reread your letter. Do you mean both Sally & Eugene have asked to stop with you. If so, I think it is the nerviest proposition I have ever heard of— & I am *ashamed* for them. Now Saxe, listen,—these are trying times. You have *your* troubles— & dollars & cents count these days—you have two children—& many obligations—so just pull yourself together & make *necessary* excuses when thoughtless people (who evidently don't know any better) attempt to impose upon you. You have plenty of *your own* relations to do that!— And *don't think Gene wants you to do this.* For *he does not!* Don't you see it puts us in an embarrassing position, too!—

I'll write soon—

Love as always,
Carlotta

Tuesday
P.S.³
Dear Saxe:

I subscribe to what Carlotta says one hundred percent. Please don't you and Dorothy get the idea that because Eugene happens to be my son you

2. Sally, Eugene, Jr.'s third wife.
3. This first postscript is in O'Neill's handwriting.

have to let his frau—or him—impose on you. You know how I feel in that matter. Tell Dorothy she should always have a few good lies on hand to ward off the invader. This is a day for preparedeness!

Gene

P.P.S.[4] I am afraid that you have an effusive manner of saying, "Now, be sure, when you want to come to New York let us know—& come & stop with us"! *Don't do this.* It is not fair to Dorothy. The kind of people who take you up on this—are *not* the kind of people you want in your house, any way.——Learn to protect your home from parasites. And never go into any-one's home that you don't want in yours! Gene & I have had many lessons to have learned this truth. Go to Childs' for your meal—it is cheaper in the end!

---

204. *To Saxe Commins from Eugene O'Neill.* TLS 1 p.
On stationery headed: Tao House / Danville / Contra Costa
County / California

April the 25th 1940

Dear Saxe,

I'm writing this from bed where I am again laid up with the after-effects of the flu. A nasty brand of the infection is this one which has been preva-lent on the Coast this year. You get over it and then find you are not over it. It seems to have the doctors a bit bewildered. My own doctor got it originally a week before I did and he still is having relapses which send him back to bed for a couple of days. Everyone who has had it has been through the same thing. It is particularly exhausting, and a piece of bad luck for me, coming on top of my low blood pressure spell. I've felt lousy practically ever since you were here and have not had the energy to write much. I work a couple of days and then get that tired, all-in feeling.

Re Gassner, will you tell him how much I appreciate his courtesy in in-scribing his book.[5] Please explain to him that I don't feel up to reading it now, and probably won't get around to it for many months—not until I finish the latest play I've started[6] because I never read plays or books on drama when I'm on the job.

Please explain this to Bennett, too, will you? (aside, as in "Strange Inter-lude") Jesus, what a couple of pals Bennett and Saxe are to send me an 800

4. This second postscript is in Carlotta's handwriting.
5. *Masters of the Drama* by John Gassner (New York: Random House, 1940), with a sixteen-page chapter on O'Neill.
6. *Long Day's Journey into Night.*

page book on the drama which weighs about ten pounds, and here I am with flu, and low blood pressure, listening to War news over the radio, and my only thought about the Art of the Drama is Fuckit! And then to make life more atrocious, Bennett has to pass on to me from one St. John Terrell a prospectus for a Workman's Theatre which, to quote Mr. Terrell's letter will "blend specialized artists with simple people using the theatre as a mixing bin," and which strikes me as a new all time low in crap!

Please tell Bennett the expurgated version to pass on to Mr. Terrell, who sounds earnest and well-meaning, is that I simply am not interested in any theatre of that kind.

And now, my pals, a parting word in a mood of deep affection and no offence: Will you kindly, until further notice, keep all books dealing with the drama and shove them far, far up your old jazbos! Jees, an old guy like me's gotta right to some peace, ain't he?

As ever,
Gene

---

205. *To Saxe Commins from Carlotta Monterey O'Neill.* ALS 4 pp. On stationery headed: Tao House / Danville / Contra Costa County / California

Saturday—
[ca. June 15, 1940]

Saxe dear/——

A thousand thanks for Lillian![7] You have saved my life!

What with the war news— & all it means— & Shane left this morning after a two weeks visit. Shane has been playing about at Art School for a year. He has little more talent than I for drawing. But it encouraged even less discipline—lying in bed— & the usual Boulton routine. He is a sweet kid—but has no mind, body or guts! It has caused Gene (who loves him deeply) and me, *worry*—& given us pause. To make a long story short Gene has talked to him frankly, firmly, and with deep affection (for the first time in his life!) & told him that he must get a job in a ship yard— or some such—& prove he has the guts to work, & the desire to help himself. "If" he does this Gene will help him—if *not*——! And I know Gene means what he says.—The "poor white" atmosphere of the ménage in New Jersey is no help to anyone. Now Oona is to be taken away from her school in Virginia (after being there 2 yrs.) & put in a school in New York as A. wants to live in N. Y. for a bit! Oh—God!—

7. *Lillian Russell: The Era of Plush* by Parker Morell (New York: Random House, 1940).

Genie is depressed today—but 'twill pass—as all emotions do.——All this entre-nous.

To get back to "Lillian." I am enjoying it no end. My only criticism is re the photographs—I think many more beautiful ones are in existence! As a kid I sat next to Lillian Russell one day in old *Martin's*— & God, she was beautiful with amazing *charm*. A peaches & cream complexion— & really *lovely*. Of course she was a "fine figure of a woman" —but that went with the era! —I *adore* the photograph of the cosy corner, don't you?—

I read *raving* notices of a book by a negro called "Native Son,"[8] & I read it & am still in a *fury*. I never hated a book so in my life. How *dare* critics go on about a book of that type in such a manner. It leads to all sorts of mis-understanding. Praising communistic lawyers of the Leibowitz[9] brand—that would stir up any trouble for publicity & money.

It's time we had a Dictator— & *we will* if people don't get sense & decency on their own hook.—

Are you feeling better?

I am very low & disintegrated. I *can't think*. Gene makes no attempt to *work*. He can't see any importance in the theatre *now!*

Our dearest love always—
Carlotta

Will write a real letter soon— Love to D. & the kids! I am getting grey!—

———

206. *To Saxe Commins from Carlotta Monterey O'Neill.* TLS 1 p.
On stationery headed: Tao House / Danville / Contra Costa
County / California

January the 21st 1941

Saxe dear,

First, Gene likes (*very much*) the cover you sent him for the new edition.[10] I do, too! It is dignified and a colour scheme that fits well with any room.

I am enclosing our *Blemie's Last Will and Testament*.[11] It is one of the most charming things Gene has ever written. Carl Van Vechten[12] is crazy

8. The Richard Wright novel is today considered a classic on the black experience in America.

9. Samuel Leibowitz, a prominent Brooklyn attorney, was a liberal in politics. In 1941 he was named to be a county court judge.

10. Random House was planning a three-volume boxed edition of O'Neill's plays.

11. The O'Neills' beloved Dalmatian had died on Dec. 17, 1940, and after they buried him on the grounds of Tao House, O'Neill wrote "Blemie's Last Will and Testament" (see Sheaffer, *O'Neill: Son and Artist*, p. 519).

12. American novelist, music critic, and photographer, who was a close friend of the O'Neills.

about it, too. Of course, anyone not a dog lover cannot give it its full value. And, as I don't like people who don't like dogs, I don't give a hoot what they think! What I want to know is this. What would it cost to have about fifty copies of this printed for us to give only to those friends of ours who knew and *really liked Blemie?* Not an expensive affair but something simple and nice. I feel this sort of thing should be done in large pages so that the whole is not more than three pages and a simple cover. Also, can this be copyrighted? If so, have you copyright cards, and would you see to this for me?

I would have written to Bennett about this, Saxe, only I felt he would be wintering someplace now, and I did not want this to go to a secretary. So, please, let me know Kiss![13] about it. I am so fond of this that I don't want anything to be done about it that is not *just right.*

Gene went to bed three days before Christmas with a damnable bronchial cold. He only got up a few days ago and is still not as he should be. If the rain would stop for more than twenty-four hours it might help us all.

I can feel the world cracking beneath my feet—so why talk of it. We are all helpless and can do nothing. It will just get worse and worse!

With our love to you
and Bennett—
Carlotta

P.S.——When you read the WILL please send it back with what the cost etc. would be for the printing. *Gene would want to go over it before it is finally printed. C. M. O'Neill*

Pardon haste—

---

207. *To Carlotta Monterey O'Neill from Saxe Commins.* TL(cc) 2 pp.

January 24, 1941

Dear Carlotta:

I make haste to answer your letter about printing Gene's beautiful memorial to Blemie. Already I have talked with a printer and he has provided me with an estimate for fifty copies. Purposely I selected a chap who is completely trustworthy and would not print a single copy beyond those ordered. He is a man of impeccable taste, the chap who designed the bindings for the Complete Plays and does all the better Random House work. I could, of course, put the whole thing on the basis of a favor to Random House and get a cheaper rate, but I preferred to ask him to do it at his regular fees.

I would make a little book about seven by ten inches of six pages, bound

---

13. Whenever Carlotta made an ink blot in her letters, it was her practice to write "Kiss!" above it.

in stiff board and covered with a tastefully ornamented paper on which a simple and dignified label bearing the title would be pasted. The six pages would comprise the following:

1. A title page, which merely carried the title itself;
2. This would be the reverse of the title page and would carry the copyright line. (I would take care of the copyright for you, but I have to ask in whose name it would be issued. This is rather important.) This page would also contain a "limit" notice, saying in effect that only fifty copies of this edition were printed; they are not for sale and they will be numbered from one to fifty;
3. The text begins here and it would carry over to four and five;
4. A left-hand page, blank.

My printer tells me that such a job would cost in the neighborhood of $100.00. I could, of course, get it done for less, but you would never have the kind of book that would satisfy you. Please let me know about this fee. If it is not too high, I shall go ahead and order the job done. All you will have to do, besides give your consent, is to tell me how you want the copyright. Of course I shall send you a set of the proofs for correction and revision before it goes to press.

I think I have covered everything. There is nothing to add of a personal nature. We are all well, and I am buried in work. It is a great opiate against all the hurts of the world.

Devotedly,
Saxe Commins

P.S. I will hold the little manuscript locked in my desk until I hear from you.
SC:LJ

––––––

208. *To Saxe Commins from Carlotta Monterey O'Neill.*
WIRE 1 p. [Columbia]

[February 28, 1941]

INADI82 17—Danville Calif 28 1105A
Saxe Commins—
   Care Random House 20 East 57 St—
The new addition[14] is grand job Gene not feeling very well Will write soon Our love—

Carlotta

Saxe Commins

14. Misprint for edition. Reference is to the new three-volume boxed edition of O'Neill's plays.

209. *To Saxe Commins from Eugene O'Neill.* TLS 1 p.
On stationery headed: Tao House / Danville / Contra Costa
County / California

March the 2nd 1941

Dear Saxe,

I am feeling lousy cum laude physically, to say nothing of mentally, so this will be merely a line to tell you how much I like the appearance of the new three volume set. It won't sell, of course, what with the cheap competition of the Doubleday-Doran and Giant Nine Plays,[15] but it serves a good purpose in getting all the plays gathered together.

I hope to hell you are coming out here on your vacation. It's just as well you didn't make it up to this time. It has been one of the—if not, *the*—rainiest season on record. Terrible stuff to take! I'm longing for Spring to come—or would be if I didn't dread so much what Hitler may do with it![16]

Come out if you possibly can. It will be a charitable act—a boon to us to have you here—and ruin you at "Sorry."[17]

Love from us to you, Dorothy, and the kids.

As ever,
Gene

210. *To Dorothy Commins from Carlotta Monterey O'Neill.* ALS 3 pp.
On stationery headed: Tao House / Danville / Contra Costa
County / California

May 1st 1941

Dearest Dorothy,—

"Lullabies"[18] reached us this morning. What a charming book—& dear God, what labor went into it. I should think *thousands* should be sold. Do let me know how the sales go.—

Of course, in these days of war & hate there is no value (in the majority's eyes) in beauty, charm or loveliness. But, let us hope that our schools & teachers (mostly Reds!) will, at least, see the value of your book & use it.

15. Both the Garden City Publishing Company (Doubleday, Doran) and Random House had reissued the *Nine Plays* volume, the former in 1940 and the latter, as a Modern Library Giant, in 1941.
16. The Nazis were widely expected to launch an invasion of England in the spring.
17. A parlor game.
18. *Lullabies of Many Lands* by Dorothy Commins, published by Harper Brothers in the spring of 1941.

Gene & I thank you so much for sending us a copy & with such a valued inscription.

Life goes on. Work & chores—looking after Gene & *trying* to forget, for an hour now & then, the hideous state of this world.—At times my head aches so with worry I feel unable to cope with what is in store for all of us, —& envy those who have gone before.

The winter has been long & wet—Gene not well. And, naturally, today's danger of all loss of freedom—*living* & *writing*—gives Gene little peace of mind.—

Politicians go on playing politics—propaganda everywhere. But *truth* is kept from us all. And I see no way out!

Forgive this letter—I hope I am unduly alarmed.

Again, our deep thanks for "Lullabies" & our dearest love always to you, & Saxe, & the kids!

> God bless you all!
> Love—
> *Carlotta*

---

211. *To Saxe Commins from Eugene O'Neill.* TLS 1 p.
On stationery headed: Tao House / Danville / Contra Costa
County / California

> *November the 4th*
> *1941*

Dear Saxe,

I am a prize bum not to have thanked you before this for the Pascal book.[19] Meant to, and kept saying mañana. You know how it is. I certainly appreciated your sending it, and I think you did a grand job with the Introduction. My sincere congrats.

How are your mother and father now? Better, I hope. And is there any chance of your getting out here on vacation? You're due for one, aren't you? Do try and make it! So much to talk about that is too long for letters. A beautiful world, eh? —and getting prettier every minute!

I've written no less than seven—count them!—detailed outlines for non-Cycle plays this year.[20] All grand ideas, too, I think. But I can't seem to de-

19. *Pensées: The Provincial Letters* by Blaise Pascal, with an introduction by Saxe Commins, published by the Modern Library in 1941.

20. According to O'Neill's diary, he worked on outlines or scenarios for the following plays in 1941: "Time Grandfather Was Dead"; "Gag's End," also titled "Blind-Alley Guy"; "The 13th Apostle," a story of Christ vs. Satan; "Malatesta Seeks Surcease," a comedy; *Hughie,* part of a series of short plays with the general title of "By Way of Obit"; "Rudie," another part of the series; *A Moon for the Misbegotten. Moon* and *Hughie* were the only ones of the above that O'Neill ever completed.

cide which I want to do first. Too much distraction in the air. Too much tragedy. And my health uncertain. It's hard to settle down to the hard labor of day after day plugging at one thing.

Want you to read "Long Day's Journey Into Night." Better than "The Iceman Cometh." Entirely different. Best thing I've done or ever can do, I believe. But it will have to wait until you come here. Only one typed copy—and anyway, this is a play I don't want to send anywhere or have anyone read, for the present, except three or four people. No one except Carlotta has read it.

Will you thank Bennett for sending "Storm"[21] to me—and save me a letter. Frankly, a lot of it bored me. A good idea, but the author hasn't the stuff. Too much informative journalistic writing in it. The subject needs the Conrad of "Typhoon." The author's "Ordeal by Hunger" was a much better piece of work, I think.

Our love to Dorothy and the kids. And to you! Try and come out!

As ever,

Gene

Saxe was able to go to California to work with O'Neill on the manuscript of *Long Day's Journey into Night*. He later recorded his memories of that visit:

The earliest opportunity to leave New York for California came in January 1942. Arrangements were made at Random House whereby I could remain with the O'Neills until work on the manuscript of *Long Day's Journey into Night* would be completed and I could return with the finished play.

At Oakland, California, I was met at the railroad station by Herbert Freeman, a one-time South Carolina football player and for many years man servant, chauffeur, and family retainer of the O'Neills. He had been with them since their Sea Island days and was worshipfully devoted to Gene. When we arrived at Tao House in Danville, Contra Costa County, I was greeted with cordiality, with a shy warmth from Gene and a visible relaxation of her habitually imperious manner by Carlotta.

For the sixteen days of my visit rain fell almost constantly and we were virtually prisoners in a palace. When the sun appeared from behind the grim clouds for a little while, we walked about the spacious estate up a narrow trail to the crest of a hill from which there was a spectacular view to the northeast of mist-veiled Mount Diablo, an im-

21. *Storm* by George Stewart (New York: Random House, 1941).

posing mountain peak of the coastal range. We seldom ventured beyond the trestled entrance to the road leading to the house.

Only twice did we leave the grounds. The first time was when Gene was driven to Oakland by Freeman for treatment by his physician and I went along for the ride, and the second when we celebrated the completion of our work with a dinner party for three in San Francisco. Otherwise we remained in isolation and devoted ourselves during the daytime to our labors, I at typing four copies of *Long Day's Journey into Night* from the version mentioned in Gene's letter. This typescript bore many interlinear additions and corrections in Gene's microscopic handwriting. While I pecked away with two fingers on the typewriter, Gene occupied himself with other scripts in his study and Carlotta, a compulsively fastidious housekeeper, busied herself with her own chores. . . . At night we played "Sorry" for the standard stake of a quarter a game or we sat in front of the fire and talked about a remote world going up in flames. Such news as we heard on the radio was bleak and disheartening. America had been at war for a month and the bulletins from two fronts were then dismal. They repetitiously announced setbacks and withdrawals on land and sea. Rigid blackouts were in force on the West Coast for fear of Japanese assaults by sea and air. . . .

My stay at Tao House was pleasant and congenial and made unselfconscious by affection. Gene and I worked steadily and, I like to believe, to good purpose. When questions were raised about vague or indecipherable words or phrases in his minute handwriting, they were answered patiently and painstakingly even if the queries were captious or preposterous. Discovery of an inconsistency or unconscious repetition or the suggestion of a transposition or change in syntax or accent always brought out how amenable Gene was to recommendations and grateful for a second, objective eye. He never seemed to mind how irrelevant or absurd an editorial comment might be because he was convinced that the chances of overlooking anything would thus be reduced. Unlike many writers, he was not so blindly in love with every word he had written that he would want to slur over possible imperfections in what he cherished most. Even observations which showed my own stupidity were welcomed because they provided an opportunity to explain and clarify intent and effect.

In this manner we worked together for more than two weeks and often during that time the subject of posthumous publication and production was discussed. *Long Day's Journey into Night,* he had become convinced, should be kept from the public until everyone involved, particularly the members of his family, was dead or old enough not to be hurt or even disturbed by it. After debating various lengths of time, he fixed a period of twenty-five years after his own death for publication and production. The time lapse settled, he asked me to have a legal statement embodying his wishes drawn up when I returned to New York.

Four typewritten copies were made of the play, two for deposit in Washington with the Register of Copyrights, one for himself and one for me to carry back to New York for safekeeping in the Random House vault. It should be explained that plays in manuscript form, unlike books of fiction and nonfiction, qualify for copyright as unpublished works and may be registered therefore at any time before publication.

Our task completed, I left Oakland on "The Lark" for Los Angeles on the night of 8 February 1942, carrying with me one copy of *Long Day's Journey into Night*. My stopover in Los Angeles was prolonged beyond my expectations because of a sudden death in the family and I remained two days longer than I had intended in order to attend the funeral. Immediately after it I left for New York.

There I consulted with Horace Manges, making known to him what O'Neill required, and asked him to draw up a document which would explicitly set forth his wishes concerning the posthumous publication and production of the play. When he had the statement formulated, it was mailed to O'Neill for his signature.

29 November 1945[22]

Random House, Inc.
20 East 57th Street
New York 22, N.Y.

Gentlemen:

I am this day depositing with you, on condition that it not be opened by you until twenty-five years after my death, a sealed copy of the manuscript of an original play which I have written, entitled *Long Day's Journey into Night*.

I should like to have you publish this play under the same terms as those set forth in our agreement dated 30 June 1933 (in which you are referred to under your former corporate name of The Modern Library, Inc.) as amended and extended, except, however, in the following respects:

1. Publication shall not take place until twenty-five (25) years after my death.
2. No advance shall be payable prior to said publication date, at

22. Saxe apparently has conflated two occasions in this account. It was the original which O'Neill deposited with Random House in 1945, when he came to New York to attend rehearsals of *The Iceman Cometh*. Saxe had previously deposited a copy there in February 1942.

which time an advance of Five Thousand Dollars ($5,000) shall be paid.

3. Copyright in the United States and Canada shall be taken out in your name.

4. Where the term "Author" is used in our prior agreement, it shall, after my death, apply to my Executors or Administrators, to whom all payments hereunder shall be made.

If the foregoing terms are acceptable to you, will you kindly sign and return to me the enclosed copy of this letter.

Sincerely yours,
Eugene O'Neill

Accepted: 29 November 1945
Random House, Inc.
By (signed) Bennett A. Cerf

On the return of this letter, signed, from California, it was attached to the carefully wrapped and heavily wax-sealed package containing the typescript of *Long Day's Journey into Night* and deposited in the Random House safe. There it remained undisturbed with a copy of a one-act play entitled *Hughie* for twelve years. No one was permitted to touch or move it. The secret of its contents remained sealed with the five people who had read it—the author, his wife, his son, the critic Russel Crouse, who was allowed to examine O'Neill's copy on the occasion of his visit to Tao House, and myself.

---

212. *To Dorothy Commins from Saxe Commins.* ALS 2 pp.
On stationery headed: Tao House / Danville /
Contra Costa County / California

Friday 6 P. M.
[January 23, 1942]

Darling,

How it has rained! From the moment of my arrival the skies have been emptying themselves, and we have not put foot out of doors. That does not mean we have been entirely inactive, if talk goes as an activity. Gene and I have been inseparable except for the time this morning given to the reading of the new play. Only briefly can I tell you that it is the most deeply moving, intimate, and certainly the most revealing thing he has ever written. It is by far the most tragic of his plays, and so personal that it is doubtful if it can be produced during his lifetime. I have volunteered to type it out for him, and happy I am to do so in order to study it more closely and, for sentimental reasons, to have even so little a finger in it. So tomorrow morning I shall begin what will probably be a week's labor of love.

My reception continues to be more than cordial; it is spontaneously warm and affectionate and trusting. I really love being here.

My only anxiety is about you and the kids. Believe me when I tell you that I've hardly given a thought to Random House, except to wonder why I have always taken it as a life-and-death consecration. Even you do not realize how much work and faith and heartache have gone into that job. It is the only way I could approach it because I am the kind of guy I am, and too it is my career and my responsibility in life. It doesn't matter if no one is aware of it or gives a damn. That's where I have struck such roots as I have and only there can I grow and find a purpose.

It is now a little after nine in New York. The kids are in bed, but probably not yet asleep. I follow their activities from hour to hour. When I looked at my watch at 5 this morning I saw them eating breakfast, hurrying Ruth[23] and generally making the daily flurry before starting off for school. I miss such little things.

So far there has been no mail. Maybe tomorrow's post will bring the first letter, if you have written. If you haven't I shall be bitterly disappointed. I want to know how the concert went on Tuesday last, how you are managing, but, above all, what the children are doing. Maybe, even, there will be mail from them. Kiss them both for me.

Naturally, I shall have no real news for you until I reach Los Angeles. Here we are completely isolated. We can only talk and read and occasionally listen to the radio. It is ideal for resting purposes and for feeding up the spirit. I am genuinely happy to be here. Never have Gene and I been as close. XXXX for Franny & Puge.[24]

> With all my love
> Saxe

---

213. *To Dorothy Commins from Carlotta Monterey O'Neill.* ALS 2 pp. On stationery headed: Tao House / Danville / Contra Costa County / California

> Saturday
> [January 24, 1942]

Dearest Dorothy,—

I wired you of Saxe's safe arrival— & to thank you for your lovely handkerchieves. You should not be so generous! But I do love having them!—

23. A maid in the Commins household.
24. The Comminses' affectionate nickname for their son Eugene.

It is such a happy time, for us, to have Saxe here. He is such a lamb, and as a house-guest, God's gift to the O'Neills!

Gene & I are up to our necks getting out income tax data. A job we both hate— & also a most depressing job. Saxie is typing from my copy (none too perfectly done!) another new play of Gene's. The best & most tragic he has ever done—"Long Day's Journey Into Night."

It is pouring rain— & the wind howling. But, God be thanked, we have a warm house & we love each other!—

The war looks *ghastly*. Will this country realize (*each one of us*) that *man* must become more decent, honest & charitable before peace can ever come to the human race again?— The way of life we loved is as dead as the Pharaohs! Now, we must create a simpler way, with God in our hearts.

Our dearest love to you & the children—

Bless you dear—
Carlotta

---

214. To Saxe Commins from Eugene O'Neill. TLS 1 p. [Columbia]
On stationery headed: Tao House / Danville /
Contra Costa County / California

March 25th 1942

Dear Saxe:

Herewith enclosed, a letter from Whit Burnett which explains itself. What is your opinion on the importance of this projected anthology?[25] I have written Burnett, gratefully declining, but if you and Random House think it's important, you could contact Burnett and ask how much space in the book he can offer. "5000 words" length is no yardstick for a play. I would refuse to write any explanation of why I chose what I chose, in any event. As I explained to Burnett, my main reason for declining is I would have to read all my old plays again—a tough job when you feel punk—or anytime. Wouldn't give him anything from new stuff.

Let me have your frank dope on this.

Love from us,
Gene

P.S. Please return his letter when you write.

25. Burnett, founding editor of *Story* magazine, was planning an anthology, *This Is My Best,* to be published in 1942, and had asked O'Neill to choose the best of his work for inclusion.

----

215. To Eugene O'Neill from Saxe Commins. TL(cc) 1 p. [Columbia]

March 27, 1942

Mr. Eugene O'Neill
Tao House
Danville
Contra Costa County
California

Dear Gene:

I hasten to answer your question about the Whit Burnett anthology. I don't see how you could have done otherwise than to have declined gratefully, under all the circumstances. Not only is the fee ridiculous, but I cannot be persuaded that the project is as important as he makes it sound. I know Burnett very well and he's a nice enough guy, but for my dough I'd rather have somebody with a little more flair. What he asks, of course, is worth at least $200.00, for all the trouble it involves. So far as Random House is concerned, we go all the way with you in declining. His letter, naturally, makes the project seem of world-shaking importance, but I can't see how a book of snippets representing the work of one hundred authors can mean very much.

I had lunch with Gene Junior today and found him in marvelous shape. He came in to deliver a lecture before about three hundred and fifty girls at Hunter College. We had two hours together before he had to get up in front of that mob. My admiration for him rose because he was not a bit nervous with that ordeal ahead of him.

I'll be writing you a long letter from home soon.

Always,

sc: eg

----

216. To Eugene O'Neill from Saxe Commins. TL(cc) 1 p. [Columbia]

April 14, 1942

Eugene O'Neill

Dear Gene:

I managed to pick up an out-of-print Modern Library copy of Max Stirner's THE EGO AND HIS OWN. It's a little shabby I'm afraid, but the only one to be had for love or money. I got it for love. At any rate the text is complete and will serve your purposes.

Always,

217. *To Saxe Commins from Eugene O'Neill.* TLS 1 p.
On stationery headed: Tao House / Danville /
Contra Costa County / California

May the 24th 1942

Dear Saxe:

Re Whit Burnett's Anthology, he now offers me enough space to make it worth while—offers to include all of "The Moon Of The Caribbees," which Nathan suggested to him as something I might approve. But I don't. These old sea one-acters are stale stuff, especially since the movie.[26] I've chosen Act One, Scene Three of "The Great God Brown."[27]

My comment, to be published with it, explains why and is as follows: "Rereading "The Great God Brown," written in 1925, which I haven't looked at for ten years or more, I still consider this play one of the most interesting and moving I have written. It has its faults, of course, but for me, at least, it does succeed in conveying a sense of the tragic mystery drama of Life revealed through the lives in the play. And this, I think, is the real test of whether any play, however excellent its structure, characterization, dialogue plot, social significance, or what not—is true drama or just another play.

I choose this particular scene for the anthology because it is one of the best and the most self-sufficient when taken out of its context."

I've made it a condition that I receive proof on the above to read over—also that I can make cuts and corrections in the published text of this scene. There is one bad error in the stage directions. It makes one sentence describing Cybel completely meaningless. It must always have been there since I find it in the Liveright first edition. Last word of this sentence should obviously be "cud" not "end." End means nothing.

If Burnett agrees to these conditions and my foreword I'll send you book containing my revisions of this scene to give him.

Please tell Bennett about this.

Love from us to you, Dorothy and the kids—and many thanks for the Greek Historians[28]—a grand publishing job! Congrats!

As ever,
Gene

26. *The Long Voyage Home*, Dudley Nichols's 1940 film adaptation of the four S. S. Glencairn one-act plays.
27. O'Neill chose the first meeting between Dion Anthony and Cybel.
28. *The Greek Historians* by Francis R. B. Godolphin (New York: Random House, 1942).

---

218. *To Eugene O'Neill from Saxe Commins.* TL(cc) 1 p. [Columbia]

May 28, 1942

Dear Gene:

I am dictating this reply to your letter in reference to the Burnett anthology. Trust me to see the whole thing through. I called up Burnett yesterday, but he was out of town and his secretary said that he would call me back, which he hasn't done yet. No doubt he will get in touch with me and let me handle it from this end.

I will be writing you a long letter from home over the week-end.

You will be interested to learn that Donald Klopfer reports for duty as a captain in the aviation service in Santa Ana, California. He leaves on Saturday. Everyone here is sunk at the prospect of trying to get along without him. For me, particularly, it will be hard to take.

Always,

Mr. Eugene O'Neill

---

219. *To Saxe Commins from Eugene O'Neill.* TLS 1 p.
On stationery headed: Tao House / Danville /
Contra Costa County / California

June the 8th 1942

Dear Saxe:

Here's an important request, having to do with my alimony burden. Will you whisper in Bennett's ear that it would be a great favor, if whatever is coming to me on semi-annual statement your accounting department is now getting out, *was not sent to Madden until after August first*. I suppose it can be easily arranged so statement to Madden with cheque be delayed until that time. My alimony year ends July 31st. Enough said. You get it.

Of course, this is hush-hush stuff. I know you will know how to handle it.

Much gratitude—and love from us to you, Dorothy, and the kids.

As ever,
Gene

P.S. Corresponding statement last year was sent out July 8th, so it only means delaying matters a little over three weeks.

220. *To Saxe Commins from Eugene O'Neill.* TLS 1 p.
On stationery headed: Tao House / Danville /
Contra Costa County / California

July the 7th 1942

Dear Saxe:

Recently I sent Nathan a script of "Hughie" to read. He seems to have liked it a lot. I've written him to turn the script over to you. Will you get in touch with him and then put the script in the Random House safe with "The Iceman Cometh"? I'd like one script to be held in New York—just in case.

Bennett can read it, if he wants to. You can explain it's only one of a series of seven or eight but will give him idea of method, etc.—that it was written over a year ago—everything I told you about series. Haven't written another since but am still keen on them.

We're just recovering from a heat-wave—over 100 outside front door *under an awning.* Usually the dry heat here doesn't bother me but this time it knocked me flat. The old blood pressure sank below 100 and that means I felt lower physically and mentally than you can imagine—a regular coma of depression which wasn't helped a bit by the news from Russia, Egypt, etc.

Love from us to you, Dorothy and the kids.

As ever,
Gene

221. *To Saxe Commins from Carlotta Monterey O'Neill.**
On stationery headed: Tao House / Danville /
Contra Costa County / California

July 7th 1942

Dear Saxe:

The "Hughie" Nathan has was typed by my child.[29] It's not so hot. Before it is shown to Cerf it ought to be edited!!!

Gene had another flop (from heat, this time) and even the old lady is not feeling so hot. Oh, well—a hundred years from now all will be well. I have,

29. Cynthia Stram. After Freeman, their "man of all work," entered the Marines, Carlotta was forced to take on more of the household chores and hired her daughter, whose husband was crippled from rheumatic fever and unable to work, to do most of the secretarial work.

at least, got Gene's original longhand scripts all safe and sound and where the owners are pleased to have them.[30] That is a good job done.

WEINBERGER is due about Thursday, Entre-nous, it is like having the Boultons for a visit. That's all I'll hear.

Love as always,
Carlotta

---

222. *To Dorothy Commins from Eugene O'Neill.* TLS 1 p.
On stationery headed: Tao House / Danville /
Contra Costa County / California

August 22nd 1942

Dear Dorothy:

And what a lousy correspondent I am! A million apologies for my laziness. The only excuse I have is that I've waited to hear from the Guggenheim people before writing you, knowing from previous experience that they send a printed form on which you have to write your recommendation of the candidate. Why the delay, I wonder? You had better make sure, if you can, that they know they are to refer to me.[31]

I don't know what you mean by "tone of conceit." I'd say you were too darn modest in what you wrote. The reason I asked Saxe to do it—not you—is simply that I felt he would know what things to emphasize and not omit anything.

Much love from us to you and Saxe and the kids!

As ever,
Gene

30. The scripts were divided for safekeeping between the Yale University Library, Princeton University's Firestone Library, and the Museum of the City of New York.

31. Dorothy Commins was applying for a Guggenheim Fellowship and had asked O'Neill to write a recommendation for her. He apparently had Saxe write the letter for him, and he signed it.

223. *To Saxe Commins from Eugene O'Neill.* WIRE 1 p. [Columbia]

[August 25, 1942]

NBG1923 60—Danville Calif 25 1037A
Saxe Commins, Care Random House—
    20 East 57 St—
Whit Burnett has sent me proof of Great God Brown scene but not of foreword I wrote to explain my choice of this scene. Must have this to make corrections or revisions He agreed to this or I would never have consented to be represented in anthology. Will you get in touch with him and make it strong. Many thanks—

Gene

224. *To Eugene O'Neill from Saxe Commins.* WIRE(copy) 1 p. [Columbia]

November 9, 1942

Eugene O'Neill
Tao House
Danville
Contra Costa County
California .

Script[32] in safe weekend letter on way all best

Saxe

225. *To Eugene O'Neill from Saxe Commins.* TL(cc) 1 p. [Columbia]

February 16, 1943
Dear Gene:

The enclosed speaks for itself. I send it to you, even though it is marked confidential, with Julian Boyd's[33] consent.

I recall that when he and I first discussed placing the manuscripts in the archives of the Princeton Library Boyd then suggested the possibility of the conference of an honorary degree by Princeton University. I told him at once that you were very reluctant about coming East because of your health and your work. Immediately afterward, as I understand, Boyd spoke to President Dodds,[34] and he was eager to sound you out on the proposal.

32. *Long Day's Journey into Night.*
33. Head librarian of Princeton University.
34. Harold W. Dodds, president of Princeton University.

Now as you see the matter has come up again, and the same problem of travel recurs. As I understand it, Princeton never gives honorary degrees in absentia, although I suppose an exception could be made in case of illness and inability to come East. I'm quite sure that Boyd would try to persuade the authorities at Princeton to grant that exception, if you are interested. Please write me exactly how you feel about the whole matter, and I shall communicate your decision directly to Boyd.

There's no news to add to the little I sent Carlotta last night except, as always,

My love,

SC: jb

---

226. *To Saxe Commins from Eugene O'Neill.* TLS 1 p.
On stationery headed: Tao House / Danville /
Contra Costa County / California

Feb. 24th 1943

Dear Saxe:

About the Princeton Honorary degree matter, you know what I think of honorary degrees. Crap cum laude. This, of course, is for your private ear.

For Boyd's ear, tell him that while I appreciate the honor, it would be a great favor to me if he would forget it. Because my nerves are too rotten for such ceremony. It's a torture, not a pleasure. I made up my mind after the Yale ordeal in '26, never again. I've refused more than one since then, and I went through with that one because it meant so much to Professor Baker[35] and I know how hard he had worked to get it for me. I was his best known pupil, and Yale was really honoring him through me. In short, I was on a spot, liking him as much as I did. And my nerves were a lot less terrible then—not to speak of general health.

Boyd will understand, I know. Also President Dodds. It's the flesh that is weak, etc.

Besides I couldn't make the trip East. And I would not let them break their in absentia rules for me, even if they wanted to. Granting honorary degrees are desirable, it is a good rule for them to stick to.

Well, that's that. You will know how to put it to Boyd. I really do appre-

---

35. George Pierce Baker, who had been O'Neill's playwriting teacher in English 47 at Harvard in 1914–15, had left Harvard in 1925 to head a newly formed drama department at Yale. On June 23, 1926, Yale had conferred an honorary Doctor of Literature degree on O'Neill.

ciate his wish. Degrees mean something to him. For me, the game is not worth the candle.

Love from us to you and Dorothy and the kids—

As ever,
Gene

———————

227. *To Dorothy Commins from Carlotta Monterey O'Neill.* TLS 1 p.
On stationery headed: Tao House / Danville /
Contra Costa County / California

April the 11th 1943

Dorothy dearest:

Your letter upset us no end. It is a damn shame! But I honestly feel that a great deal of politics has got into the Guggenheim business, as in everything else. So, for God's sake, *don't* feel that it has anything to do with you as an artist or a woman. It is just that you are too sincere, too honest, too well mannered, too decent to play the alleys and by-ways! If you get what I mean! If one is not a politician or a Laborite one is scum! And wait until the war is over—and see just *how* very scummy the artist will be considered. We are entering a very ugly era, my dear, so prepare your shell—and join the "untouchables" with us!

Please, dear Dorothy, try not to feel sunk with this disappointment. Go on, as you always have, be brave and honest as only you know how to be. *There is a job to be done* and we must do it—*no matter what.* And no one cares how deeply our hearts ache. Each of us must round out our own soul's good—no one can help us in that. I don't want to sound the preacher, but you are too fine within to allow the politicians to disturb the inner you. So head up and let your work go on.

Somehow Tao House goes on. The days are very full and the nights are welcome. All the young men of our valley are gone. There is no labor outside of shipyards. The morals of the young gals from twelve to twenty is enough to make your hair stand on end! Disease is rampant. God, what a mess!

Gene is marvellous—considering. He is trying to help outside with pruning, etc. and it also helps him to forget.

Buck up, my dear, we still have our homes. A bed to sleep in, and a sort-of freedom. Also, we *know* we are honest, that helps such a lot!

Our dearest love to you, and Saxie, and the kids—

As always,
Carlotta

---

228. *To Saxe Commins from Eugene O'Neill.* TLS I p.
On stationery headed: Tao House / Danville /
Contra Costa County / California

June the 30th 1943

Dear Saxe:

A favor. Can you find out about how much is due me on the next statement? You will understand why I want to know whether the payment should
be made as usual, or as last year, deferred until after August 15th.

What's the matter with Bennett? Carlotta wrote him some time ago—re
Freeman and mystery stories we pass on to the Marine Barracks in Frisco.
No reply to date. Is he ill or on vacation or what?

No servant. Carlotta does the cooking and I wipe the dishes. Now Roberts
is leaving us. Tough to keep Tao House above water. May have to close up
or sell out. Carlotta's health is bad. So is mine.

You've read about my charming young daughter, I expect.[36] Nice! Especially the bit about her mother being there to aid and abet. Two of a kind.
Well, I had severed relations with Oona before this—for many other reasons.
Probably the papers here on the Coast played it up and gave many details
you didn't get in the East. True, too. A friend from Hollywood was here a
few days ago. He told us stuff he knew for a fact from a friend who had an
apartment right under the one A. had rented in her name, where Chaplin hid
out—drunken parties, etc. As I've said, a nice thoroughly Hollywood affair! I
am grateful to the Press for their treatment of me. They left me out as much
as they could and did not try very hard to corner me personally.

Well, to hell with it. But, as you can imagine, it had its effect on me and
that was not helpful.

Love from us to you, Dorothy and the kids.

As ever,
Gene

36. Oona O'Neill had come to Hollywood with her mother and had met and fallen
in love with Charlie Chaplin. Oona was eighteen, Chaplin three times her age, thrice
married and divorced, and at the time embroiled in a paternity suit. Despite these ob-
stacles, they were married on June 16, 1943, and had one of the most secure and happy
marriages in show business, producing eight children.

229. *To Eugene O'Neill from Saxe Commins.* TLS 1 p. [Columbia]
On stationery headed: Random House The Modern Library /
20 East Fifty-seventh Street New York / Saxe Commins, Editor

October 20, 1943

Mr. Eugene O'Neill
Tao House
Danville
Contra Costa County, Calif.

Dear Gene:

This is a business letter as you will see from the enclosed. The Council on Books in Wartime, as you probably know, is set up to distribute books to soldiers and sailors free of all charge. They usually print about 50,000 copies at a crack, in a format such as LORD JIM, a copy of which I am sending you separately. All publishers and authors are cooperating with this wartime effort.

As you see from the enclosed letter, the royalty is one cent a copy which is equally divided between publisher and author. Please let me know how you feel about the Council's doing an edition of the plays listed. They are doing a book edited with an introduction by me on the essays of Charles Lamb.

I hope to have a letter from Carlotta soon. I want above everything to know how you both are.

Always,
Saxe

SC:awb

Yes. Gene says okay with him—love Carlotta. Have written note—[37]

---

230. *To Saxe Commins from Eugene O'Neill.* ALS 1 p.
On stationery headed: Tao House / Danville /
Contra Costa County / California

[Dec. 16th 1943]

Dear Saxe:

The enclosed is to get the kids something from old (and shaky) Uncle Gene. Love and Merry Christmas to you & Dorothy and them!

Write us you're coming out! Your last chance! We've put the rancho up for sale. Too much of a burden & worry. It has us licked.

Gene

37. This is written in Carlotta's handwriting on the text of Saxe's letter.

231. *To Saxe Commins from Eugene O'Neill.* TLS 2 pp.

July 12th 1944

Dear Saxe:

I've just been writing to Arthur Quinn, dean of the College, University of Pennsylvania. You've probably heard of him. He wrote *History of the American Theatre,* etc. —a lot on my stuff, lectures on it, etc. I've corresponded with him since the early twenties, and he has always been an appreciative and intelligent critic. He wants to read *The Iceman Cometh.* I should have let him have a script long ago. Haven't anything but my working copy here, others in storage. So I have told him to see you and you will loan him the Random House copy. He writes me he will be in or near New York for a week beginning July 23rd. So expect him, will you? He seemed a bit diffident about Random House because he knew no one there, but I've told him you are one of my oldest friends, etc. and would show him any courtesy, etc. I think you will find him a good guy. He has always seemed so to me, and also a genuine theatre lover. I know he will be careful with the script and see that it gets back to you at his earliest possible.

Carlotta seems better now that she is taking x-ray treatments for her throat. By a process of elimination, the Docs have been trying to find the basic infection behind all the infection and pain she has gone through in the past five months. Appears to be a wheat allergy of long standing affecting her throat and possibly a chronic strep throat, too. She has really been through a hellish time. As for me, city life[38] has not improved my Parkinson's,[39] as you can guess. I have recurrent bad spells of it, when my nerves are a torture and the accompanying mental depression is a worse torture. It is hard to take philosophically, knowing nothing can be done for it except ineffective sedatives.

Love from us to you and Dorothy and the kids.

As ever
Gene

P.S. Are you looking forward to the approaching Peace treaty with Germany as a good Liberal should—full of forgetfullness of the past and dopey visions

38. From Tao House the O'Neill's had moved to a suite at the Hotel Fairmont in San Francisco in late Feb. 1943, and then to a larger suite at the Huntington Hotel, also in San Francisco.

39. In Feb. 1942, shortly after he completed the first draft of *A Moon for the Misbegotten,* O'Neill's doctor diagnosed the tremor in his hands that had troubled him since childhood but had worsened recently as Parkinson's disease. Thereafter, the tremor came and went; some days it bothered him hardly at all, but often it was so bad he could not hold a pencil. At his death an autopsy revealed that his trembling had primarily been caused by a familial tremor that had, in his later years, been only slightly aggravated by a mild case of Parkinson's (see Sheaffer, *O'Neill: Son and Artist,* p. 670).

of an end of wars? I imagine not! And neither am I. I fear they will not allow our article writers and radio commentators into the little locked room where the same old game is played by three or four professional swindlers—that is, alleged statesmen—who will sell the future of peoples down the river of power politics. My greatest hope for the coming little arrangement, if I had any hope, would be that we could bring Talleyrand[40] back to life to be our representative. Then we could at least be sure that it would be the others who would come out of the secret little room without their pants and holding the sack! Dear old Talleyrand, Prince of Diplomacy! He came before his time. In this realistic age, he would have had unrestricted scope for his genius—and his intelligence, which his modern imitators so sadly lack.

---

232. *To Eugene O'Neill from Saxe Commins.* TL(CC) 1 p.

July 14, 1944

Dear Gene:

I hasten to assure you that Arthur Quinn will get the warmest kind of reception from me. I've always wanted to meet him and this is by far the best way of doing so. The script is in the safe and will be taken out for him only.

I am greatly relieved to learn that Carlotta is a little better. It's time that your luck turned and that you had a respite from all the torment of illness and pain. The maldistribution on that count has always been beyond my understanding. It's not fair!

I'd like to talk at great length with you on my attitude toward the coming peace. A blanket statement in a letter must cover too much and too little. Only a talk would clarify for us the meanings possible in realism itself. Whose realism? The politicians? The moralists? The manipulators of cartels? There is no Talleyrand in sight; there are Roosevelt, Churchill, Stalin, Chiang Kai-shek, or maybe even—and God forbid!—Tom Dewey.[41] Are these men realists? Have they ever been exposed to the concept that we knew in our youth of the good European, with its implication of the unswerving internationalist? I have a theory which is convenient. I call it the theory of the anti-climax. Expecting the let-down, on all planes and in all events, I shall be spared too much bitterness and disappointment. I'd like to believe, however, that someone will come along who can crystallize the moral conscience of the world and give it reality in the terms of the peace. That, how-

40. Charles Maurice de Talleyrand (1754–1838), French statesman and diplomat who achieved his greatest diplomatic successes at the Congress of Vienna in 1815.

41. Thomas E. Dewey, governor of New York from 1942 to 1950 and unsuccessful Republican candidate for president against Roosevelt in 1944 and Harry S Truman in 1948.

ever, is a vain hope. We will see, I fear, a grab-bag dressed up with ribbons bearing fancy shibboleths and new names for the balance of power, national greed, sovereignty and hegemony. Then again we face the eternal recurrence.

See how impossible it is to write out what needs hours and hours of talk. That's one of the reasons why I want you to come East.

All love to you both
always,

---

233. *To Saxe Commins from Eugene O'Neill.* TLS 1 p.

December 14th, 1944

Dear Saxe:

Just a line to say how damned sorry I am to learn of your recent illness. It must be nice having various tubes down your gullet. Carlotta had a bit of that some months ago. She didn't like it.

Enclosed is for our Christmas something for the kids—with the love and blessing of the old Uncle Gene they never saw.

"I am not well," and I wish it was "Strong drink has put my system on the blink"— Some fun in that. In this, nothing.

Love to you, Dorothy and the kids.

As ever,
Gene

1075 California Street, San Francisco 8 —California[42]

---

234. *To Saxe Commins from Eugene O'Neill.* TLS 1 p.

Sept 16th 1945

Dear Saxe:

Note enclosed. It will be a favor if you will answer this for me. I do not remember the Professor Cordell one hundred dollar fee for "Anna Christie." That must have come through Madden and I must have had some particularly good reason for being lenient with him.[43]

---

42. The address of the Huntington Hotel.

43. Probably refers to William Howard Cordell's reprinting of *"Anna Christie"* in his and Kathryn (Coe) Cordell's *A New Edition of the Pulitzer Prize Plays* (New York: Random House, 1940).

If you see fit to give this Fulton guy a break it's all right with me, and it's equally all right if you don't.[44]

I wonder how Professors in our university English Departments think authors and publishers live? In fact I wonder why the hell professors in our English Departments live?

With much love to you, Dorothy, and the kids—and again congratulations for the Washington Irving article[45]—

> As ever,
> Gene

---

235. *To Eugene O'Neill from Saxe Commins.* TL(cc) 1 p. [Columbia]

February 25, 1946

Mr. Eugene O'Neill
Hotel Barclay
48th St. & Lexington Ave.
New York, N. Y.[46]

Dear Gene:

Here is an exact typescript of the assignment of copyright from Horace Liveright, Inc. to you. It gives you the date of publication, date of registration and copyright classification and number. Working from this list, we would automatically take care of the renewals of each play before the expiration of the twenty-eight-year period.

Today I have written to the Register of Copyrights about the chances for recovering plays that have been copyrighted, but not published or produced. As soon as I hear, we'll do what we can to get the scripts back.

> All best,
> Saxe Commins

SC:MB
Enc.

---

44. Reference is to Albert Rondthaler Fulton's request to reprint *Beyond the Horizon* in his forthcoming anthology, *Drama and Theatre, Illustrated by Seven Modern Plays* (New York: Holt, 1946). O'Neill's play was included.

45. Probably the introduction Commins wrote to *Selected Writings of Washington Irving*, which he edited for the Modern Library and which was published in 1945.

46. The O'Neills had moved back to the East Coast in Oct. 1945, settling in a two-room suite at the Barclay, while the playwright prepared for the Broadway premiere of *The Iceman Cometh*.

Upon the O'Neills' return to New York in fall, 1945, Saxe began to see them regularly in their suite at the Hotel Barclay. His account of that period follows:

At dinner there one evening I was witness to a painfully embarrassing display of cruelty and vindictiveness. It was not the first time that I had been made privy to domestic scenes of spite and violence on one side and a tormented meekness on the other. The origins of the sparks that detonated this explosion of malevolence could only be sought by an examination into the nature of evil.

Gene had brought with him from California a varied collection of manuscripts, the harvest of many years of intensive work. Principally they were finished plays, notes in long hand running to 125,000 words, tentative drafts, character sketches, scene divisions, snatches of dialogue, stage directions and the like for the nine plays of the cycle in progress on the general theme of the tyranny of possessions and the consequence to those possessed by them. Among the completed plays was *A Touch of the Poet* which dealt with the founder of the family that was to proliferate from his seed through many generations to become the symbols of O'Neill's pervasive theme of the havoc wrought by the passion for possession. Of incidental interest was the choice of the name of the leading character in *A Touch of the Poet*. He was called Melody, a man who had fought under Wellington in the Peninsular Wars and had migrated to Boston, there to establish himself as a tavern keeper. The name was given him after a talk we had long before the writing of the play about prizefighters remembered from our youth. One of them, a Negro lightweight out of Boston, bore the mellifluous professional name of Honey Melody. After repeating it many times and delighting in its euphony, O'Neill said it would be a fine name for a character he had in mind.[47]

Our dinner was a dismal affair; eaten in silence and gloom. It was all too apparent from Gene's nervous anxiety and Carlotta's angry gibes that something serious had occurred. When the table was cleared I learned the cause of the tension; the manuscripts were lost. They had disappeared mysteriously during the day and there was no clue to their whereabouts.

We tried to recapitulate every event and every contingency from the time the manuscripts were last handled to the moment when it was discovered that they were missing. Gene was certain that he had not taken them out of the hotel suite when he went that morning to the offices of the Theatre Guild. He was sure that he had locked the door and de-

47. O'Neill later called one of Cornelius Melody's grandsons—a character in *More Stately Mansions*—Honey Harford.

livered the key at the desk the few times he was obliged to leave the hotel. He recalled how he had packed the manuscripts in the trunk in California and how he reassured himself about their safety when his baggage was brought to their hotel rooms in New York. For a few days after that he simply assumed that they were where last he had seen them.

Carlotta disclaimed having seen the manuscripts at any time since they had left California and made matters worse by insinuations that Gene's memory was failing him, that he was growing senile and was less than aware of what he was doing most of the time. I ventured the suggestion that we make another thorough search of the suite and perhaps, like Poe's purloined letter, we would find what we were seeking in the most obvious of places. Whereupon we went through every trunk, closet, cupboard and bureau drawer in the apartment, all to no avail. Carlotta taunted us while we explored likely and unlikely places of concealment, omitting only an examination of the drawers in which she kept her lingerie and other items of a personal nature. When we stopped there, she insisted with growing resentment that we should not let delicacy deter us and she flung open the bureau in which she kept her underwear. Gingerly and embarrassedly we removed every garment, but still no manuscript came into view.

As the search continued, Gene's nervousness manifested itself in an uncontrollable tremor of his hands and a quivering of his lips. He was trying desperately to prod his memory and thus solve the mystery of the missing manuscripts, but he was completely blocked. Our systematic examination of the apartment convinced us that they had disappeared without a trace. We gave up the search and I went home.

Two days later when Gene and I were alone for a moment, he whispered to me that the manuscripts had been found and begged me to forget the entire unhappy episode. He explained, as if he were trying to condone a sick child's perverse behavior, that Carlotta had taken them out of the apartment and hidden them to punish him for reasons totally obscure to him. She knew where the manuscripts were during all the time of his torment and of the vain search. Only Strindberg, he observed grimly, would understand his predicament and know the motivations for such wantonly calculated cruelty.

When Edward Sheldon died in 1946,[48] the O'Neills gave up their suite at the Hotel Barclay and rented and refurbished his penthouse apartment. The elevator door opened directly upon a large hallway, to

48. Playwright Sheldon, author of *Salvation Nell, The Boss,* and *Romance,* suffered for the last thirty years of his life—he died at sixty—from acute arthritis and total blindness. During that period he regularly received visitors and carried on his business lying completely immobilized on a sort of catafalque in his penthouse apartment at Eighty-Fourth Street and Madison Avenue. Carlotta had visited Sheldon on several occasions.

the right of which was Carlotta's room, furnished with a canopied bed, a blue-black paneled mirror, an elaborate dressing table and deep closets for clothes. A glazed porcelain Chinese hip-high idol stood a grotesque guard at the foot of her bed.

Gene's room, farther down the hall, was austerely furnished. In the drawers of his natural-wood desk were kept his manuscripts. At this desk we worked on the texts and proofs of his plays. A Victrola and a cabinet containing many jazz records stood against the wall beside his dresser. In the hallway near at hand were ceiling-high shelves stacked with phonograph discs.

The large living room, where Sheldon held court from his raised bier for so many years, served as a library and dining room. Its walls were lined with books and its tables covered in neat array with current magazines. A French door led to a spacious roof garden, canopied for about a quarter of its length with a large roll awning. From this roof could be seen the Metropolitan Museum of Art, Central Park and the towering apartment buildings that framed it to the west.

It was to this apartment, always associated with the living corpse of Edward Sheldon, that I came two or three times each week, either to work or to talk haphazardly about events and ideas and books and, for the most part, a past summoned to remembrance by a phrase or a name or any one of the accidental keys that open the locks of speech and thought and communion. Our own home at the time was on East Ninety-fifth Street, only eleven short blocks away, and with or without invitation we visited each other in neighborly fashion. Neither of us had many other visitors.

Where Ned Sheldon had lain in state as a procession of callers came and went, we, the seeing and living, sat in isolation with an invisible wall around us, believing hopefully that we could exclude the world. Gene, always seclusive, now built even higher barriers against intrusion. His physical affliction, Parkinson's disease, had advanced considerably and the tremor of his hands and his slowness of speech were so manifest that he became more and more conscious of the impression they made on others. To avoid explanations and apologies he withdrew farther and farther into silence and self-effacement. Occasionally I would bring my children to visit him and now and then he and Carlotta would come to our home for dinner. . . .

Those were the quiet times. Friends and neighbors were at peace. It was the calm before a great storm. When it blew, the hurricane left a wake of destruction.

We were at dinner in the room in which Ned Sheldon's ghostly presence still lingered. Carlotta, Gene and I had moved to more comfortable chairs away from the table to drink coffee. The telephone bell rang and

Carlotta answered it. The tone of her voice underwent an abrupt change when she heard the name of the caller; it was all too apparent that her annoyance was mounting. Holding her hand over the mouth-piece, she turned to Gene and said icily: "It's one of your friends, I won't talk to her." Thereupon she began to pace the floor nervously while muttering to herself.

Timidly Gene went to the telephone. All I could hear was his share of the conversation. It went somewhat like this: He said "Hello" and waited a little while. Then he said: "Of course, Fitzi, I'll do anything I can . . . Will one hundred be enough? I'll be glad to make it more . . . are you sure? . . . I'll mail you the check right away . . . Let's hope it's not as serious as you fear . . . Count on me." Then he hung up.

While he was talking, Carlotta continued her restless pacing of the floor, wringing her hands and working up a seething rage. She was close to hysteria, her eyes blazing and her voice hoarsely incoherent with words of imprecation. When Gene came away from the telephone, her rage had mounted to fury. All of Gene's former friends were roundly cursed, blamed for his illness and branded as parasites and hangers-on. Fitzi, particularly, was singled out as the worst miscreant, as a bum and scrounger who was interested only in preying on Gene. This was M. Eleanor Fitzgerald, the friend and consoler and steadfast encourager during the days of poverty and anonymity. Mildly and placatingly Gene tried to say that Fitzi had helped him when he was in need and now he could do little less than try to repay her for her many kindnesses. She was sick and in desperate need of help and even if she was all and more than Carlotta charged, he still was bound to lend a hand. Patiently he tried to explain that the call came from Mount Sinai Hospital, where Fitzi had been taken after suffering severe abdominal pains. At first glance the doctors suspected a malignant growth and there would have to be X-ray examination and perhaps even an exploratory operation. Meanwhile Fitzi had to find enough money to pay the deposit demanded by the hospital before admission to cover the initial costs of room, nurses, laboratory fees and the like. But Fitzi was without funds and in desperation she had called Gene and she was right in doing so, Gene tried patiently to explain. She had helped him when he had known trouble and the least he could do was to respond to the appeal of someone who had befriended him.

So reasonable a statement, instead of abating the storm, lashed it into an even greater fury. Carlotta cursed Fitzi in language that was far less than ladylike and gave special emphasis to a word that for her had the worst possible connotation—bohemian! That epithet coming from Carlotta had an obscene inflection; it represented all that was evil and reprehensible to a person who made great pretensions to an aristocratic

lineage. She, the lady, abandoning refinement, heaped abuse upon contempt for the people Gene knew during his days of struggle; they were
criminals, blood-suckers, thieves, bastards, scum—and bohemians. As the
tirade gained momentum, Gene tried vainly to defend them and himself,
to explain old loyalties and to justify his past. This brought on another
eruption.

I cowered in my chair, not saying a word and hoping against hope
that a favorable opportunity for a quiet exit would present itself. It came
when a servant entered the room to clear the coffee cups. I pleaded that
I was tired, that I had to go to work early next morning, that my family
were waiting up for me and stuttered in that vein as I meekly backed
out of the room to the elevator. I walked a short distance to my home,
embarrassed for having been a silent witness to a family upheaval and
quite ashamed of myself for having made no effort to mediate the quarrel
or, worst of all, for failing to speak up in behalf of Fitzi who had always
been kind to me.

The following morning I was wakened early by a telephone call. It
was Gene asking me to come over without delay to his apartment. On
my arrival I saw no sign of Carlotta. I soon learned from Gene what had
happened after I had left the night before. Immediately after the elevator
door had been closed behind me, Carlotta renewed her attack on Gene's
friends with increased virulence, heaping the major portion of her hatred
on Fitzi. The outburst continued for a long time, a one-sided harangue
in which the central theme was Gene's weakness and cowardice in tol-
erating his bohemian friends. He remained silent, but that silence lent
fuel to the fire and at its height it culminated in an explosion of violence.

Carlotta rushed into Gene's room and lifted the glass that covered his
dressing table over her head and crashed it to the floor where it broke
into hundred of splinters. Underneath this glass Gene had kept the *only*
picture he had of his mother and himself as a baby. Carlotta, now at
the summit of her frenzy, snatched the picture and tore it into bits,
crying, "Your mother was a whore!"

This was the last straw. Gene slapped her face. Whereupon she
screamed maniacally and ran to her own room. There she hastily packed
a bag, dressed for the street and made a melodramatic exit, swearing she
would never return.

Gene waited for dawn to call me. Soon after my arrival and after
having learned from him the sequence of events that led to the wild
parting, we took counsel. First of all, someone would have to stay with
Gene and we immediately thought of Walter Casey, a boyhood friend
from New London and a man of unswerving devotion. Within an hour
after we called him, Casey arrived with a handbag containing his clothes
and toilet articles. He understood the situation without detailed explana-

tions and began to take charge by preparing breakfast. I was then able to go to work and left for my office with a somewhat easier mind.

Within twenty-four hours we were aware of the presence of detectives assigned to watch the apartment and whoever came or left. Always in pairs, the sleuths stood guard on the street corner. They employed a mysterious system of waving white handkerchiefs, to what end none of us could guess.

Gene's remorse over the night's quarrel was pitiful and in a sense degrading. He reproached himself for having lost his temper and, because of that, his wife. There were, he pleaded, extenuating circumstances which we could not possibly understand. There was guilt on both sides and the marriage of two quiveringly sensitive people required an expansion of forbearance. It was he who should have exercised greater control and no matter what the provocation should have shown more tolerance.

The Parkinson tremor became more and more acute. Alarmed, we called Dr. Shirley Fisk, whose offices were nearby on Fifth Avenue. When he arrived we explained the entire situation to him. He prescribed sedatives and urged that someone remain at Gene's side twenty-four hours a day. He also recommended frequent cups of black coffee as a means for controlling the agitation of his arms and legs. But more important, Gene was to be watched constantly lest he come by an injury, accidentally or self-inflicted.

For ten days Casey and I alternated on sentry duty. We sat in the kitchen percolating coffee and trying to formulate plans for the future. Most of all, Gene insisted on discussing measures whereby he could learn where Carlotta was hidden. He wanted to hire a detective and actually did so, only to learn that his lady was, for the time, incommunicado at a mid-town hotel.

On the night of January 28, 1948, I became sleepy as the hours dragged by. At midnight I asked Casey whether he could remain in charge while I went home for some rest. He assured me that there was no need for me to wait, that he was certain that Gene would sleep well into the morning and that even he could retire for a few hours. So I went home, thinking of little else but the comfort of my bed.

I was awakened at six in the morning. Dr. Fisk was on the phone. He urged me to dress quickly and come over at once, for Gene had fallen a few hours before and broken his arm. The doctor had been summoned by Casey after the accident and he had found Gene on the floor of his bedroom with Casey leaning over him, afraid to move him lest he do him further injury.

While I was on my way to the apartment Dr. Fisk ordered a Keefe and Keefe ambulance. It arrived soon after I did and after the doctor had briefly outlined what had happened and what had to be done. Apparently Gene had tried to walk in the dark to the bathroom and had slipped on the highly glossed floor and fallen over a low stool, fracturing his right arm as he wildly tried to break his fall. Now all that could be done would require hospital facilities. At the moment he was in a semi-comatose condition because of the injection given him by Dr. Fisk but still suffering severe pain.

The ambulance arrived and Gene was bundled onto a stretcher and carried down the elevator. Its siren screaming, the ambulance, with Dr. Fisk and me seated beside Gene, drove heedless of red-light traffic signals to Doctors Hospital on East Eighty-seventh Street. While Gene was being trundled into the X-ray room, I registered for him, paid the ambulance fee and declared myself next of kin on the hospital admission form.

The X-ray plates revealed a compound fracture of the humerus. An orthopedic specialist was summoned and he and Dr. Fisk reduced the fracture and applied a plaster of Paris splint from the shoulder to the wrist. In spite of the acute pain in setting and splinting the broken arm, there was no word of complaint from Gene. Only the haunted, melancholy eyes showed his suffering. Once in bed and made relatively comfortable by his French-Canadian nurse, he fell asleep under heavy sedation.

For a few days his only visitors were Casey and I, and we always came separately. Casey was reluctant to leave the apartment unoccupied because he was concerned most of all about the manuscripts in the desk drawers. Gene was especially worried about them because the elevator door opened directly upon the apartment and he feared that such easy access would tempt a thief—or somebody. He then asked me to have Casey take all the manuscripts out of his desk and bring them to Random House, where they could be placed safely in the company vault.[49]

I did as I was asked and telephoned Casey. At about 11 in the morning he drove up in a taxicab to the Fifty-first Street entrance to Random House and with the aid of the driver carried in two cartons containing all of Gene's manuscripts. They were deposited in the vault and labels were attached to them on which were written notices that these boxes were not to be moved or opened by anyone but Eugene O'Neill or me. That done and the vault locked, Casey went back to the apartment.

I tried to do something about earning my pay. While thus engaged in the mid-afternoon my telephone bell rang. A blast assaulted my ear. It was Carlotta's voice. "What do you mean, you thief, by stealing my manuscripts! I caught you this time. I'll send you to jail. My detectives

49. O'Neill was also fearful that, as he put it to Saxe, "Carlotta in her frenzy might do with my manuscripts what she did with the only picture I had of my mother and myself as a baby." She had destroyed the picture.

saw it all. They followed Casey. They know you engineered it. I know how to handle the likes of you!"

"Just a minute, Carlotta," I managed to interrupt. "I didn't steal Gene's manuscripts. Don't you know that he has been in Doctors' Hospital for several days with a broken arm? He asked me to put them in a safe place. That is all."

"You are a liar, and so is Gene. He couldn't tell the truth. I don't give a damn what happened to him."

There followed a cascade of curses. The veneer of the lady had been rubbed off and the mind and the language of the show girl were exposed. The tirade became an outpouring of obscenities.

I tried to stop it by interjecting that she could say anything she pleased about me, but she had no right to revile Gene in this way. He was sick and helpless and unable to defend himself. These last days had been ghastly for him and now, alone in the hospital with a broken arm, he deserved the utmost consideration. Whereupon she reacted against me with all the hatred and evil she could compress into three words.

"You— —bastard!" she screamed into the phone and banged her receiver into its cradle.

Stunned, I sat looking at the telephone in bewilderment and chagrin. Then I wrote out from memory as accurately as possible a transcript of what had been said over the telephone, omitting the grosser obscenities.

---

236. *To Eugene O'Neill from Saxe Commins.* TL(cc) 1 p.

COPY

February 26, 1948

Dear Gene,

At 2:30 this afternoon—five minutes ago—Carlotta called me at the office. I want to set down, while it is still fresh in my mind the exact conversation, so that there will be no distortion later.

After identifying herself, she asked:

"Have you given those scripts to Dodds of Princeton or whatever his name is?"

"What scripts?" I asked.

"The ones Gene has been lying about. You know what a God-damned liar he is."

"I won't listen to that, Carlotta. Gene is not a liar; he has never lied, and you know it."

"He has always been a liar. Did you take those scripts out of the desk?"

"You can't talk that way to me. I did not take *any* scripts out of the desk."

"I've got enough on you to send you to jail after all you've said about me."

"Carlotta, I've never mentioned your name to anyone. You ought to know that. I've always treated you with respect and I deserve a little from you."

"Respect, hell. God-damn you, I'll show you. I'll have you in jail where you've belonged for years."

"Please, Carlotta, what is it that you want?"

"Don't lie to me. You know you took those scripts out of the desk."

"I did not."

"Well, they're either in Random House or Princeton and you know it."

"Don't ask me about them. They are not mine."

There followed a string of abusively vulgar epithets and the phone was violently slammed down.

The fact that Carlotta called me about the scripts indicates that she knows about their removal from the desk and that she is in a state of sick bitterness about it. Her virulent language can only be explained by her state of agitation and a deep-seated illness. Her hatred is now turned toward me and with great violence.

What else could I have done, Gene, but tell her that I did not take the scripts? Without authorization from you, I cannot even mention them. Under the circumstances, I want you to know and approve of whatever I say or do whenever it touches you.

Always

Saxe's memoir continues:

That night at the hospital I showed Gene what I had written and asked him whether, under the circumstances, I was to come to see him again or stay away altogether. He read the sheet of paper slowly and then paused for a long time.

"Try to understand," he said, "She's sick, terribly sick. Don't you leave me too."

I promised I would not.

---

237. *To Eugene O'Neill from Saxe Commins.* ALS 1 p.
On stationery headed: Random House, Inc. The Modern Library /
457 Madison Avenue / New York 22, N.Y. / Saxe Commins, Editor

Dear Gene, March 2, 1948

I have been giving much tormented thought to the possibility that my frequent visits to the hospital and my daily phone calls of inquiry might have been causing you embarrassment. Nothing, as you must know, could be farther from my mind or heart. Yet if it will save you the slightest need of explanation, I shall stay away until you summon me. All I want you to know is that as long as I live I'll be available, when the chips are down or at any other time, on the moment of your call.

> With all devotion
> Saxe

Shortly after this episode, the O'Neills were reconciled and planned to resume life together someplace on the New England coast. They arrived in Boston late in the spring of 1948 and soon purchased a small cottage at the tip of Marblehead Neck, twenty miles north of Boston. While they were having their new home remodeled, they spent several months in a suite of rooms at the Ritz-Carlton Hotel. From there, Gene wrote to Saxe.

---

238. *To Saxe Commins from Eugene O'Neill.* ALS 2 pp.
On stationery headed: The Ritz-Carlton / Boston 17, Massachusetts

July 26 '48

Dear Saxe:

Much gratitude for the inscribed book.[50] I feel as if I'd read it already, you've told me so much about it, but I know I will have a new pleasure in reading it.

The big news with us, which I meant to write you long ago, is that we had the good luck to get in first on the sale of a house *right on the ocean* near Marblehead—first sale of waterfront property in it's vicinity for many years. Carlotta bought this out of her reserve fund. It is a tiny house with little rooms, the upstairs ones with sloping eaves—built in 1880. Reminds me of the first home my father bought in New London, also on the waterfront when I was a kid. We both love this new place. Of course, a lot has had to be done to modernize it—as to kitchen, etc. and to thoroughly insulate it for an all year round home—our last. Everything to cut down overhead and make it a cinch to run with just a cook. No car. We won't need one. The aim is to simplify living and gain as much security for our old age as is pos-

50. *Basic Writings of George Washington,* edited and with an introduction by Saxe Commins (New York: Random House, 1948). Saxe's inscription read, "To Gene, through all the years with unchanging love and devotion, always Saxe, July 9, 1948."

sible. I feel I shall be able to write again, and again have some roots—of seaweed—with my feet in a New England sea. It is like coming home, in a way, and I feel happier than in many years, although we are still stuck here in a hotel impatiently awaiting the completion of the work on the place.

As to health, we are both much better and will be better still when we are in our home. My arm isn't right yet and won't be for six months, they say, but it steadily improves. No swimming this summer, of course. But next year—! The tremor is better, too, but I'm just cursed with it for life, I guess, and the best to hope for is to circumvent it. This letter, for example, is written during a good spell, and its not so bad, eh? And why complain when the world itself is one vast tremor.

All best to you, Dorothy & the kids!

As ever,

Gene

P.S. Remember me to Bennett, Haas,[51] Klopfer

---

239. *To Dorothy Commins from Carlotta Monterey O'Neill.* TLS 1 p.
On stationery headed: Point O'Rocks Lane Marblehead Neck, Massachusetts

October the 21st 1948

Dear Dorothy:

Gene has asked me to tell you how pleased he was to receive your birthday wire.[52] You were sweet to remember him.

When it was time for Gene to leave the hospital it was necessary to make a home for him—and away from New York which he grew to loathe, as I did! So, we came to New England (that I have always loved) and I have been doing my best to make a home. Am afraid I have lost my resiliency to this and that, but the home will be finished in another week or so. It is the smallest house I have ever seen! (Which we both wanted) And cost the most! I had the beautiful idea that if I sold all the securities I had left I would have enough to re-do some little house and, when finished, go to Master O'Neill and say, "Here, young man is a home for you all ready made!" But, like everything I have attempted with the Master it did not work out that way. I bought a very small house for $25,000.00 being told $25,000.00 more would put it in condition. To make a long story short I put all my money in it, then

51. Robert Haas, who had joined Cerf and Klopfer as Random House partners.

52. Once O'Neill and Carlotta were reunited, after his stay in the hospital and move to Boston, Saxe was barred from O'Neill's life by Carlotta. Saxe, knowing that she would intercept any birthday greeting from him, had Dorothy send one in her own name. O'Neill's birthday was October 16.

was forced to go to Gene for $15,000.00 and now I have to mortgage the place for $20,000.00 to pay the last payment.[53] I am stoney—Gene hard-up—but, we have a home!

Life goes on, and what more can one say! I hope things go well with you and yours. And, again, let me thank you for your remembrance of Gene.

As always,
Carlotta

———

Saxe's memoir contains the rest of the sad ending to the O'Neills' story:

All communication was cut off and even matters pertaining to Gene's work had to be transmitted through Miss Jane Rubin of the office of his literary agent, Richard Madden. I had been purged, as had all of his old friends and, most unfortunately as it turned out, his children, Shane, Oona, and Eugene, Jr. The son who bore his name was, more than anyone else, in desperate need of communication with his father.

Young Gene was then undergoing a time of adversity. His three marriages had failed miserably. His academic career, in the beginning rich in promise, was in decline. He had given up his post at Yale University as an Assistant Professor of Greek and the Classics, a position he had attained after a notable scholastic record as an undergraduate. The promise, unfortunately, was greater than the performance, and both he and the university were disappointed. . . .

Through the good offices of Professor [Whitney J.] Oates, young O'Neill was tendered a place in the Classics Department at Princeton in 1947, but the experiment, after a year's trial, did not succeed. He then drifted from one institution of learning to another, including Fairleigh-Dickinson college in Rutherford, New Jersey, and the New School for Social Research in New York, and dropped gradually in status until he reached the bottom of the academic ladder.

A bearded giant of a man, perhaps six foot three in height and massively built, he had a basso-profundo voice of which he was inordinately proud. He made himself believe that with a little training he could become Chaliapin's successor. With his resonant voice to recommend him, he sought engagements with radio networks and actually found some

53. Casa Genotta, built in the depth of the Depression with nonunion help, cost about $100,000 (today it would take several million for such a residence); Tao House, including house, some 150 acres, swimming pool and road-building, also came to about $100,000. The Marblehead place, relatively small and ordinary, cost so much, nearly $90,000, not only because home-building costs soared after World War II but because the O'Neills were in a hurry to move in, something that led to extra expense for overtime labor.

radio assignments as a reader of books for the benefit of the housebound. He also appeared occasionally on the program known as "Invitation to Learning," a weekly half hour informal discussion of the world's great books. Always in need of money, the earnings he came by so infrequently and precariously were never enough for his needs. Let it be said for him that in the face of heartbreaking discouragements he tried his skills at whatever presented itself and never betrayed his love of scholarship.

He had bought a small piece of land near Woodstock, New York, on the Ohmayo Mountain where he hoped to build a home. It carried a mortgage of $4,000, sponsored by the endorsement of his father. The time came when the mortgage was due for renewal and all that was required was a re-endorsement. That formality, he was confident, would be observed without difficulty. As the due date approached he made every possible effort to communicate with his father, but to no avail. Letters remained unanswered, telegrams were ignored, telephone calls never went beyond the vigilant monitor and guard at Marblehead. In a panic he appealed to whoever might have access, but every avenue of approach was blocked. He persuaded W. E. Aronberg, O'Neill's attorney in New York, to intercede but his messages were intercepted and never relayed to the father. Desperate, the junior O'Neill tried to raise the money by appeals to his friends, but they were as impecunious as he.

He came to my office on Thursday, September 21, 1950, to seek my counsel, even though he knew that I had been forbidden communication of any kind with his father. He told me of all the stratagems he had used to break through the barrier and how he was always repulsed and turned back. His hatred of Carlotta was almost maniacal; it was she, he insisted, who was the cause of his desperation. If only he could have the mortgage renewed and find some work, his problems would be on the way to solution. He was a scholar of considerable reputation among his peers; he had a voice of deep sonority and great appeal; he was a strong man and could do manual labor. He asked me to try to induce five or six book publishers to underwrite a radio program in which he could offer thumbnail comment and criticism of current books in a weekly broadcast. This was indeed clutching at a straw, for even if he was qualified by scholarship, voice and judgement, the problem still remained to bring five or six publishers into accord, a thirteenth Herculean labor. Nonetheless I promised to do what I could and actually explained the proposal to a few publishers, all of whom merely wondered whether I had taken leave of my wits.

When he left me on that Thursday, there was no way of foretelling from his despair that it would carry him as far as it did. On the following Monday afternoon at about three o'clock, a telephone call from Woodstock brought the hysterical voice of Frank Meyer, a neighbor of young Gene and the man from whom he had bought his land, crying out: "Gene has just killed himself. He slashed his wrists and ankles. My wife found him dead at the bottom of the stairs in his house."

Would I notify his father?

In my own panic dread of such an assignment, trying either to evade the delicate task or to act as rationally as possible, it seemed to me then that a doctor or a lawyer should be asked to perform it. I forthwith telephoned Bill Aronberg to convey the shocking news and to seek his advice more than to shift the burden onto him. He said without hesitation that it was his duty as O'Neill's lawyer to notify him of the disaster. After all, he was, he said, on a retainer and this was his responsibility, not mine. He promised that he would telephone Marblehead and then call me back to report how the father withstood the shock.

A half hour later his call came and I realized at once from the tone of his voice that he was disturbed and blazing with anger. He said he wanted to give me a verbatim report of his long-distance conversation.

When Carlotta answered the telephone, Bill Aronberg said: "Hello, Carlotta. This is Bill Aronberg. I have terrible news for you. Try to be brave and break this gently to Gene. Young Gene has just committed suicide."

Whereupon Carlotta answered: "How dare you invade our privacy?" and slammed the receiver down. That was the entire conversation.

Young O'Neill was beyond insult and injury. No inquest could reveal that he died as much from a thwarted effort at communication as by his own hand. A note found near his body tried to convey a sardonic if somewhat theatrical last message of bluster and defiance. It read: "Never let it be said of an O'Neill that he failed to empty the bottle. Ave atque vale!"

Less than five months after young Gene had written his final hail and farewell, Bill Aronberg, still Eugene O'Neill's lawyer, Lawrence Langner, director of the Theatre Guild, and I were involved in what Carlotta chose to call a conspiracy to kidnap and transport her husband from Salem, Massachusetts, to New York City. Also implicated in the "criminal conspiracy" was the late Dr. Merrill Moore, physician and psychiatrist and the only begetter of thousands of sonnets.

The sad episode had its beginning in Marblehead in the first week of February, 1951. What I know of that act in the tragic drama that was his life came to me from Eugene O'Neill's own lips as he lay immobilized in a bed in the Salem Hospital. This is what I learned from him when I was summoned to his bedside:

On the cold February night of the 5th he and Carlotta had had a quarrel, the nature of which he would not divulge. At any rate, to escape her wrath, he explained, he walked out of the house, coatless, and wandered in the darkness about the grounds of their Marblehead home, following the path that led from the door to the road. The night was colder than he at first thought and he decided to return for an overcoat. As he approached the door he mistook one of the stones, sharply angled at the top, which lined the driveway for a shadow. Unheedingly he stepped on it and fell, stunned by a sharp pain in his knee as he lay sprawled on the ground. On trying to rise, he discovered that his leg would not support him and fell again. He realized at once, from the pain and his inability to flex his leg, that serious damage had been done to his knee.

He began to call for help. There was no answer. For an hour he lay on the roadway, helpless and unable to move, crying all the while for aid. With no coat on his back, he suffered from the severe cold and felt, besides the pain, fear of the consequences of long exposure. He continued to cry for help and finally the door of their house was opened. Carlotta stood framed in its small rectangular proscenium, her figure lighted by the vestibule lamp. She made no move. After a long silence, she delivered in histrionic tones these lines:

"How the mighty have fallen! The master is lying low. Now where is all your greatness?"

Wherewith she closed the door.

Fortunately, the doctor who had been due an hour earlier to administer medicine to allay Gene's Parkinson's tremor was late. When he arrived, he heard Gene's cries from the path and hastened to his side. At a glance he could tell that the knee had been broken and nothing less than hospitalization could be of any help. He threw his own overcoat over Gene and went into the house to summon an ambulance from Salem. While telephoning it was apparent to him that he had two patients, not one, for Carlotta was in a state of hysteria.

When the ambulance arrived he had Gene placed on the stretcher and lifted into the vehicle. He tried to persuade Carlotta to accompany them to the hospital, but she refused. In the very early morning she was seen wandering on the road by a policeman making his habitual rounds. Carlotta demanded that he take her to her husband in the hospital. [The two preceding sentences are from Saxe's notes and were not part of his memoir.]

While in the lobby, she created a scene, screaming maledictions on Gene's head, insulting the doctors and nurses, and threatening them with arrests and lawsuits and whatever else came into her disturbed mind. So great was the disturbance caused by her wild behavior that the police were called. They merely escorted her outside the building and appealed to her to calm down. Outdoors she continued her incoherent tirade and it reached such a peak of violence that the police decided to call a psychiatrist. He, at first ignorant of Carlotta's identity, saw the urgency of the situation and at once had her committed to a hospital for mental patients. The psychiatrist was the poet Merrill Moore.

That is how matters stood when I arrived by train from New York. Gene, in severe pain and trembling with nervous shock, his leg encased in a plaster cast that stretched from mid-thigh to ankle, lay on his hospital bed and pieced out the story for me haltingly and with desperate sadness. Little could be done for him now beyond attending to his needs, making him comfortable and trying to assure him that the doctors and the nurses of the hospital staff were eager to serve him with all the facilities at their command. Before I left he made me promise that I would come to him as often as possible.

Once a week thereafter I went to Salem from New York, by air rather than by train, because it was quicker and more convenient to travel by taxi from the Boston airport to Salem than to go by train to Boston, drive across the city, take another train to Salem and then be transported by taxi to the hospital.

Each visit brought more and more confirmation that, although Gene's knee was healing under the cast, his nervous condition was steadily becoming more aggravated. Consultation with Dr. Frederick B. Mayo and other physicians in Salem ended with their recommendation that the wisest course would be to take Gene to New York, where he would have his own physician and the best possible orthopedic and neurological care. When first told of the doctors' counsel, he vetoed the plan because he was gravely concerned about Carlotta. He had learned that she had taken steps to gain release from the institution to which she had been committed. Since she was not a voluntary patient and because she had been admitted in an emergency by a psychiatrist, she was within her rights to demand immediate dismissal. This was accomplished without any intervention on Gene's part and Carlotta left her hospital for parts unknown.

The doctors in Salem again urged upon Gene the wisdom and necessity of going to New York and he was finally persuaded to undertake the trip. Bill Aronberg, Lawrence Langner and I arranged ways and means of bringing about the transfer. We decided, with the doctors' consent, to engage a trained nurse as a traveling companion, take a room on the train to which he would be brought in a wheelchair with his physician in attendance and run the risk of his withstanding the journey to New York.

Aronberg, Langner and I met him at the Grand Central Station and with the aid of the nurse carried him to a waiting wheelchair. A limousine was in readiness to drive us to a Madison Avenue hotel where we were joined by Russel Crouse, a staunch old friend whose good sense and reliability in any crisis were always unfailing.

Within a few hours it became evident to the nurse and to us that a hotel room would not be adequate for his needs. The nurse had to return to Salem and we would have to engage three shifts of nurses to take her place. Then, too, sleeping quarters and food would have to be provided for them. Under these circumstances we agreed to telephone Doctors Hospital to arrange for a room and to call Dr. Fisk who was again to be in charge and would select an orthopedic specialist.

The nurse from Salem and our entire group attending, we accompanied Gene to Doctors Hospital where he was assigned a comfortable room overlooking the East River. He remained there for a month. X-rays showed that his knee was healing satisfactorily, but his general physical and nervous condition had undergone obvious deterioration. He was down to ninety-seven pounds.

Every day for four weeks we visited together for at least one hour, usually in the evening after work. His nights, he told me, were hideous, haunted by spectres and delusional terrors, asleep or awake. He was taking frequent doses of chloral hydrate at the time, both to reduce the Parkinson tremor and to induce sleep. Once, while I was with him, he sprang from the bed before I could grasp him and cowered in a far corner of the room nearest the door, crying out: "She's on the window sill. She's coming toward me. Please keep her away!" Whereupon he scraped the wall with his fingernails, trying vainly to get a finger hold so that he could climb the wall, cast and all, and escape whatever was pursuing him in his overwrought, phantom-ridden mind.

It was not entirely a sick fantasy that she was near. Upon her insistence and certainly within her legal rights, Carlotta was released from the sanitarium to which she had been committed by Dr. Moore and, after a brief delay, came to New York. There she engaged a room in Doctors Hospital underneath Gene's. Several times during my visits she telephoned him. Whenever she did so I waited in the hall until the conversation came to an end. It was all too manifest that she was regaining control.

Even in the face of Gene's imminent return to captivity, our group tried to make plans for an uncertain future. Bennett and Phyllis Cerf found and were about to sign a lease for a New York apartment for Gene to which he could move upon his dismissal from the hospital. This plan was vetoed and the option on the apartment was dropped. My wife and I had gained his half-consent to setting up an establishment in Princeton, New Jersey, where we would try to minister to his needs.

Carlotta's appearance summarily disposed of this notion. Other friends generously suggested alternatives, to all of which he listened patiently but would not respond affirmatively or negatively. All of us soon began to realize that our good intentions only paved the way to nowhere.

As Gene grew a little stronger, he began to analyze or, more properly, to explain and rationalize his predicament. He realized, as we were beginning to do, that the tie that bound him to Carlotta was too firm to undo. Yet he was acutely aware that submission meant the final severance from all his old friends and repudiation of his own past. He realized that he would need constant care, would have to be fed and nursed and guarded. On that score alone he was unwilling to impose upon his friends. There was, on the other hand, the risk of other quarrels with Carlotta and perhaps other broken limbs. Consideration, too, had to be given to his Parkinson affliction; it had advanced to the point where he could not possibly live without close moment-to-moment help.

Essential as this was, it cut a deep wound into his pride. After all, Carlotta had lived with him and it for almost a quarter of a century, and when she was not in a state of acute disturbance, she could be competent and devoted and even sacrificial in her imperious and managerial way. Hers was not a radiant future, he argued as much to convince himself as me, and she had relinquished a life of ease as a woman of conspicuous beauty in order to be at his side through all those years, for better or for worse. As the wife of a famous man (he smiled wanly at the use of the adjective), she had expected to be surrounded by all that wealth and recognition could bring. But, instead, the latter years had been bitter for both of them, and not only was he sick and unproductive, but so was she and hers was a peculiar sickness only he could understand and had to forgive. Together, they might help each other; apart there could only be even greater torture and then dissolution. And, finally, his chief article of faith was that doom had to be his companion to his last hour.

---

240. *To Bennett Cerf and Saxe Commins from Eugene O'Neill.* TL 1 p.
On stationery headed: Random House, Inc. The Modern Library /
457 Madison Avenue New York 22, N.Y. / Bennett A. Cerf, President

March 17, 1951

Dear Bennett and Saxe:
Please let this note serve as my official permission to Random House to pub-

lish, prior to production, individually or together, my two plays, A MOON
FOR THE MISBEGOTTEN and A TOUCH OF THE POET. I rely on your judgment
as to the appropriate publication date and the general format of the book.[54]

Sincerely,

Engene O'Neill

Saxe and I visited O'Neill on May 16, 1951, the day before he left New York
to return to Boston and to Carlotta. Saxe had brought with him a letter which
Oona, long estranged from her father, had asked him to relay to him. Saxe
gave it to O'Neill, who put it under his pillow; whether he ever read it is
uncertain. Oona never received a reply. As we were leaving, O'Neill put his
arms around Saxe and said, "Oh, Saxe! Goodbye, my brother!" It was so
utterly sad I could not suppress my tears.

We never saw or heard from the O'Neills again. Accompanied by a nurse,
O'Neill arrived in Boston on May 17, 1951, and went straight to the Hotel
Shelton, where Carlotta awaited him in a two-room suite that became his
final home. There, in isolation and loneliness, death came to O'Neill on
November 27, 1953. Carlotta outlived him by seventeen years and survived
to orchestrate the O'Neill "revival" of the 1950s by releasing the rights to
Long Day's Journey into Night (which won for O'Neill his fourth Pulitzer
Prize), *A Touch of the Poet, More Stately Mansions,* and *Hughie.* She died
on November 18, 1970.

After we saw O'Neill for the last time, Saxe wrote to Oona about our visit.
He wrote her again after O'Neill's death.

241. *To Oona O'Neill Chaplin from Saxe Commins.* ALS 2 pp.
On stationery headed: Random House, Inc. The Modern Library /
457 Madison Avenue New York 22, N.Y. / Saxe Commins, Editor

May 16, 1951

Dear Mrs. Chaplin,

Last evening I delivered your letter to your father. It came just in time,
for tomorrow he goes by train, accompanied by a trained nurse, to Boston,
where he will rejoin his wife. Had your letter come a day later I doubt
whether it would have reached him.

54. Random House published *A Moon for the Misbegotten* in 1952. After O'Neill's
death Carlotta gave the publication rights of *A Touch of the Poet* and *Long Day's
Journey into Night* to Yale University, and they were published in 1957 and 1956,
respectively, by Yale University Press.

I had gone to the hospital last night to say a last good-bye. It is doubtful that I will be permitted to see him again. But that is as it must be. The important consideration is that your father is well on the road to recovery. His leg is entirely healed; his tremor is immensely improved; his speech is clearer; his strength is returning and his will to live has been restored.

It would be impossible to recite all the facts and their interpretation in a single letter. You will have to wait for the return of Dudley Nichols[55] from Europe. He will be able to give you the essentials and do so with the fairness and understanding so characteristic of him.

I saw your father virtually every day since his arrival in New York. I went twice to Salem, Massachusetts, to be with him in the hospital there. When he first came to New York the doctors and his friends had grave fears that he would not live. But those anxieties are, happily, past and now he is doing what he wants to do, namely go back to what may be happiness for him or perhaps even death. In any case, it is what he wants and that is all-important.

His friends, acting with the purest motives of devotion, did what they could and, in my opinion, saved his life. Now they must withdraw completely and perhaps even face the prospect of being accused of acting against his interests and wishes. No one knows the best course. It must be enough to have done what seemed right at the time, out of love. My hope is that your father's strength will be restored completely, so that he can work again in all serenity. He has had more than anyone should be asked to bear of torture and physical hurt.

When he goes to Boston tomorrow it will mark a kind of end of thirty-five years of friendship. It will be very difficult for me to communicate with him.

Long, long ago in that friendship I knew you when you were a very little girl. It was in Bermuda that I knew you best, even if you cannot remember. Only once did I see you after that, when one night in Princeton you sat directly back of me in the McArter theatre during a Paul Robeson performance of Othello.[56] You were with Agnes, your mother, and it was hardly the occasion to tell you how fond I had been of you when you were a child.

Dudley has told me wonderful things about you and I was immensely pleased to learn that you are a happy and a completely fulfilled woman.

If ever you come to New York, please communicate with me. I'd like to be able to tell you more about your father than can possibly be compressed into

55. Nichols, a leading Hollywood screenwriter who had been responsible for adapting the S. S. Glencairn plays for the movies as *The Long Voyage Home* (1940) and for the film version of *Mourning Becomes Electra* (1947), was also a close friend of O'Neill's in the late 1930s and 1940s.

56. Following the Princeton engagement, the Theatre Guild production of *Othello*, costarring Robeson with Jose Ferrer and Uta Hagen and designed by Robert Edmond Jones, gave 296 performances in the 1943–44 season, a phenomenal Broadway run for Shakespeare.

a letter of this kind. I'd like very much to see you. If ever I get to California I shall get in touch with you in the hope of having a long talk about the most meaningful friendship of my life.

Sincerely
Saxe Commins

---

242. *To Oona O'Neill Chaplin from Saxe Commins.* TLS I p.
On stationery headed: 85 Elm Road / Princeton, New Jersey

December 1, 1953

Dear Oona,

I address you so familiarly because I knew you when you were a little girl and it was then and for many years afterward that I loved your father and counted him my best friend. We worked together, thought and dreamed together, and in the end it all had to come to naught. You may even remember having sent a letter through me for your father when he was sick in Doctor's Hospital. I delivered it somewhat surreptitiously and waited until he read it[57] before saying good-bye to him for the last time. I was forbidden ever to see him again, and for what reason I do not know and probably never will.

But I was not alone in the general proscription. All his friends, one by one, were kept outside the wall built around him.

Right now it is very, very important that I tell you how deeply I've felt the enforced alienation by a will not your father's. You have probably felt it yourself, as I have reason to know.

But even all that is to be forgotten. Gene is now beyond being forbidden; he is beyond fear. I've been told that his passing was peaceful and painless. That, at least, is something gained. The torment is over. The gentlest and noblest man I ever knew is finally at rest. There is nothing any of us can do except revere his memory and be very proud and very sad, too, that so fine a spirit became a prisoner and never knew freedom until he died.

I send my love to you who hardly know me but must somehow remember me from the years long gone by as Gene's friend.

Yours
Saxe Commins

I obtained your address from Professor Albert Einstein.[58]

57. Saxe said he waited while O'Neill read Oona's letter out of regard for her feelings.
58. Professor Einstein, who lived in Princeton, was a friend of both the Commins family and the Chaplins.

The conclusion of Saxe's memoir provides a fitting epilogue to the O'Neill story:

When after his death in November of 1953, Eugene O'Neill's will was probated in Boston on December 24th of that year, it was revealed that he had disowned his two surviving children, Shane and Oona, and had named his widow as his sole beneficiary and executrix. The sentence cutting off his two children read:

"I purposely exclude from any interest in my estate under this will my son Shane O'Neill and my daughter Oona O'Neill Chaplin and I exclude their issue, now or hereafter born."

The reason for this exclusion was incomprehensible at the time and gave rise to surprise and wonder. But it was not long before the mystery was solved.

In mid-1954, Bennett Cerf, President of Random House, was called on the telephone by Carlotta O'Neill and asked whether he had read the copy of *Long Day's Journey into Night* which had been hidden for so many years in the company safe. To this he answered that indeed he had not because he was not allowed legally to do so and therefore he had never so much as seen nor opened the package; the seals were still intact and he had no intention of breaking them. In reply to this, Mrs. O'Neill said she wished he would read it at once because she wanted it published as soon as it was possible to do so. Before Cerf consented to read it, he wanted, he told her, to think about the matter and would then call her back.

He immediately consulted with me and asked my views. I suggested that he learn from our lawyer, Horace Manges, whether this violation of a dead man's wishes would be legally, if not morally, condonable, and second, that he insist upon a public statement, to be printed on the jacket and within the book itself, signed by the widow, to the effect that publication rights were granted with her full authorization. The last suggestion was offered with the view of averting the possibility that Random House or Bennett Cerf might be accused of vandalism. We were clearly faced with the alternative of undertaking publication with clean hands or relinquishing our right to do so altogether.

When Cerf communicated this decision to Mrs. O'Neill, she exploded with fury and vented most of her wrath on me, accusing me of having instigated a plot against her, of having ruined all the O'Neill plays on which I had worked with him and charging me with about as many crimes as are included in the penal code. To which, with characteristic loyalty, Cerf replied in a letter that was as gratifying as it was bolstering to my vanity. This letter alone, if I could live up to it, was a solace for the hurt inflicted by the unforeseen termination of a nearly forty-year friendship. For Cerf's act of devotion I hold him in high esteem, but even in greater respect for his determination not to compromise his principles as a publisher by violating a dead man's wishes.

We were shocked when we learned from our attorney that a strict interpretation of the law provided that the instructions of the deceased may be superseded by those of the *sole* beneficiary and executrix of a will. Therefore, Mrs. O'Neill was within her legal rights if she caused to be produced and published a play for which there had been a legal, if no longer binding, stipulation against such publication or production. There was no mention of the restricting document or the wish itself in the will.

At last the mystery was solved. Now it became clear why Eugene O'Neill had been *induced* to disown his two surviving children. Had they been legitimate heirs in the eyes of the law, the widow would not then have been sole beneficiary and the claim, within a strict interpretation of the law, to the right to produce and publish *Long Day's Journey into Night* before the stipulated time, which would have been in 1978, would have elapsed.

Astounded and bewildered by this development we could not at first let ourselves believe that, legally or morally, such a flouting of a dead man's wishes, explicitly stated in a signed document, would be permissible or justifiable. Unfortunately, we were laboring under moral illusions only, but our legal misapprehensions were more decisively against us.

Lawyers for Mrs. O'Neill overruled our naive contentions and confirmed the opinion of the attorney retained by Random House. That made it unanimous. Two distinguished members of the Boston Bar, successors to many colleagues who had been hired and fired by the relict of the playwright, called on Bennett Cerf to reach a determination about the publication of the posthumous play. Their errand was quickly accomplished; Cerf relinquished all rights to publication.

These counsellors were the successors to Mr. Melville Cane, poet and essayist and an able and trustworthy lawyer, one of the many who had served their terms and been rejected. Long ago Cane and I had had a brief encounter in which at first I was the victim of his client's wrath. He was to feel its lash much later.

For more than ten years Mrs. O'Neill and I had maintained in our joint names a large safe-deposit box in the Manufacturers Trust Company which had its banking offices at 57th Street and Fifth Avenue. In it were stored many manuscripts, certificates of stock, mementoes and some rather expensive jewelry. During the time the O'Neills lived in France and California, letters, cables and telegrams came to New York asking me to remove certain items from the box and ship them wherever they were at the time. Sometimes I was asked to add things to the contents of the box. But no article of mine was ever placed in this receptacle, nor did I ever have occasion to use it for my own purposes. The reason for the joint rental of the safety-deposit box was so that I could always have access to it and deposit or withdraw anything the O'Neills might request.

Once an anxious series of telegrams and letters came from Mrs. O'Neill. She was nervously concerned about the loss of some valuable jewelry. Reference to the inventory of jewels locked in the box revealed that they were quite safe and intact. Her telegram on receiving the good news expressed happiness, relief and gratitude at my having found them where they were all the time. There also came the request to ship all the jewels in the safety box in the bank to California by registered mail. This was done and the acknowledgment of their receipt was in the language of rejoicing.

During the first of two separations between the O'Neills—once when his arm was broken and then his leg—I received a peremptory letter from Melville Cane. He demanded that I relinquish my key to his client's safety-deposit box and made the statement that my access to it was not only questionable but also suspicious. The implication was that I planned to make off with its contents. To this letter I replied with a bitter reproach to him for impugning my honesty and also with a full explanation of the circumstances under which the box had been rented and used for more than a decade. The key was enclosed with the letter.

Gene was in Doctors Hospital at the time convalescing from a fractured arm. I brought him Cane's letter and the carbon copy of my reply. He was furious. His anger expressed itself in a rather irrelevant but humorous manner. First of all, he disparaged Cane's literary work and then rebuked me for not writing a more scathing response. Then, with a broad grin on his face, he asked me whether we had in our offices printed rejection slips for manuscripts that were not worthy of a personal letter. When I told him that we had such standard forms and used them only for the utterly hopeless manuscripts submitted to us, he said that what I should have done was to let one of those printed rejection slips serve as my answer to his letter.

Fortunately my little contretemps with Melville Cane was resolved many years later when he was no longer Mrs. O'Neill's attorney. He remembered our exchange of letters and at last could explain why he had to act as a lawyer under the orders of his client. He knew all along, he said, that I had never used the safety box for my own purposes and was certain that I had discharged my part of the bargain scrupulously. We later came to respect each other with genuine understanding.

Now Melville Cane belongs to that growing company of lawyers who were given rejection slips by Mrs. O'Neill. The two gentlemen from

Boston who called on Bennett Cerf about the publication by Random House of *Long Day's Journey into Night* were also honored in this manner and can now consider themselves alumni. They were succeeded by a constellation of attorneys whose names on their letterheads are an awesome directory. It was they who arranged for the posthumous publication of the play by Yale University Press, after Random House had relinquished all rights to it, *twenty-two years* before Eugene O'Neill had intended to issue it.

For several years prior to his death in 1953, Eugene O'Neill had contributed manuscripts, notes and correspondence to the archives of the Yale University Library. After his death all his papers were given to Yale for safekeeping and for the ultimate use of scholars. Under these circumstances and even if a quid pro quo was not involved, it was logical and certainly legal, regardless of the moral distinctions entailed, to override the author's living wish and have Yale University Press publish *Long Day's Journey into Night* with deserved success.

When the play was produced in 1956, first in Stockholm and then in New York, the question of the propriety of bringing it to the stage was overshadowed by the unanimous acclaim of the critics and the wholehearted support of the public. O'Neill's own misgivings about the effect his work would have on the reputations of the dead and the susceptibilities of the living proved in the end to be baseless. The play was accepted, as it so richly merited, not as a rattling of skeletons in a family closet, but as a work of art dealing with a universal rather than a personal experience. It has been, from all accounts, magnificently acted and produced. I have never seen the play in whose history I was, in a strange sense, an unlisted member of the cast acting an anonymous role.

INDEX

About the editor

Dorothy Commins is a musician and the
author of *All about the Symphony Orchestra*
and *Lullabies of the World,* as well as
What Is an Editor? Saxe Commins at Work.

———————————————

Library of Congress Cataloging-in-Publication Data
O'Neill, Eugene, 1888–1953.
"Love and admiration and respect."
Includes bibliographical references and index.
1. O'Neill, Eugene, 1888–1953—Correspondence.
2. Commins, Saxe—Correspondence.   3. Dramatists,
American—20th century—Correspondence.   4. Editors—
United States—Correspondence.   I. Commins, Saxe.
II. Commins, Dorothy.   III. Title
PS3529.N5Z484   1986   812'.52   [B]   86–6195
ISBN 0–8223–0668–9